LITERACY IN THE ROMAN WORLD

JOURNAL OF ROMAN ARCHAEOLOGY

SUPPLEMENTARY SERIES NUMBER 3

GENERAL EDITOR: J. H. HUMPHREY

AN INTERNATIONAL JOURNAL

Literacy
in the
Roman world

Mary Beard
Alan K. Bowman
Mireille Corbier
Tim Cornell
James L. Franklin, Jr.
Ann Hanson
Keith Hopkins
Nicholas Horsfall

ANN ARBOR, MI
1991

TABLE OF CONTENTS

Preface

William Harris' *Ancient literacy* (Harvard University Press, 1989)[1] is an important and thorough survey of a great deal of material relating to this important subject. Its publication has prompted scholars to reevaluate and reformulate their views. Because the topic of literacy is multifarious and wide-ranging, it seemed appropriate to provide more space than is normally given to a review in a scholarly journal.[2] Several scholars, each with their own long-standing and rather different interests in the subject of literacy in the Roman world, were therefore invited to adopt Harris' book as the starting-point for their own discussions of literacy in the Roman world.[3] Eight scholars kindly responded in good time, and it is worth noting that the contributors have hardly challenged Harris' basic point, that levels of literacy in Graeco-Roman antiquity were never high. The contributors were given complete latitude regarding the aspects of the book and of the topic on which they wished to focus, except only that the emphasis was to be Roman rather than Greek or Hellenistic. No effort has been made to impose any kind of consensus upon the discussions, except that the focus was to be upon the Roman world — Roman in the geographical as well as the chronological sense. Included therefore is the earliest material from Etruria and archaic Latium, the Greek East in the Roman period, as well as late antiquity. Archaic and Classical Greece, which constitute an important part of Harris' book, were not intended to be covered. Each contributor speaks for him- or herself. Editing has been directed chiefly at achieving some minimal consistency of format and style. Because the journal regularly accepts contributions in other languages, the contribution by Mireille Corbier has not been translated.

---

1   408 pp. , 8 illustrations, cloth $35, ISBN 0-674-03380-9; the book is available as of August 1991 in paperback ($15.95, ISBN 0-674-03381-7).

2   Reviews of this book have so far appeared in *New Republic* (April 2, 1990, by G. W. Bowersock), *Times Higher Education Supplement* (13 April, 1990, p.22 by David Rankin), *Times Literary Supplement* (July 6-12, 1990, p.736 by Greg Woolf), *Chronique d'Egypte* 65 (1990) pp.174-75 (by Alfons Wouters), and in *Classical Review* 1991.1, pp.168-69 (by E. Kenney).

3   Throughout the chapters which follow, page references to W. V. Harris, *Ancient literacy*, take the form simply of "Harris p.xxx".

It has seemed best to issue the discussions together in the supplementary series of this journal because they may well prove to be of interest to some who are not regular subscribers to the annual numbers of the journal itself. The editorial board of the *Journal of Roman Archaeology* is most grateful to the contributors for allowing their discussions to be published in this way.

The editorial board is most grateful to Margaretta Fulton, Humanities Editor at the Harvard University Press, for kindly and promptly providing numerous review copies of the book *Ancient literacy*. I am grateful to Alison Griffith for assistance with typesetting and proofreading.

J. H. Humphrey

The tyranny of the evidence: a discussion of the possible uses of literacy in Etruria and Latium in the archaic age

Tim Cornell

1. Introduction

The great strength of W. V. Harris' book on ancient literacy is that it does not attempt to go beyond the evidence. Harris' wide-ranging survey of the epigraphic and literary material from all of Graeco-Roman antiquity leads him to conclude that mass literacy was never achieved in classical times: the available evidence simply will not support it. His arguments are vigorous and persuasive, and few would now be likely to challenge his basic conclusion, that the ability to read and write never extended beyond a small proportion of the population.

In the case of archaic Italy and Rome down to the middle republic, to which he devotes a brief but important chapter, Harris is extremely negative. Very few people, he believes, could read or write in central Italy during the archaic period. "No serious consideration supports the notion that reading ability was widespread by the end of the sixth century, if such an expression means literacy among more than, say, 5% of the male citizens" (p.151).

This general conclusion is unexceptionable; but Harris goes on to suggest that such literacy as there was in archaic Italy was of little historical significance, and had only a limited range of uses. It was restricted mainly to the religious sphere, and had no significant social, commercial or political functions. Harris casts doubt on the authenticity of archaic documents referred to (and sometimes quoted) in literary sources; and in general he argues that "Rome is unlikely to have given wide functions or diffusion to the written word". In support of this contention, he cites the extreme paucity of contemporary epigraphic documents: "the earliest surviving Latin inscriptions other than graffiti are consistent with this view. These are not at all numerous ..." (p.151).

At this point, the common-sense argument starts to wear thin. The paucity of direct evidence may be consistent with the idea of low-level literacy with limited functions, but it cannot be said to prove it, or even to make it probable. In this paper I hope to show that Harris, along with other English-speaking scholars who have recently touched upon this subject,[1] has not taken sufficient account of the nature of the surviving evidence, and of why and how it has come down to us. It is my firm belief that the evidence we have does not give a true impression of the extent and diffusion of writing in archaic Etruria and Latium; that, in fact, writing may have served a wide variety of public and private functions, and that its historical importance is considerable; and, finally, that the many references to archaic documents in later literature deserve to be taken seriously, and imply an important rôle for public documents in early Rome.[2]

2. The earliest texts

The art of writing was introduced into Italy by the Greeks, whose first settlements on the coast of southern Italy date from the early 8th c. The use of the Greek alphabet by the indigenous peoples of the peninsula can now be dated before 700.[3] The earliest examples attest the use of single alphabetic signs to represent numerals or some other form of reckoning or identification. The earliest inscribed texts in Etruscan go back to the beginning of the 7th c. At present, the total number of 7th-c. Etruscan texts amounts to about 120, and a further 800 or so can be dated to the 6th and 5th c.[4] Some of these are epitaphs carved in stone on the tombs of the aristocracy, but most are inscriptions on movable objects deposited in tombs or dedicated at sanctuaries. In Latium the pattern is rather different. A handful of inscriptions (perhaps about 10) can be dated to the 7th c. (only a minority of them

---

1   For example, S. Stoddart and J. Whitley, "The social context of literacy in archaic Greece and Etruria," *Antiquity* 62 (1988) 761-72; and N. Spivey and S. Stoddart, *Etruscan Italy* (London 1990) 106-8. R. M. Ogilvie, *The Cambridge Ancient History*[2] VII.2 (Cambridge 1989) 11 ff., is extremely cautious about early inscriptions. His statement — "it is surprising how little actual epigraphic material survives from the period 600-250. This may be a fact of chance; or it may be that writing was at first an aristocratic and hieratical phenomenon" — may be taken as typical of the sceptical position I am criticising.

2   All dates in this chapter are B.C.

3   G. Colonna, "L'écriture dans l'Italie centrale à l'époque archaique," *Revue de la société des élèves, anciens élèves et amis de la section des sciences religieuses de l'École Pratique des Hautes Études* (1988) 22-31.

4   Colonna, ibid. 25; Stoddart and Whitley (supra n.2) 767, give a figure of 620 Etruscan inscriptions from the period 710-500.

are from tombs), and between 60 and 70 to the 6th and 5th c.[5] Many of these are graffiti, consisting in some cases of only one or two letters. The majority are from sanctuaries, although some were found in areas of habitation. Very few, if any, of the 6th- and 5th-c. inscriptions come from tombs.

In Latium, as in Etruria, the majority of inscriptions are on movable items, usually pots. Many are 'speaking objects' (*oggetti parlanti*). That is, the object is made to address the reader in the first person, as in *ego fulfios* ("I [belong to] Fulvius") on a bucchero vase dating, probably, from the 5th c. (*CIL* 1[2], 479).[6] The texts record ownership, as in the quoted example, or gift-giving.[7] Formulae such as *duenos med feced* ... (" a good man made me ...", from the famous 'duenos' vase) are not craftsmen's signatures, but rather have a 'causative' sense. Hence: "a good man caused me to be made ..." (in Italian, *fece fare*).[8] This pattern is repeated, with a much greater range of examples, in Etruria. The inscribed objects themselves are often valuable artefacts or prestige articles, of precious metal or fine pottery (sometimes imported Greek painted vases), and most of them were found in aristocratic contexts such as princely tombs.

These facts have led scholars to draw the following conclusions:
1. In archaic Italy, literacy was confined to a narrow social group and to a restricted range of functions. Writing was used principally as a means of reinforcing the prestige and standing of an aristocratic élite. In the

---

5   J. Poucet, "L'écrit et l'écriture dans la Rome des premiers siècles," *Latomus* 48 (1989) 287. Many of these texts are listed in the corpus of archaic Latin inscriptions edited by G. Colonna, "Le iscrizioni strumentali latine del VI e V secolo a.C.," in C. M. Stibbe *et al., Lapis Satricanus* (The Hague 1980) 53-69. Of these, nos. 29 and 34 are probably earlier than 600. Other 7th-c. Latin inscriptions include the Manios fibula and the Vetusia inscription from Praeneste (both discussed below), and the red impasto bowl from a tomb at Osteria dell'Osa discussed by G. Colonna, *Archeologia Laziale* 3 (1980) 51-55.

6   This is no. 37a in Colonna (supra n.5). The vase was acquired in Rome by G. Pansa in the 1880s, and in 1899 was in the possession of H. Dressel, but its present whereabouts are unknown. See Colonna's note *ad loc.* with further references. A parallel text is Colonna no. 36: *eqo Kanaios* (from Ardea, 6th c.). This formula (with its peculiar grammar!) continues into the middle republic. Cf. *CIL* I[2] 2, 462: *eco C. Antonius*, with Colonna's comments, ibid. 68-69. On 'speaking objects' in general see L. Agostiniani, *Le iscrizioni parlanti dell'antica Italia* (Firenze 1982).

7   M. Cristofani, "Il 'dono' in Etruria arcaica," *PP* 30 (1975) 132-52.

8   G. Colonna, "Duenos," *StEtr* 47 (1979) 163-72.

earliest period, according to one recent study,[9] literacy "fitted into the pre-existing social structure as a marker of ideological power". There is no evidence that it was used as a commercial or administrative tool. In the 6th c. it may have been employed more extensively in activities such as pottery manufacture and accounting,[10] but it continued to be used predominantly as a way of defining and enhancing the élite, not only privately but also publicly, through the use of openly-displayed tomb inscriptions and dedications in sanctuaries. The functions of writing were nowhere near as diversified as in archaic Greece, where it was used in a variety of élite activities, including literature, and by craftsmen and artisans, who advertised themselves by signing their products.

2. Secondly, if Etruria lagged behind Greece, Latium lagged behind Etruria. The quantity and quality of material from Rome and other Latin sites cannot compare with that from major Etruscan centres such as Caere, Vulci, and Tarquinii. The epigraphic evidence is consistent with the widely-held notion of Latium as a provincial adjunct on the periphery of the Etruscan cultural sphere. This view may derive support from the fact that some of the inscriptions found in Rome and elsewhere in Latium are written in Etruscan, and from the belief that the Latins used an Etruscan version of the alphabet. A suitable historical context for the introduction of literacy into Latium is provided by the theory that in the last quarter of the 7th c. Rome and Latium fell under Etruscan rule, which lasted until the end of the 6th c. The decline of Etruscan power in Latium would then account for a decrease in the use of writing, which may have occurred around 500.[11]

3. The significance of the surviving sample

Unfortunately, these conclusions are based on mistaken premises and cannot be accepted. The principal objection is that the evidence we possess is not a representative sample of the written material that once existed. On the contrary, the evidence is heavily biased, and cannot possibly justify the statistical inferences that have been drawn from it. Scholars sometimes use phrases like 'the accident of survival' in referring to archaeological evidence, which tends to be concentrated in certain categories (such as pottery) and unevenly distributed between different types of site (cemeteries, sanctuaries, urban centres, rural

---

9   Stoddart & Whitley (supra n.2) 769.
10   Ibid. 770.
11   Harris, 151: "There may have been some decrease in the use of writing as Etruscan power and influence declined about 500."

settlements, etc.).[12] In fact, these biases are not the result of accident, but rather of identifiable circumstances and conditions which favour the survival and recovery of certain classes of objects in particular kinds of site. The point is so elementary that it is unnecessary to elaborate; the physical properties of the materials, climate and soil conditions, the differing levels of archaeological activity between different regions, the preferences and preoccupations of archaeologists (e.g. their alleged obsession with cemeteries), and other such factors, are well known to all, although it is surprising how frequently scholars fail to take them into account.

One fact that deserves emphasis, however, because it has special relevance here, is that the sample is often self-selected. I am referring here to the importance of tombs and votive deposits, which have yielded so many of the known Etruscan and Latin inscriptions from the archaic period. Grave goods and dedications buried in votive deposits survive because they were deliberately deposited and sealed in antiquity, and have remained intact until modern times. It is this fact, and not the supposed fascination of archaeologists with death and religion, that accounts for the archaeological importance of cemeteries and sanctuaries. Habitation sites are more problematic because they tend to contain nothing but the worthless débris that people are prepared to leave behind. It is hardly surprising that inscriptions carved on objects of value are not often found in habitation sites.

Let us examine some of the specific inferences about literacy that have been drawn from the central Italian material. In the 7th c., the use of writing is said to have been confined to a funerary context.[13] What this means is that almost all of the evidence comes from tombs. That the inference is mistaken is virtually certain. Are we seriously to assume that literacy in 7th-c. central Italy was a skill similar to coffin-making or grave-digging, called upon only when somebody died? Secondly, the notion that writing was used only in the service of an aristocratic élite is based on the fact that most surviving inscriptions are on prestige objects in aristocratic tombs (which we assume to be aristocratic because they contain prestige objects). In this instance it is, of course, perfectly possible that the inference corresponds to some

---

12   Stoddart & Whitley (supra n.2) 763-64 are aware of this objection, but dismiss it as "the old argument about the hazards of survival". To me, arguments have much in common with jokes: the old ones are often the best.

13   Stoddart & Whitley, ibid. 769: "[Writing] was a tool of elite legitimization almost entirely restricted to a funerary context."

extent with reality; but the evidence cannot be said to prove it. Writing may have fulfilled all kinds of other purposes in daily life that are not represented in the evidence we have. Thirdly, the fact that many 6th-c. inscriptions (including the great majority of those from Latium) come from votive deposits does not necessarily indicate that writing was now being used for a wider variety of purposes (although that may of course have been happening); still less that, in Latium, writing was largely confined to the religious sphere. What it indicates is that communal sanctuaries became important in the 6th c., as we know from material discovered in votive deposits; this development was no doubt connected with the rise of city-states, a phenomenon that is itself intimately bound up with literacy (*pace* the assertions of some modern scholars). Once again, if the evidence of early Latin texts is largely confined to the religious sphere, that is a comment on the evidence, not on the possible uses of writing in early Latium. This brings us to the fourth point, the paucity of evidence from 7th- and 6th-c. Latium in comparison with that from the major Etruscan centres. Does this show that Rome and Latium were lagging behind?

Quite apart from the obvious imbalances between Latium and Etruria which would make any serious comparison difficult,[14] there is a particular source of bias in the process of self-selection which completely undermines the argument in this case. The best way to illustrate this point is to approach it obliquely through a study of one particular site, which is situated on the margins of Etruria and Latium. This site is the Etruscan city of Veii. The epigraphic record of Veii is unusual and instructive, and can be used to highlight the errors that arise from statistical inferences drawn from a biased selection of data.

4. The case of Veii

Veii was one of the most powerful and important of the Etruscan cities in the archaic age, but it has so far yielded very little in the way of epigraphic material. Indeed, in the early part of the present century

---

[14]   Etruria was a large region containing many urban centres, most of which are now deserted and whose cemeteries have been extensively investigated. Latium was smaller, and in the 6th c. its only major urban centre was Rome, which has been continuously inhabited since antiquity and offers only limited scope for archaeological investigation. Statistical analysis of data from different sites should never in any event be based on a direct comparison of absolute quantities. Cf. the remarks of S. C. Humphreys, *Anthropology and the Greeks* (London 1978) 118 and 291, n.42.

it was believed that the population of Veii was not Etruscan-speaking;[15] rather, it was supposed that the Veientines spoke a dialect of Latin akin to that of the Faliscans, to whom they were closely allied in culture and politics.[16] Scholars were prepared to concede, at most, the presence of a small Etruscan-speaking ruling class. This notion seems less absurd when we remember that it was once fashionable to believe that the Etruscans were a conquering minority who had migrated to Etruria from the Near East during the Iron Age, and whose influence and control did not penetrate very deeply into the communities on the outer fringes of Etruria, of which Veii, the southernmost city, could be considered one. The theory was at least consistent with the fact that, before 1930, Veii had yielded very few Etruscan inscriptions.[17]

Nowadays matters are very different, partly because the conquering minority theory has been abandoned, but mainly because of discoveries of Etruscan inscriptions at Veii. In 1930, G. Q. Giglioli published no fewer than 47 inscribed potsherds that had been unearthed during the excavations of the sanctuary at Portonaccio.[18] They belong to a votive deposit containing material ranging from the 7th to the early 5th c.; most of the inscriptions are dated to the 6th c. Further excavations at the same site produced another 13 inscriptions, including the famous dedication by Avile Vipiiennas (known to later Roman tradition as Aulus Vibenna).[19] Subsequent discoveries of Etruscan texts from Veii include a fragment of an inscribed vase (6th c.) from the sanctuary site

---

15   L. R. Taylor, *Local cults of Etruria* (Rome 1923) 8; and T. Frank, *Roman buildings of the republic* (Rome 1924) 114 ff.

16   During its final war with Rome (405-396), Veii was helped by the Capenates and Faliscans, but received little or no assistance from the other Etruscan cities. Cf. my comments in *CAH* (supra n.1) 300.

17   As far as I am aware, only one or two texts had been published before 1930. They include the Tite Latines inscription, published in *NSc* (1889) 61 (and see further infra n.24), and an inscribed fragment from Piazza d'Armi, published in *NSc* (1922) 400.

18   G. Q. Giglioli, *NSc* (1930) 302-45. Additional fragments from this collection were published by M. Pallottino, *StEtr* 20 (1948-49) 251-53, and by G. Colonna, *StEtr* 51 (1983) 236. A selection can be found in *TLE*[2], 34-48.

19   Published by M. Pallottino, *StEtr* 13 (1939) 455-65. Two further additions in V. Martelli Antonioli, *StEtr* 39 (1971) 357-58. On the Aulus Vibenna vase see J. Heurgon "La coupe d'Aulus Vibenna," *Mélanges Carcopino* (Paris 1966) 515-28 (=*Scripta varia* [Brussels 1986] 273 ff.), and, most recently, C. Ampolo in A. Momigliano and A. Schiavone (edd.), *Storia di Roma* I (Turino 1988) 206-8.

at Piazza d'Armi,[20] and the casual find, on the acropolis, of an inscribed fragment provisionally dated to the 7th c. by P. Forlini.[21]

Five other important texts are known from Veii; all of them are very early (7th c.), and they are the only Veientine inscriptions to have been found in tombs. They are: (1) a spiral amphora from tomb 4 of the Monte Campanile cemetery, which was excavated in 1914, dating to the last quarter of the 7th c.;[22] (2) a 7th-c. inscription from tomb 8 of the Riserva del Bagno necropolis;[23] (3) a bucchero amphora from tomb 17 of the Picazzano cemetery, dating from the last quarter of the 7th c., with the inscription *mi tites latines*;[24] (4) an inscribed Etrusco-Corinthian aryballos from a chamber tomb at Casale del Fosso, dated by F. Buranelli to the end of the 7th c;[25] and (5) an oinochoe, dating from the beginning of the 7th c., bearing the inscription *mi aviles aukanas/ qutumuza*.[26]

The last of these inscriptions is, if correctly dated, one of the earliest-known Etruscan texts; Veii thus joins Caere, Tarquinii and Vulci as one of the few sites that have so far produced texts dating from the period around 700.[27]

What this brief survey reveals is that the 'epigraphic profile' of Veii is quite unlike that of the other cities of southern Etruria, where tombs account for the majority of Etruscan inscriptions; on the other hand it is remarkably similar to the pattern found in Rome and Latium, where, out of some 70 archaic inscriptions, no more than about 6 very early examples come from tombs; the rest come from other contexts, principally votive deposits. At Veii the five 7th-c. inscriptions from tombs have to be set against the other 60 or so which are mostly from sanctuaries. The parallelism is striking, and is almost certainly due to the same cause. It should be noted that in other ways too Veii resembles

---

20   G. Colonna, *StEtr* 39 (1971) 343-44.

21   *StEtr* 51 (1983) 236.

22   A. De Santis, *StEtr* 51 (1983) 239-43.

23   F. Buranelli, *StEtr* 50 (1982) 91-102.

24   G. Colonna in *Civiltà del Lazio primitivo* (Roma 1976) 376 and cf. supra n.17.

25   *StEtr* 47 (1979) 317-18.

26   G. Colonna, *StEtr* 49 (1981) 258-59.

27   Cf. Colonna, ibid. The two-part name (*praenomen + nomen gentilicium*) is exceptional in such an early text. Cf. Colonna, *StEtr* 45 (1977) 176 f. For other early Etruscan inscriptions see G. Colonna, *MEFR* 80 (1970) 637-72 (Caere); M. Cristofani, *AnnPisa* ser. 3.1 (1971) 295-99 (Tarquinii); id., *ArchCl* 25-26 (1973-74) 151-65 (Vulci).

Rome and the other Latin centres in contrast to the rest of Etruria.[28] Parallel developments in architecture, sculpture and ceramic production, symbolised by the tradition that a Veientine sculptor was commissioned to make the cult statue of Jupiter for the 6th-c. Capitoline temple in Rome, are borne out by archaeological evidence — most strikingly by the series of architectonic friezes of the Rome–Veii–Velletri series, so called because friezes made from the same mould have been found at all 3 sites.[29]

But the clearest sign that Veii belonged culturally with Latium rather than with the rest of Etruria is the changing character of its funerary practices. Whereas in other Etruscan cities elaborate burials with expensive tomb furnishings continued throughout the 6th and 5th c., at Veii and in Latium there was a distinct change. In the late orientalising period (c.630–c.580) a marked decrease can be observed in the quality and quantity of grave goods, and after about 580 they disappear altogether. For the next 200 years or so the Veientines, like the Latins, buried their dead in simple graves without any accompanying goods or artefacts. The reason for the change is almost certainly cultural and ideological rather than economic. The disappearance of grave goods is unlikely to be the result of worsening economic conditions or a decline in prosperity; there is no sign of any such decline in the rest of the evidence from Veii or from Rome, but rather the contrary. This was, after all, the age of the 'grande Roma dei Tarquini'.[30] In any case economic constraints might deter people from burying treasure with the dead, but would not stop them from including cheap artefacts such as pottery.

The evidence clearly bears witness to a change in funerary custom, arising from some kind of development in people's notions about death and the proper rituals to be followed in disposing of the dead.[31] The

---

28   J. B. Ward Perkins, *PBSR* 29 (1961) 39 ff.; M. Torelli, *DialArch* 8 (1974-75) 57 f.

29   A. Andrén, *Architectural terracottas from Etrusco-Italic temples* (Lund 1940).

30   This unfortunate phrase, coined by G. Pasquali (*Nuova Antologia* [16 August, 1936] 405-16 = *Terze Pagine Stravaganti* [Firenze 1942] 1-24), has become a cliché of modern scholarship. In the summer of 1990, it was used as the title of a grandiose exhibition in Rome timed to coincide with the World Cup Finals (see the catalogue, *La grande Roma dei Tarquini*, M. Cristofani [ed.] [Roma 1990]). On Pasquali and the origins of the phrase notice C. Ampolo in E. Campanile (ed.), *Alle origini di Roma* (Pisa 1988) 77-88.

31   This important point was established conclusively in an excellent paper by G. Colonna, *PP* 32 (1977) 131-65; cf. id., *Archeologia Laziale* 4 (1981) 229-

precise nature of this shift need not concern us here; the important point is its archaeological effects. As far as the epigraphic evidence is concerned, it is immediately obvious why the number of inscriptions from the rich cemeteries of Tarquinii, Caere and Vulci is far greater than from Veii, Rome or any other Latin centre. The imbalance has nothing to do with the level of literacy, attitude to the written word, or 'epigraphic habit' of the various cities; rather it is due entirely to their different burial customs, which have given us samples with completely different biases.

5. The earliest Latin inscriptions, and Etruscan influence in Latium

In view of these facts the surprising thing about the epigraphic evidence from Veii and the Latin cities is not that it is so meagre, but rather that there is so much of it. This prompts me to make a number of further observations. First, there is no good reason to think that Rome and Latium lagged behind Etruria in the adoption and use of writing. The two earliest Latin inscriptions are from Praeneste and date from the first half of the 7th c. Both are controversial. One, consisting of the name *Vetusia* inscribed on a silver bowl from the Bernardini tomb, is held by some to be Etruscan rather than Latin,[32] but this interpretation seems unlikely to me (see further below); the other, the celebrated 'Manios' fibula, is widely reckoned to be a fake. This is not the place for a full discussion of the fibula; I would merely say that the arguments that have been raised against it strike me as inconclusive at best, and as inadequate to prove the case, whereas the linguistic arguments in favour of its authenticity are overwhelming.[33] It there-

32; C. Ampolo, *AION, ArchStAnt* 6 (1984) 71-102; and most recently A. Naso in *La grande Roma dei Tarquini* (ibid.) 249-51.

32   M. Torelli, *DialArch* 1 (1967) 38-45. According to M. Pallottino, *StEtr* 35 (1967) 568-69, the people who commissioned, inscribed and used the bowl were "certissimamente" Etruscans and not Latins.

33   M. Guarducci, "La cosiddetta fibula prenestina," *MemLinc* Ser.8. 24. 4 (1980) 413-574; "La c.d. fib. pren.: elementi nuovi," *MemLinc* Ser.8. 28. 2 (1984). Her case rests principally on a scientific test purporting to show that before it was engraved the fibula had been treated by a process unknown before the 19th c. But it is doubtful if such a test could be reliable or conclusive. The other arguments are far less compelling, while some are frankly preposterous, for instance her suggestion (*MemLinc* Ser. 8. 28. 2 [1984]) that the letter forms of the inscription resemble the handwriting of W. Helbig, the supposed forger. Linguistic aspects are discussed most recently by R. Coleman, *PCPS* n.s. 36 (1990) 17-19, making a strong case for the authenticity of the text.

fore seems reasonable to treat it as genuine in the absence of conclusive evidence to the contrary. Other inscriptions dating from before 600 have been found at Rome, Ficana and Osteria dell'Osa.[34]

Secondly, the idea that the Romans learned to write from the Etruscans is not proven. There are indeed grounds for thinking that they adopted the alphabet directly from the Greeks, a perfectly reasonable assumption, given the evidence we now have for the presence of Greeks in early Rome. One of the earliest inscriptions from Rome appears to be the signature of a Greek, a certain Kleiklos, engraved on a Corinthian vase from Tomb 125 of the Esquiline cemetery (c.640).[35] Moreover, the fact that the Latins made use of Greek letters not used by the Etruscans (Δ=d, O=o, and X=ks) is best explained by direct Greek influence. On the other hand Etruscan influence is indicated by the use of the Greek C (Gamma) to represent the unvoiced velar consonant as well as the voiced G sound, even though Latin continued to use K and Q in early texts. The use of C to represent a K sound is found already in the very early 'duenos' vase (early 6th c?),[36] but in the Forum cippus (c.580) C is used to represent the voiced G sound (recei = regi), and K is used throughout for the unvoiced velar (sakros = sacer; kalatorem = calatorem; kapiad = capiat).

It is probably wrong to look for a single line of transmission for the alphabet; rather, we should imagine a period of experiment in the years after 700 in which the native peoples of central Italy sought to use the alphabet to represent the sounds of their own languages. It is not a question of one version of the alphabet being adopted for a particular language by some centralised authority and fixed for all time; rather, the alphabet was and is a universal instrument which can be used to represent the words of any language by anyone who wishes. In the early 7th c., when there was no recognised or agreed system, the precise way in which letters were used to represent particular sounds would vary from person to person, depending on who they were, what languages they spoke, and how they had been taught.

---

34 G. Colonna, Lapis Satricanus (supra n.5) nos. 29 (Roma) and 34 (Ficana); cf. id., ArchLaz 3 (1980) 51-55 (Osteria dell'Osa). Reports have been circulating for some time of the discovery at Osteria dell'Osa of a (Latin?) inscription dating from the beginning of the 8th c. If so, it would be the earliest alphabetic text so far discovered anywhere. The discovery is briefly alluded to by M. Cristofani, La grande Roma (supra n.30) 16.

35 H. Dressel, AdI (1880) 288f.; Colonna (supra n.24) 375; H. Solin, ZPE 51 (1983) 180-82.

36 Colonna (supra n.8); Cristofani (supra n.30) 20, with further bibliography.

For this reason I cannot accept that the Vetusia inscription is 'Etruscan'. The name itself appears to be Latin; the simplest interpretation is that Vetusia (in classical Latin it would be written 'Veturia'[37]) was a woman belonging to the Roman *gens Veturia*, a patrician clan, and that she was the wife of the Praenestine aristocrat buried in the Bernardini tomb. Intermarriage between the aristocrats of different communities was typical of the 'horizontal social mobility' of the archaic period, and survived in later times among the Latins in the form of the *ius conubii*.[38] This interpretation is especially attractive in view of possible links between the Veturii and Praeneste in the early republic,[39] and is surely more likely than the alternative, that *Vetusia* is the genitive of an Etruscan masculine name *Vetus*.[40] The question of whether the name is Latin or Etruscan is in any case independent of whether the script is 'Latin' or 'Etruscan'.[41] I use quotation marks because at this date the distinction may be quite meaningless. It is doubtful whether we can speak of a recognised Etruscan alphabet, or a

---

37   This change occurs by means of a well-known sound shift which philologists call rhotacism. As it happens, Livy refers to it in connection with this very name: ... *T. Veturium Geminum, sive ille Vetusius fuit* (3.8.2) (462 B.C.).

38   On horizontal mobility see C. Ampolo, *DialArch* 4-5 (1970-71) 37-68; ibid. 9-10 (1976-77) 333-45; and in *Gli Etruschi e Roma* (Festschrift Pallottino) (Roma 1981) 45-70; on the *ius conubii* see F. de Visscher, *RIDA* ser. 2.1 (1952) 401-22 (Études de droit romain public et privé 3 [Milano 1966]) 147-67. As far as Vetusia is concerned, Colonna suggested that she might be the wife of the Praenestine aristocrat buried in the Bernardini Tomb, but nevertheless calls her "una dama etrusca" (supra n.24, p.374).

39   Praeneste defected to Rome in 499 B.C., the consulship of P. Veturius Cicurinus. Cf. Torelli (supra n.32). Torelli's argument, that the *gens Veturia* migrated from Praeneste to Rome in this year (like the Claudii in 504), does not strictly fit the evidence, since Veturius Cicurinus was already consul in Rome.

40   Thus Torelli (supra n.32). Doubts were expressed by M. Cristofani, *Prospettiva* 5 (1976) 64. The standard work on the Bernardini Tomb is F. Canciani, F. W. von Hase, *La Tomba Bernardini di Palestrina* (Latium Vetus 2, Roma 1979) 39-40, which has a full discussion of the Vetusia inscription (with bibliography).

41   Actually, the matter is more complicated, since it requires an assessment of at least 4 distinct variables: the name, the script, the person who inscribed it, and the person who ordered it to be inscribed. Even if we arbitrarily confined ourselves to 2 alternatives (Latin or Etruscan), we should be faced with $2^4=16$ possible answers. If we allowed a third alternative (e.g. Greek), there would be $3^4=81$ possible answers!

recognised Latin alphabet, in the first half of the 7th c. All we can say is that the inscription was engraved by someone who knew the phonetic values of the various Greek signs and used them to write 'Vetusia'. The first letter is represented by a digamma (F), which is taken by some to indicate that the inscription must be 'Etruscan', since in later Latin this sign was used for the labio-dental fricative — that is, f.[42] But the argument is clearly anachronistic; in any case we know from the contemporary Manios fibula that at this date the f sound was represented by the combination FH (manios med fhefhaked numasioi — Manius me fecit Numerio). Moreover, A. L. Prosdocimi has pointed out that the use of F = f presupposes an earlier stage when FH = uh, which in turn presupposes an original stage when F = u.[43]

The inscription may therefore be taken as Latin, in the sense that it records a Latin name written on an object found in a tomb at Praeneste, a Latin city. Admittedly Praeneste was once generally assumed to be 'Etruscan' in this period; this was because of its rich orientalising tombs, which bear a close resemblance to those found at Etruscan centres such as Vetulonia, Tarquinii and Caere. In particular, the fabulous Regolini-Galassi tomb at Caere contained orientalising objects very similar to those found in the Bernardini tomb at Praeneste. This caused archaeologists to suppose that such 'princely tombs' were characteristically Etruscan, and consequently that Praeneste was dominated by conquering Etruscan warlords in the 7th c. The same argument was applied to Campania, where princely tombs are attested; even at Cumae, a Greek city, the discovery of a princely tomb of the standard type was thought to reveal Etruscan interlopers.[44] The theory was ultimately based on the old-fashioned view of Etruscan origins. The oriental character of the finds in the princely tombs, and indeed the whole orientalising phenomenon in Italy, was explained by the eastern provenance of the Etruscans.

It scarcely needs saying today that such a theory is untenable. It is not simply that the ancient tradition concerning the eastern origin of the Etruscans is now generally rejected; more important is the fact that the orientalising phenomenon in Italy is now recognised as the cultural side of a profound social change that resulted from contacts between the native communities and the Greek colonies.[45] For the present purpose it

42   Torelli (supra n.32) 39.
43   A. L. Prosdocimi, StEtr 47 (1979) 381-83.
44   See the important discussion by M. W. Frederiksen in D. and F. R. Ridgway (edd.), Italy before the Romans (London 1979) 291 ff.
45   Ibid. 292; cf. A. Rathje, ibid. 145-83.

is enough to notice that the Etruscans, Latins and native Campanians were all equally exposed to oriental culture and 'orientalising' Greek culture during the late 8th and 7th c. There is no need to assign any priority to the Etruscans in the development of a Tyrrhenian cultural *koiné*. To return again to the problem of the princely tombs: the recent discovery of similar tombs at Decima, Satricum, Pratica di Mare and other Latin sites has shown that those of Praeneste are not as exceptional as was once thought, and that local élites in Latium had achieved a level of wealth that enabled them to deal on equal terms with their Etruscan and Greek counterparts.[46]

Modern research has also begun to undermine the idea of Etruscan rule in Latium during the 7th and 6th c. There is no serious evidence to support this notion, and in my opinion Giovanni Colonna was right to describe it as "nothing other than a modern myth".[47] The same is true, more generally, of the widely held belief in Etruscan cultural hegemony. Etruscan influence is commonly invoked to explain developments in Roman architecture, craft production, military technique, religion, social organisation and political institutions.[48] But this imperialist (or neo-colonialist) explanation has recently begun to give way to an alternative model which stresses parallel development and change through processes of exchange and interaction.[49] The presence of Etruscan elements in the population of Rome and other Latin communities is best explained, not as evidence of foreign occupation, but as a function of an open society that permitted the free mobility of individuals and groups across ethnic and linguistic frontiers. In the Etruscan cities inscriptions have revealed the presence of persons of Greek, Latin and Italic origin occupying positions of high social rank, and attest to the same process in the opposite direction.[50] In these circumstances, the art of writing should also be seen as something that

---

46   T. J. Cornell, *Archaeological Reports* 21 (1979-80) 77-78.

47   G. Colonna in *Gli Etruschi e Roma* (supra n.38) 165.

48   An extreme version of this theory in R. M. Ogilvie, *Early Rome and the Etruscans* (London 1976), where it is assumed that the Etruscans were responsible for every major change in Rome in the 6th c. Cf. my remarks in *CR* 29 (1979) 106-9.

49   The pioneer in this field was S. Mazzarino, *Dalla monarchia allo stato repubblicano* (Catania 1945). A good example of the use of an 'interaction' model is the volume on "La formazione della città nel Lazio," *DialArch* n.s.2 (1980). In general see the important collection of papers edited by C. Renfrew and J. Cherry, *Peer polity interaction and socio-political change* (Cambridge 1986).

50   See C. Ampolo, *DialArch* 9-10 (1976-77) 333ff.

spread throughout the Tyrrhenian lowland zone by a process of interaction as various ethnic and linguistic communities reacted, each in its own way, to the stimulus of Greek colonisation and trade.

6. Escaping from the surviving sample: some suggestions

So far we have established that the surviving epigraphic evidence from archaic central Italy is a biased sample. What we happen to possess is wholly determined by the peculiar circumstances that have caused the preservation of certain types of artefact in a limited number of archaeological contexts. The data are misleading because they do not faithfully represent the full range of uses to which writing was put in archaic Etruria and Latium, or even the nature of the epigraphic habit of these societies. Latium was probably not a poor relation of Etruria; it adopted the alphabet in its own way and for its own purposes. Equally, it is not necessarily true that Etruria lagged behind most of the Greek world in its use of writing in the archaic age.[51]

The next step in the argument is more problematic. Is there any way of assessing the situation more positively? Can we identify areas where writing was important in archaic central Italy, but which are not well represented in the surviving evidence? The discussion that follows is inevitably rather speculative, but there are some slight indications which point a way forward. In any event the picture that is offered here has every chance of coming closer to the truth than studies that share the biases of the existing epigraphic evidence. There seem to me to be 4 main areas in which progress is possible.

1. Inscriptions from everyday contexts

I begin with an observation that does not take us very far, but nevertheless seems worth making. The point is simply to draw attention to epigraphic documents from contexts other than tombs and votive deposits. The material is very meagre, but it may be more significant than it looks at first sight. Several early inscriptions from Latium were found in domestic contexts in areas of habitation. They include 3 items

---

51 J. Bundgaard, *AnalRom* 3 (1965) 40, writes: "[the] number of inscriptions in Etruscan from before 500 B.C. ... compare[s] favourably with even the principal Greek regions where writing flourished: Ionia, Attica, Corinth. The art of writing spread like wildfire in Etruria as it did in Greece." I think this is probably true. Athens may be an exception; when scholars speak of Greece in connection with literacy they usually mean Athens. This is an example of what Keith Hopkins calls 'the Everest fallacy' ("Everest is a typical mountain").

from the settlement at Acqua Acetosa on the Via Laurentina just outside Rome.[52] Two of these were found in rubbish pits in the courtyard of a 6th-c. building; they consist of graffiti scratched on vases and probably represent personal names. The third example was scratched on a fragment of tile. The text reads ---]etartispo[... and is of uncertain meaning, but may contain part of a name. The important point about these examples is that they evidently do not have a funerary or religious function. They may be craftsmen's signatures; at any rate they are evidence that writing was not confined to aristocratic circles. The pots are of no value, and what kind of aristocrat would scratch his name on a tile?[53]

In 1965 earth-moving operations at a place called Casale Pian Roseto, about 2 km. north of the site of ancient Veii, revealed a mysterious subterranean building dating from the beginning of the 4th c. It was found to contain a dump of Etruscan pottery of the 6th and 5th c. At least 27 fragments had graffiti scratched on them, mostly consisting of only a few letters, although on one the full name of the owner was preserved: mi larisal patavas ("I [belong to] Laris Patavas").[54] What needs to be emphasised here is that the material turned up purely by chance. It is the merest accident that we possess it at all; on the other hand it is clear that finds of this type could be made at any time. Secondly, we should note the mundane character of the material. It is a most uninteresting site, and its discovery has aroused little scholarly attention. There is nothing remarkable about the inscribed fragments other than that they are inscribed. But that is precisely the point. They imply that writing on pottery was a normal feature of daily life, practised for everyday purposes by ordinary people. The precise function of these examples can only be guessed at. The most obvious answer is that writing was used for identification and enumeration in a commercial context (i.e. as some form of stock control).[55]

---

52   Colonna, "Iscrizioni strumentali" (supra n. 5) nos. 31-33. F. Cordano and C. De Simone, "Graffiti e iscrizioni provenienti dall'Acqua Acetosa Laurentina," PP 36 (1981) 128 ff.; A. Bedini in La grande Roma dei Tarquini (supra n.30) 175, 177.

53   Colonna, ibid. 69, describes the writers as "gente modesta", which must be correct, in spite of Harris' scepticism (Harris 151 n.11).

54   M. Torelli, StEtr 38 (1969) 323-30; a full report of the excavation is in L. Murray-Threipland and M. Torelli, PBSR 38 (1970) 62-121.

55   Note also the fragment found in the fill of a ditch at Ficana, on which is scratched the numeral xxxxxiiii (Colonna, "Iscrizioni strumentali" [supra n.5] no.34).

2. *The use of perishable materials*

The second possibility to be considered is that most day-to-day writing was on perishable material, and that inscriptions carved on pottery, metal or stone were exceptions rather than the rule. Unprejudiced reflection might well suggest that this conclusion is inherently probable; and there is, as it happens, some evidence in its favour. The most important item is the famous ivory writing tablet from Marsiliana d'Albegna, dating from the first half of the 7th c. [56] The tablet has a recessed area which would have been coated with wax to form a convenient (and replaceable) writing surface. Tablets of this kind were widely used in Roman times for day-to-day purposes such as keeping accounts.

The Marsiliana d'Albegna find shows that this practice went back to the 7th c. That it is a single isolated example is irrelevant; the surprising thing is that we should have any examples at all. Normally such tablets were made of wood, and have therefore failed to survive. The preservation of the Marsiliana d'Albegna tablet is due to unusual circumstances: first, it is made of ivory, which gave it special value as a prestige artefact, and incidentally ensured its survival; and secondly, it evidently had a particular significance for the person who owned it, and for this reason it was buried with him. An alphabet is engraved around the border of the tablet, which was clearly designed as a teaching aid for a beginner. The natural assumption is that the deceased aristocrat took pride in his rudimentary ability to write, which at this early date was probably a novel and striking accomplishment. This single example proves that waxed writing tablets were known in archaic Etruria, and it is perfectly reasonable to assume that this convenient medium came to be widely used in daily life. There is also evidence from 6th-c. Etruria for the use of *tabulae ansatae*, that is, concave wooden tablets with notches at each end, which enable 2 tablets to be placed together with the writing on the inside, and then tied with string and sealed. Such tablets were common in Roman times, and their characteristic shape (see fig.1) came to be used as a surround for *tituli* on inscribed monuments. There could hardly be a better symbol of the primacy of the wooden writing tablet, and the fact, obvious enough to anyone with any imagination, that epigraphy is a secondary development.

---

56   J. Bungård, "Why did the art of writing spread to the west? Reflexions on the alphabet of Marsiliana," *AnalRom* 3 (1965) 11-72.

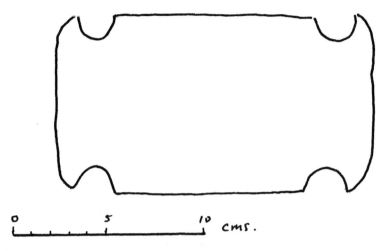

Fig.1.

The Etruscan evidence consists of bucchero imitations of such tablets from 6th-c. tombs in the Chiusi region. More than 20 examples were mentioned by J. A. Bundgård, whose important study of this whole subject remains a classic.[57] It is no good saying that in this case, too, the evidence is isolated and of limited quantity. The evidence is confined to the area around Chiusi solely because of that city's funerary ideology. It was only at Chiusi that the practice developed of burying not the actual belongings of the deceased, but bucchero imitations of them. The examples that survive in this way can therefore be taken as symbolic representations of objects that were in common use in Chiusi; and if they were common in Chiusi they were probably common in the rest of Etruria.

3. The use of writing in public life

Thirdly we may consider the possibility that writing in archaic Italy had a public and administrative function. As we shall see, the literary sources provide most of the evidence for this; but there is at least one item of monumental evidence (apart from surviving public inscriptions, such as the Forum cippus, on which more below). In an important study G. Colonna drew attention to a 5th-c. funerary relief from Chiusi showing a public scribe seated next to two magistrates at a prize-giving ceremony.[58] He is writing on a hinged wooden tablet, while athletes, dancers and musicians parade in front of the dais on

---

57   Ibid. 22-23; 63-64, n.22.

58   G. Colonna, "Scriba cum rege sedens," in *L'Italie préromaine et la Rome républicaine (Mélanges J. Heurgon)* (Roma 1976) 187-95.

which he and the magistrates are sitting. The act of writing in this scene clearly has an official function, and Colonna may well be right that the scribe was compiling, for the purpose of permanent record, a list of victors. At all events the monument is proof of something that we should in any case have been entitled to assume, namely that writing was a necessary feature of the normal running of the state.

The city-state is characterised by formal and artificial institutions, and the public organisation of time and space. The definition of a citizen body, subdivided for different purposes into a variety of different kinds of groups according to age, wealth and place of residence, would seem to be inconceivable without writing; and indeed the classic theory of Goody and Watt, that literacy itself facilitates this kind of rational organisation, remains attractive, in spite of the criticisms that have been levelled against it.[59] In the case of Rome, it is difficult to imagine the institution of the religious calendar, normally dated to the 6th c., except in written form; the same can be said of the census, which goes back at least to the 5th c., and probably to the 6th. But the principal evidence for the public function of written documents in early Rome comes from the literary sources, and it is to these that I now turn.

4. References to writing in literary texts

Our narrative sources contain many references to the use of writing from the very beginnings of Roman history. Tradition ascribes the introduction of letters to Evander, the Arcadian hero who settled on the Palatine centuries before the founding of the city. Romulus and Remus were sent to school at Gabii, where they learned Greek (Dion. Hal. 1.84.5). Such stories show that the Romans had some awareness of the Greek origins of alphabetic literacy, and possibly that Gabii was reckoned to be an early centre of culture in Latium. But few would be prepared to go further than that, and the ultimate verdict must be that such stories are fictitious.[60] The same is probably true of casual

---

59   J. Goody and I. Watt, "The consequences of literacy," *Comp. Studies in Soc. Hist.* 5 (1962-63) 304-45 (reprinted in Goody [ed.], *Literacy in traditional societies* [Cambridge 1968] 27-68); cf. O. Murray, *Early Greece* (London 1980) 91-99. Criticism in P. Cartledge, *JHS* 98 (1978) 37; B. V. Street, *Literacy in theory and practice* (Cambridge 1984) 44-65; Harris, 40-42.

60   The exception is E. Peruzzi, who attempts to reconstruct the nature of early Roman society on the basis of the literary narratives, which he takes to be historically reliable in every detail. His discussion of literacy in early Rome, from the time of Evander onwards (including an account of

references to writing in the narrative accounts of the monarchy, for instance the elaborate correspondence of Tarquinius Superbus mentioned by Dionysius of Halicarnassus (4.57-58). There is nothing impossible about an exchange of private letters at this date, but it is nonetheless doubtful if Dionysius' account is based on authentic evidence.

Even so we must guard against excessive scepticism. Sometimes our tradition can be shown to contain authentic elements. An example of this is the Etruscan scribe who features in the story of Mucius Scaevola. Mucius, it will be remembered, made a daring attempt on the life of Lars Porsenna, but failed to recognise the king and mistakenly killed the scribe who was sitting next to him (Livy 2.12.7; Dion. Hal. 5.28.2). By comparing this interesting story with archaic Etruscan monuments (especially the funerary stele from Chiusi mentioned in the previous section), Colonna demonstrated that in this instance the annalistic tradition has somehow managed to preserve a genuine detail of Etruscan institutional practice.[61]

The most important passages, however, are those which refer to ancient documents such as laws and treaties. Some of these have a right to be considered authentic. A famous example is the treaty between Rome and Carthage quoted by Polybius (3.22), and dated by him to the first year of the republic (509). Admittedly some scholars (including Mommsen) have disputed Polybius' date, but the historical arguments in its favour are extremely strong, and are supported by the most recent archaeological finds. All in all there is every reason to concur with the majority of contemporary scholars in accepting the text as that of a genuine document of the late 6th c.[62] Monumental laws include the *lex Furia Pinaria* of 472, referred to by Varro (*ap.* Macrob. *Sat.* 1.13.21) as a *lex antiquissima* inscribed on a column of bronze; the *lex Icilia de Aventino publicando* of 456, recorded on a bronze stele in the temple of Aventine Diana (Dion. Hal. 10.32.4; cf. Livy 3.31); and the "ancient law written in antique letters and words" (*lex vetusta...priscis litteris verbisque scripta*) requiring the *praetor maximus* to bang a nail into the

---

Romulus' schooldays), can be found in *Le origini di Roma* II: *Le lettere* (Bologna 1973).

61   Colonna (supra n.58).

62   I have stated my views on this question at greater length in *CAH* VII[2].2 (Cambridge 1989) 253-57. Cf. C. Ampolo, "I due primi trattati romanocartaginesi e le loro clausole relative al commercio" in *Flotte e commercio greco, cartaginese ed etrusco* (Atti Convegno Ravello 1987) (not yet available to me); id. in E. Campanile (ed.), *Alle origini di Roma* (Pisa 1988) 82-84.

wall of the Capitolium on the Ides of September (Cincius *ap.* Livy 7.3.5). In a recent study C. Ampolo has listed 11 such documents mentioned by Roman historians and antiquarians, all of which can be regarded as genuine archaic texts of the 6th and 5th c.[63]

Public documents are also mentioned in the legendary accounts of the early kings, however, and such references may be thought to undermine the general veracity of the annalistic sources on this question.[64] For example Romulus' treaty with Veii was engraved on stelai, according to Dionysius of Halicarnassus (2.55.6); and the Sabines allegedly set up pillars in temples which bore the terms of their treaty with Tarquinius Priscus (Dion. Hal. 3.33.1). But it should be noted that Dionysius of Halicarnassus does not claim to have seen these inscriptions, nor does he say that they survived into the historical period. Indeed in 3.36.4 he observes that the oak boards on which Ancus Marcius had inscribed the priestly ordinances of Numa had long since perished.

Even so it is not necessary to assume that all these alleged documents of the early monarchic period were annalistic fabrications; some of them could have been based on reality. Here it is instructive to consider two further instances of this type: the epitaph of Hostus Hostilius and Romulus' *Res Gestae*. According to Dionysius of Halicarnassus, Hostus Hostilius was a companion of Romulus and the grandfather of Tullus Hostilius. On his death he was buried "in the principal part of the Forum and honoured with a monument and an inscription testifying to his valour" (Dion. Hal. 3.1.2). Dionysius also tells us that Romulus, after his second triumph, dedicated a bronze quadriga to Vulcan, "and

---

63 C. Ampolo, "La storiografia su Roma arcaica e i documenti," in E. Gabba (ed.), *Tria Corda: scritti in onore di Arnaldo Momigliano* (Como 1983) 9-26, especially 15-16; cf. id. in *Popoli e civiltà dell'Italia antica* (Roma 1986) 420-22. The list is as follows: (1) The regulations for the shrine of Diana on the Aventine, set up by Servius Tullius (Dion. Hal. 4.26.5); (2) The treaty with Gabii preserved in the temple of Semo Sancus (Dion. Hal. 4.58.4); (3) The first treaty with Carthage (Polyb. 3.22); (4) The treaty of Sp. Cassius (Cicero, *Balb.* 53; Dion. Hal. 6.95); (5) The *lex Icilia de Aventino publicando* (Dion. Hal. 10.32.4); (6) The treaty with Ardea (Livy 4.7.10; Dion. Hal. 11.62); (7) The inscription on the corslet of Lars Tolumnius, dedicated by Cornelius Cossus in 426 (Livy 4.20.7); (8) The *lex Furia Pinaria* (Varro *ap.* Macrobius, *Sat.* 1.13.21); (9) The law about the Praetor Maximus and the *clavus annalis* (Livy 7.3.5); (10) The inscription recording the dedication of a statue to Ceres from the property of Sp. Cassius (Livy 2.41.10); (11) The inscription in Greek characters set up at the Volcanal (Dion. Hal. 2.54.2; 3.1.2; and see further below).

64 For discussion of this material see J. Poucet (supra n.5) 294 ff.

near it set up a statue of himself and an inscription in Greek characters setting forth his deeds" (Dion. Hal. 2.54.2).

Recent studies seem to have confirmed what one might have suspected in any case, namely that these 2 passages are describing a single monument.[65] It has also been shown that another passage of Dionysius of Halicarnassus, concerning the tomb of Faustulus, the foster-father of Romulus and Remus, is yet a third description of the same monumental complex. This conclusion follows from F. Coarelli's studies of the topography and history of the Comitium, and the identification, which appears to be certain, of the sanctuary of the *Niger Lapis* with the Volcanal.[66] Confirmation is provided by an entry in Festus (p.184L s.v. *Niger lapis*) which, though fragmentary, clearly offers 3 alternative explanations of the site, associating it either with Romulus, Faustulus, or Hostus Hostilius:

Niger lapis in comitio locum funestum significat, ut ali, Romuli morti destinatum, sed non usu ob in... <Fau>stulum nutri<cium eius, ut ali dicunt, Hos>tilium avum Tu<lli Hostili Romanorum regis>, cuius familiae...

From this it follows that the famous inscribed cippus, unearthed by Boni in 1899 beneath the area of black paving in the Comitium, is none other than the inscription twice referred to by Dionysius of Halicarnassus, and identified by him as Romulus' *Res Gestae* in the one place and as the epitaph of Hostus Hostilius in the other.

The identification prompts both positive and negative comments. First, it is a salutary reminder that we should not glibly dismiss references to ancient documents, however unlikely they may look, as mere 'inventions' or 'analistic fictions'. We have in this instance clear proof that Dionysius of Halicarnassus was referring to a genuine archaic inscription, which not only survived on public display until the late republic, but is at least partially still extant. What is disturbing is that Dionysius' sources[67] should have been so grossly mistaken in their

---

65   C. Ampolo (supra n.63) 19 ff.; F. Coarelli, *PP* 32 (1977) 215 ff.; id., *Il foro romano: periodo arcaico* (Roma 1983) 167 ff.

66   F. Coarelli, ibid.

67   We can be fairly confident that it was his sources, not Dionysius himself. The sanctuary was partially demolished in the time of Sulla; the inscription, which until then had been visible to passers by, was truncated; and the whole monument covered by a basalt paving (the *Niger Lapis*). Whether the surviving part of the inscription was subsequently accessible in the time of Augustus, and whether Dionysius himself would have been able to see it (which is not necessarily the same thing), we cannot know. In

interpretation of the text and its monumental setting. The inscription on the Forum cippus is extremely obscure; but if anything is certain about the text, it is that it contains neither Romulus' *Res Gestae* nor an honorific epitaph of Hostus Hostilius.[68]

The implication must be that the sources of Dionysius of Halicarnassus were unable to make sense of the inscription, and that their interpretation of it was a guess based on their notion of the monument as a whole. For some reason they believed that the site was a death-laden spot (*locus funestus*) — either a tomb or a place associated with the death of Romulus.[69] Its location in the centre of the city probably helped to suggest a connection with the founder,[70] although it is possible, as Coarelli has suggested, that the connection of the Volcanal with Romulus is very ancient, and goes back to the time when the sanctuary was first founded at the beginning of the 6th c.[71] If so, the interpretation of the inscription offered by the sources of Dionysius, while still a guess, was not entirely arbitrary.[72]

It will not come as a surprise to anyone who has studied the inscription that Romans of the 1st c. B.C. were unable to understand it. Indeed, as M. Cristofani has recently commented, one wonders whether it was intelligible even at the time when it was first exhibited in the early 6th c.[73] A serious problem might seem to arise here. If Romans of the

---

any event, it is certain that Dionysius' knowledge of the site was second-hand, because he himself does not seem to have realised that the tomb of Faustulus, the triumphal inscription of Romulus, and the tomb of Hostus Hostilius were one and the same monument.

68 Recent discussions of the Forum cippus include R. E. A. Palmer, *The king and the comitium* (Historia Einzelschrift 11, Wiesbaden 1969); G. Dumézil, *Mariages indo-européens à Rome* (Paris 1979) 259-93; F. Coarelli, *Il foro romano* 1 (supra n.65) 178-88; R. Wachter, *Altlateinischer Inschriften* (Bern 1987) 66-69.

69 Festus p.184 L says it was "appointed for the death of Romulus" (*Romuli morti destinatum*), whatever that may mean. On the phrase see E. Pais, *Ancient legends of Roman history* (London 1906) 281 n.16; Ampolo (supra n.63) 21 n.32.

70 Ampolo (supra n.63) 24 n.40; cf. T. J. Cornell, "Gründer" in *Reallexikon für Antike und Christentum* 12 (1983) 1107-45, especially 1139 ff.

71 Coarelli (supra n.65) 237-38; id., *Il foro romano* (supra n.65) 197-99.

72 As for the alternative interpretations, the nearby presence of the Curia Hostilia may have suggested a connection with Hostus Hostilius; the Faustulus version remains mysterious. See further in Ampolo (supra n.63) 24-25.

73 Cristofani (supra n.30) 16; 58-59.

late republic were incapable of understanding the Forum cippus, can we have any confidence in their reports of texts such as the first treaty with Carthage, the *lex Furia Pinaria*, or the *Foedus Cassianum*?

The difficulty becomes less serious when we consider the dating of the texts. The latest assessment of the stratigraphic evidence from the Comitium indicates that the inscribed cippus belongs to a layer dating to the beginning of the 6th c. — between 600 and 580.[74] But most of the documents mentioned in our sources are considerably later. The earliest of the ones with a realistic claim to be what they are said to be is the inscription set up by Servius Tullius in the Temple of Aventine Diana. The date of Servius Tullius is uncertain (the traditional dates for the kings are impossible and should on no account be relied upon), but he is probably to be placed in the second half of the 6th c. — that is, at least 50 years later than the Forum cippus. Although Dionysius of Halicarnassus says that the Aventine inscription survived down to his own day, he does not quote the text[75] but merely paraphrases its contents: it set out regulations governing relations between cities, and other matters concerning the performance of the festival and the assembly, and it listed the names of the cities taking part. The text was written in "letters which Greece used in ancient times." It could be that Dionysius or his informants were able to read the names, but that their understanding of the rest was based at least in part on guesswork. But the similarity of the reported contents of this document to those of the dedicatory inscription for the shrine of Diana at Aricia, which was copied by the Elder Cato and probably dates from the same period,[76] is remarkable and must tell in favour of the basic authenticity of Dionysius' version.

The earliest inscriptions to be quoted by our surviving sources are the treaty with Carthage and the *Foedus Cassianum*, dating from the years immediately before and after 500. This is around a century later than the Forum cippus, and it is reasonable to suppose that the art and sophistication of carving inscriptions had developed considerably in the meantime. The early 5th-c. Lapis Satricanus, with its beautifully clear lettering, gives an idea of what was possible on stone by this date; and the dedication to Castor and Pollux from Lavinium (late 6th c.) is perhaps an even better guide, since it, like the Carthage treaty and the *Foedus Cassianum*, was engraved on bronze.

---

74   Coarelli (supra n.65).
75   Nor does any other source. The quotation in Festus 164L, if it is from the Servian inscription (which is not certain), consists of just one word.
76   Cato, *Origines* 2.28 Chassignet (= fr. 58 Peter).

The evidence, taken together, suggests that the practice of inscribing public documents and displaying them in public was well established in archaic Rome; moreover, it indicates that a substantial number of archaic inscriptions survived and were still visible in the classical period. Livy's statement that all public and private records were destroyed by the Gauls in 390 (6.1) is certainly incorrect, and is probably based on a misconceived notion of the real extent of documentation in early Rome. The damage caused by the Gallic sack was probably exaggerated in the Roman tradition: the surprising thing is not that so many ancient records, buildings, monuments and relics were destroyed, but rather that so many of them survived.[77] Livy also states that "letters were few and scarce at that time" (*parvae et rarae per eadem tempora litterae fuere*), but it has to be said, first, that Livy was not necessarily an expert on such matters,[78] and secondly that by "letters" he almost certainly meant not writing as such, but rather literature, and in particular historical books.[79]

Finally, it is certain that archaic documents were consulted and used by historians and antiquarians in the 2nd and 1st c. These must have included, in addition to laws and treaties, lists of magistrates, preserved in a variety of sources, as Livy's reference to Licinius Macer and the *libri lintei* makes clear,[80] and other kinds of archival material. The *Annales Maximi* certainly went back to 400, and possibly covered the whole of the 5th c. The record of such matters as food shortages and famines in the 5th c. seems to be based on a documentary record, and the curious pattern of military campaigns during the same period is best explained in the same way.[81]

This discussion prompts the conclusion that a considerable body of archaic documents survived to the time of the late republic, and this in turn suggests that writing had an important and prominent part in the public life of Rome in the late 6th and 5th c. It is against this background that we can begin to understand the publication of the most im-

---

77 G. De Sanctis, *Storia dei Romani* I[2] (Firenze 1956) 5; cf. my comments in *CAH* VII[2].2, 308.

78 As I argued in *Roma arcaica e le recenti scoperte archeologiche* (Giornate di studio in onore di U. Coli, Milano 1980) 24 ff.

79 Thus, rightly, in my opinion, Ampolo (supra n.63) 14 n.15, citing E. Ciaceri, *Le origini di Roma* (Milano 1937) 56-57.

80 Livy 4.7.10; 23.1; 20.5 (= Licinius Macer frgs. 13-15P). Cf. R. M. Ogilvie, "Livy, Licinius Macer and the libri lintei," *JRS* 48 (1958) 40-46.

81 The pattern of warfare in the 5th c. as presented by the sources is discussed by me in *CAH* VII[2].2, 288-94.

portant of all archaic Roman documents, the 5th-c. law code known as
the Twelve Tables. The Tables, which were put together by a commission of 10 men around 450, are known to us through a large number of
quotations and references. Although some are in modernised language,
there can be little serious doubt about the authenticity of the surviving
fragments, or about the date of the legislation. The Twelve Tables are
bound to create a problem for the minimalist view, which holds that
archaic Rome was virtually illiterate and had no use for the written
word. Harris attempts to avoid the difficulty by casting a vague shad-
ow of doubt over the Twelve Tables, although he does not make his
position very clear on the question of their date and authenticity.[82]
Secondly, he attempts rather implausibly to suggest that the purpose
of the codification was to reinforce the rule of the patricians and to
strengthen their control of the law. His argument seems to be that since
hardly anyone could read, the effect of writing down the laws would be
to make them mysterious and inaccessible to the majority of citizens. It
hardly needs to be said that this thesis begs the question; it also
obliges Harris to contend, against the unanimous verdict of the sources,
that the Twelve Tables were not displayed in public. More convincing
arguments than these will be needed to persuade readers to abandon the
traditional view, that the Twelve Tables were a published document of
c.450 whose purpose was to fix the law in writing and to make it public.

Conclusions

The whole subject of literacy in central Italy during the archaic period requires further study. I have been able to deal only superficially
with some of the issues raised by this complicated question. My aim
has been simply to draw attention to aspects of the evidence which are
quantitatively negligible but which should not for that reason be
ignored or casually dismissed. It is possible that the merest scraps of
surviving material point to a range of uses for the written word in public

---

82   Harris 152-53. He speaks of the "implausibility" of a 5th-c. date for the
transmitted fragments and of the "apocryphal matter" included in
ancient accounts of the decemvirate; then, "we may suspect that the date
of the Tables was ... set too early;" on the other hand "it seems reasonable
to suppose that there was indeed a great giving of laws at some date in the
age before 390;" furthermore — a rather surprising suggestion, this, in
view of the complete lack of evidence and Harris' general scepticism —
"a number of other Latin and Etruscan cities are likely to have done
something similar in the same general period" [sc., presumably, the 5th
c.].

and private life that are not otherwise represented in our evidence. The precise significance of these uses, and their implications for the extent of literacy in the society of archaic Italy, I leave to others who are more competent than I to interpret them and to carry out the further research that is necessary. My intention has been simply to argue that the minimalist view is unacceptable. The uses of literacy in archaic Etruria and Latium were not confined to the contexts indicated by the bulk of the surviving evidence. It was not simply a matter of a few aristocrats reaching for their styluses whenever it was time for a funeral. But this caricature, ludicrous though it is, seems to be the sum total of what some modern studies are prepared to admit.

The main point is that the surviving epigraphic evidence is unrepresentative, biased and misleading. These limitations and distortions cannot be overlooked by the historian, who must engage in a constant struggle to break free of the tyranny of the evidence, and to escape from the confines of what happens to survive. The great weakness of W. V. Harris' book, I fear, is that it does not attempt to go beyond the evidence.[83]

University College, London

---

83   In the preparation of this paper I was unable to take account of M. Pandolfini and A. L. Prosdocimi, *Alfabetari e insegnamento della scrittura in Etruria e nell'Italia antica* (Firenze 1990), which has not been available to me. I am grateful to Maurizio Harari for this reference and for other helpful suggestions. I should also like to thank Michael Crawford and Rosalind Thomas, who read and commented upon an earlier draft of this paper.

Writing and religion: *Ancient Literacy* and the function of the written word in Roman religion

Question: What was the rôle of writing in Graeco-Roman paganism?

Mary Beard

Let us leave aside, for a while, our scholarly caution. Let us shelve our accustomed hesitation about bringing together, as a single object of research, all those wildly different cults, traditions, rituals, and beliefs that make up the 'paganism' of the Roman empire.[1] It is, after all, a striking virtue of William Harris' *Ancient literacy* to have taken a broad sweep, to have offered general synthetic arguments about central issues that normally remain obscured in a mass of detail. Let us follow up the implications of his arguments and ask how convincing a view Harris offers of the place of writing within pagan religious traditions; and, in particular, how convincing a context he outlines for the archaeological and epigraphic traces of that writing, which survive in such enormous quantity throughout the Roman world.

---

1   In what follows I have worked with a broad definition of Graeco-Roman paganism, concentrating on the traditional 'civic' cults of the Roman empire (including the cults of the Greek east — hence Graeco-Roman). I am confident that such a broad approach can be useful, despite the obvious differences between all the various cults of the different regions of the empire. In fact, I suspect that those differences are sometimes unhelpfully exaggerated — particularly in relation to the uses of writing. The province of Britain and its Roman(o-Celtic) cults, for example, may seem one of the areas of the empire least touched by a literate tradition, constituting a clear contrast with the Greek east and its emphasis on written forms both in cult and cultural life. But the discovery of numerous written curse-tablets at sites in Britain should warn us against constructing too sharp a contrast even here. (See for example R. Tomlin and D. Walker, *The Temple of Sulis Minerva* 2: *The finds from the sacred spring* [Oxford 1988], with an important review by J. Reynolds and T. Volk in *Britannia* 21 [1990] esp.379-82.)
I have used the Christianizing terms 'pagans' and 'paganism' throughout, for the sake of convenience, and with only a little sense of embarrassment. I have found 'pagans', in particular, useful for being gender unspecific, incorporating men and/or women.

Harris draws a sharp contrast between the functions of writing in Christianity and its functions in pagan religion.[2] That contrast is not, of course, a new insight. The 'religion of the book', the 'religion of the orthodox word', has often been seen in opposition to the 'text-free', constantly heterodox world of paganism. The opposition is an almost inevitable one — emerging directly from the term 'paganism' itself, a catch-all category for everything that is *not* (Judaeo-)Christian. But Harris brings fresh observations to support the familiar contrast. He is not only concerned with the foundations of Christianity, rooted in "a group of virtually unchangeable texts". In fact, as he notes, "writing and the book" were *not* "the main means of Christian propaganda in the first three centuries". More important for Harris is the gradual development of a more general "habit of attachment to the written word" within the early Christian communities. "Even an outsider might know that they were devoted to sacred books" — not just the scriptural texts themselves, but acts of the martyrs, learned biblical commentaries, and the letters which were the necessary means of maintaining contact and coherence between isolated groups of the like-minded. The written word, he argues, gained in Christianity a new *authority*.

Harris recognizes some overlap with pagan traditions of writing. He admits that the Christian preoccupation with texts was at least partly encouraged by "a certain Graeco-Roman tradition of awe for what was written down"; and he admits that by the 3rd c. A.D. "pagan religion also seems to have been making greater use of writing", so that the conflict between Christians and pagans came to be played out in a dazzling proliferation of written polemic. Yet, even allowing such areas of continuity, he still appears to regard traditional paganism as a set of religions in which writing was essentially peripheral. In his view, it performed some specific, often quite prominent, functions: it recorded religious dedications, magical spells, and curses; it preserved the correct text of prayers; it displayed religious law, sacred rules, and sometimes the texts of oracles; it provided among intellectual circles a vehicle for theological debate. But it never took the central, defining rôle that it came to hold within Christianity. "Ordinary people had no strong need to write or even to read in order to express their religious feelings or find out about the divine world. Visiting a shrine or uttering a prayer did not require one to read, nor did looking at a household

---

2   See especially Harris 218-21 and 298-306 (all the direct quotations from Harris in this and the next paragraph are drawn from these pages).

lararium or attending a festival." In paganism, writing was an optional extra.

The aim of this article is to take issue at a very general level with this, at first sight plausible, view. I want to show, first, that there was simply much more writing associated with the cults, rituals, and sanctuaries of Graeco-Roman paganism than Harris' argument implies; and, second, that writing played a central rôle in defining the nature of human relations with the divine, and indeed the nature of pagan deities themselves. I am not by this trying to suggest that there was no difference between the rôle of the written tradition within paganism and its rôle in early Christianity. My argument, rather, is that the contrast between paganism and Christianity should not be framed in terms of a contrast between the *marginality* of writing on the one hand and its *centrality* on the other. In no doubt very different ways, the character of *both* paganism *and* Christianity was defined in and around a written tradition.[3]

My disagreement with Harris on the functions of writing in Roman pagan religion does not follow merely from a different selection of source-material out of the vast range of potentially relevant evidence. Although I have chosen to emphasize some groups of material that Harris has passed over with little or no comment, it should be clear that the more significant reason for our disagreement lies in a funda-mental difference of approach to the nature and function of writing at a more theoretical level. Underlying Harris' discussion is the sense that writing is to be seen primarily as a practical tool, as a record (at a distance, over time) of *spoken* language. He recognizes, of course, that there are intellectual consequences in the development of a written tradition that may transcend its original practical purpose; he recognizes also that the written word can gain an awesome authority, in itself and of itself, over and above any message that it is intended to transmit. Yet most of his arguments are still founded on the idea that the function of writing is essentially practical: hence, for example, his stress on the importance of letter-writing in early Christianity — a means of communication for scattered communities who could not *speak* together; hence also his preoccupation with estimating the number of people who were able to read and write — for what use was written

---

3   I have not explicitly considered Harris' discussion of writing within the Christian tradition. Although I suspect that the clear contrast between pagan and Judaeo-Christian uses of the written word might also be questioned from the Judaeo-Christian side, I leave that for another occasion. This article is about pagan writing.

information if the vast majority of the population simply could not understand it?[4]

My own arguments are based on a different view of the nature of the written tradition. No doubt writing in antiquity, just as today, fulfilled a wide variety of practical purposes. That is not at issue. But to see writing as constantly relegated to the rôle of a utilitarian tool must misrepresent writing's potential independence from the spoken word, from the 'message' or from 'information'. A written text can have many, more important, functions to fulfil than merely to record the traces of a *voice* — whether human or divine. When discussing the set of priestly inscriptions at Rome known as the *Arval Acta*, I grouped those functions together under the broad term 'symbolic'.[5] That now seems to me an inadequate, unfortunately vague, shorthand. I would like to start to explore in the present article more precisely what those 'symbolic' functions might be — to show, for example, how writing could act to define the relationship between an individual and the divine; to constitute an identity for those who, like the gods, could not, after all, actually speak; and to hierarchize religious power.

The operation of most of these functions did not depend on a wide-scale ability to read and write. That is not to say that our estimates of levels of literacy make no difference at all to our understanding of the rôle of writing in the religions of the Roman empire. Of course, a world in which writing, religious or otherwise, can be used and actively understood only by a small group of the (largely male) élite is very different from a world of mass literacy; the functions of writing are

---

4   See Harris 25-42. Although he recognizes, and discusses, various *consequences* (especially political consequences) of literacy, his approach is essentially 'task-orientated'. This is strikingly clear in his list (pp.26-27) of the ancient uses of writing, which "probably covers the great majority of what was written down in antiquity": 42 items, each introduced by an active verb, "to indicate", "to label", "to announce", "to record", "to transmit", etc.

5   M. Beard, "Writing and ritual. A study of diversity and expansion in the Arval Acta," *PBSR* 53 (1985) 114-62. My attempts to be more specific proved to be rather tentative: I talked, for example, of the practice of writing as a means of 'validating' the ritual activity of the priests, while at the same time (disingenuously) admitting that "symbolic functions may seem to defy precision" (p.147). See also J. Scheid, *Romulus et ses Frères: le collège des frères Arvales, modèle du culte public dans la Rome des empereurs* (BEFAR 275, Roma 1990) 66-72. The same (understandable) vagueness is expressed by C. Roueché, *Aphrodisias in late antiquity* (JRS Monograph 5, London 1989) xxiii.

necessarily and obviously affected by the size and composition of the readership group. Nevertheless, the character of a religious system can still be fundamentally determined by writing and by a 'literate mentality', even in situations where very few of the practitioners of that religion are themselves literate. The simple fact, for example, that writing becomes used, even by a tiny minority, to define the calendar of rituals or sacred law inevitably changes the nature of the religion concerned. It leads, as I shall show, to a complexity in religious organisation, to literate modes of understanding human relations with the gods, that implicate and determine the religious experience of the non-literate as well as the literate. To put it simply, once a small group of individuals has chosen to use writing to define religious practice, custom or 'truth', the previous 'oral' character of that religion is irrevocably changed. Seen in this light, the number of literates within a religious community is a secondary issue.[6]

Visible writing

"Everything there will delight you, and you can also find something to read. You can study the numerous inscriptions in honour of the spring (*fons*) and of the god which many hands have written on every pillar and wall. Most of them you will admire, but some will make you laugh — though I know you are really too charitable to laugh at any of them."[7]

So Pliny ends his long description of the shrine of the god Clitumnus, in its idyllic setting near Spoletum (Spoleto) in Umbria north of Rome: after the gushing spring, the glassy pool, the trees clear-reflected in the water, after the cult statue of the god dressed in the red-bordered toga of a magistrate, the written oracles (*sortes*) and the subsidiary shrines set round the main centre, he comes finally to the fabric of the principal temple itself: it is covered apparently, ceiling to floor, with the writing of the faithful — sometimes impressive, sometimes (he suggests) laughably naïve expressions of devotion to the god and his cult.

---

6   This should not be taken as an expression of disagreement with Harris over levels of literacy. I feel fairly confident (for what my confidence is worth!) that his estimates are broadly correct.

   Behind much of my approach in this article lies a very broadly Derridean view of the primacy of writing, and the determining power of the written word over the spoken. For a clear introduction to this theoretical framework, see J. Culler, *On deconstruction: theory and criticism after structuralism* (London 1983) 89-110.

7   Pliny, *Ep.* 8.8.7 (cited by Harris 219).

The purpose of this account in the epistolary autobiography of the younger Pliny, in his creative attempts at self-representation, is all too clear. The author displays himself to his readers as a man of culture, an expert in the religious traditions of rural Italy — partly setting himself above the naïve statements of simple faith, yet at the same time respectful of honest popular piety.[8] Rather more intriguing, if as historians we are to 'trust' Pliny's description, is the prominence of the writing to which he refers. We do not now know exactly what was written on these temple-walls — perhaps, we might guess, the formal records of private vows fulfilled (*VSLM*), or, more likely, the casual inscriptions and graffiti of pious visitors.[9] But, whatever its precise content, was writing of this kind normally so striking a feature of the Roman religious world? Did the written word typically bulk so large in Graeco-Roman sanctuaries? Did it commonly extend so far beyond 'official' texts of cult regulations and sacral law?

The surviving archaeological record provides some clear parallels for Pliny's picture of the shrine of Clitumnus. The inscriptions that decorated the sanctuary of Asclepius at Epidaurus, recording the names

---

8   I stress this strategic aspect of Pliny's writing, because modern historians have tended to treat the letters as transparent social *documents*. For a neat corrective, see J. Henderson, "P·L·I·N·Y·'S Letters. A Portrait of the Artist as a Figure of Style," (partly) published in *Omnibus* 4 (1982) 31-32.

9   The temple has not been excavated (the so-called Temple of Citumnus at Spoleto being a Christian building). A. N. Sherwin-White, *The letters of Pliny. A historical and social commentary* (Oxford 1966) 458, suggests that the writing may have been inscribed votive texts (arguing, from Pliny's use of the Latin *inscripta*, that he most likely had formal inscriptions in mind). Paul Veyne, on the other hand, following Merrill and Hartleben, sees them as graffiti — "sortes de proscynèmes mi-touristiques ... et mi-dévots" (in "Autour d'un commentaire de Pline le Jeune," *Latomus* 26 [1967] 723-51, esp. 738-39). He specifically argues against Sherwin-White, that "Un ex-voto antique n'est pas une sorte de satisfecit, de texte qui se suffit à lui-même; il accompagne l'objet consacré: sa place est sur la base de l'objet ou sur l'objet même et non sur les murs du temple" (p. 738). Though note that in his later article ("Titulus Praelatus: offrande, solennisation et publicité dans les ex-voto gréco-romains," *RA* 1983, 281-300), Veyne offers a much more nuanced approach to the range of inscribed and written material associated with votives, which might allow for other possibilities, lying somewhere between graffiti and formal inscriptions on the completion of a vow.

of those cured by the god, are well known.[10] So too are the remains of the temple of Mandulis at Talmis (on the southern frontiers of Egypt), where texts in red-painted letters covered the building, proclaiming the presence of 'pilgrims', their visions and their delight in the epiphany of the god.[11] But this proliferation of writing was not just a phenomenon of the major healing sanctuaries of the east Mediterranean,[12] or of the (certainly atypical) religious world of Egypt.[13] Besides the literally thousands of inscribed stone votive texts that are such a familiar part of every major epigraphic publication, there are other, often less well-known, groups of material that force us to see *writing* as a prominent element in a variety of religious sites. Consider, for example, the small shrine of Jupiter Poeninus at the Great St. Bernard Alpine pass, where more than 50 bronze plaques have been discovered, recording the vows of travellers (both Roman and native) who journeyed safely across the Alps.[14] Consider also the remains of the fountain of Apollo in Cyrene, where on the walls and roof of one

---

10   For a brief introduction to these texts, see R. MacMullen, *Paganism in the Roman empire* (New Haven 1981) 32-33. Pausanias 2.27.3 refers to inscriptions in the temple-enclosure listing the names of those healed by the god and the diseases from which they suffered (similar to the 4th- and 3rd-c. B.C. texts fully published in V. Longo, *Aretalogie nel monde greco* I [Istituto di Filologia Classica e Medioevale, Genova 1969] 63-75, nos.1-43). The standard collection of inscriptions from Epidaurus is *IG* IV^2 (nos.380-588 for dedications from the 1st-5th c. A.D.).

11   See A. D. Nock, "A vision of Mandulis Aion," *Essays in religion and the ancient world* 1 (ed. Z. Stewart) (Oxford 1972) 357-400, esp. 358-63 (= *HThR* 27 [1934] 53-104); R. Lane Fox, *Pagans and Christians* (Harmondsworth 1986) 166-67.

12   These sanctuaries have, of course, produced large amounts of epigraphic material. See, for example, *Altertümer von Pergamon* VIII.3 (Berlin 1969), *Die Inschriften des Asklepieions* (ed. C. Habicht) esp. nos.63-144; *Inscriptiones Creticae* I, XVII (ed. M. Guarducci, Roma 1935) esp. nos.8-27 (the sanctuary of Asclepius at Lebena). F. T. Van Straten, "Daikrates' Dream," *BABesch* 51 (1976) 1-38 offers a clear analysis of a large group of these inscriptions. Material from healing shrines in the west is cited by MacMullen, *Paganism* (supra n.10) 158-59.

13   Note also the famous graffiti on the colossal statue of Memnon fully published by A. and E. Bernand, *Les inscriptions grecques et latines du Colosse de Memnon* (BIFAO 31, 1960) and acutely discussed by Lane Fox (supra n.11) 166-67.

14   *InscItal* XI.1 (Roma 1932) 27-38.

underground approach-passage almost 60 graffiti, scratched in the mud, commemorate priests or visitors to the shrine.[15]

The quantity of writing visible at Graeco-Roman sanctuaries cannot, however, be judged by the surviving material alone. Much is lost. Much was, in any case, displayed on perishable material — and, although originally perhaps as impressive as a permanent record on stone, it is recoverable now only through chance references in literary texts. In a recent article, Paul Veyne has demonstrated the importance of wooden placards (*tituli*) sometimes carried in a Roman sacrificial procession, stating the reason for the sacrifice or naming the deity to whom it was offered.[16] Although none of these objects survives (except in a couple of crude images), the practice of performing a sacrifice *titulo praelato* is mentioned on several occasions by Roman writers — once, notably, in Suetonius' account of the reign of Augustus, where it is stated that "the will of more than one householder directed that his heirs should take sacrificial victims to the Capitol and carry a placard before them as they went, inscribed with an expression of their gratitude for Augustus' having been allowed to outlive the testator."[17] Veyne reasonably conjectures that many such placards may have ended up displayed (or stored) at the sanctuary where the sacrifice was performed.[18] Other placards would no doubt also have been found there, recording not the fulfilment of a sacrifice but the earlier contract of a vow. Such, maybe, were the placards that (again according to Suetonius) displayed the vows of the loyal supporters of Caligula — who, during the emperor's illness, promised *titulo proposito* to die in his place.[19]

One common literary theme certainly creates an image of Graeco-Roman sanctuaries as full of written documents in very much this form — or yet more insubstantial ones. Juvenal, for example, writes of porticoes (presumably the porticoes of temples) 'clothed' with *libelli* containing vows to the gods for recovery from illness;[20] and he refers, on another occasion, to the knees of cult statues loaded with wax — wax

---

15 G. Oliverio, "La fonte di Apollo," *Notiziario Archeologico* 4 (1927) 215-43 (= *SEG* 9 [1944] nos.254-301). Compare the similar material from Budrasc near Cyrene, *SEG* 9 (1944) nos.727-66. For further examples of writing associated with religious sites, see MacMullen (supra n.10) 31-34 (with 157-60), and Veyne ("Titulus Praelatus" supra n.9) esp. 286-92.

16 Veyne ibid.281-86.

17 Suet., *Aug.* 59.

18 Veyne ("Titulus Praelatus" supra n.9) 288-89.

19 Suet., *Cal.*14.

20 *Sat.*12, 100-1: *legitime fixis vestitur tota libellis / porticus.*

tablets, that is, bearing petitions and prayers.[21] A similar point is made by Philostratus, in a text cited by Veyne; discussing a particular statue of a god, one of the interlocutors in Philostratus' dialogue *Heroikos* talks of worshippers not only anointing the image, but also piling it up with 'sealed' vows, presumably on folded pieces of papyrus.[22] The importance of these passages lies not so much in their literal truth, but in the imaginative picture they present of religious sites and objects inextricably linked with, even swamped by, the written word. The observer of the 'real-life' sanctuaries of the Graeco-Roman world would no doubt have seen the point of Juvenal's joke, while recognizing also, at the very least, a degree of creative exaggeration. Only from time to time did image and reality literally overlap — as in Miletus in the 3rd c. B.C. when the local authorities had to take steps to prevent worshippers at the sanctuary of Apollo Delphinion from ruining the new wooden portico by affixing private dedications, pointing out that there was a specially plastered section intended to receive such objects.[23]

It would, of course, be misleading to suggest that all Graeco-Roman sanctuaries were the same in this respect, that they all made a prominent display of the written word. There were obviously immense variations between the sites that I have been discussing, and, for example, the excavated temples of Pompeii and Herculaneum — where (even allowing for the disappearance of some perishable materials)

---

21 *Sat.*10, 54-55: *ergo supervacua aut quae perniciosa petuntur / propter quae fas est genua incerare deorum.* It is possible, alternatively, that Juvenal is referring to prayers on papyrus attached to the cult statue with knobs of wax (see C. Gnilka, "Das Einwaschen der Götterbilder," *JbAC* 7 [1964] 52-53).

22 *Heroikos* p.141 (Kayser). Though note that Veyne ("Titulus Praelatus" supra n.9) is occasionally a little over optimistic in his search for references to religious writing. So, for example, he treats Tac., *Hist.*3.74 (*aramque posuit casus suos in marmore expressam*) as if it obviously referred to a *written* account of Domitian's escape from the Vitellian forces, rather than (as it is usually understood) a sculptured relief (p.292, with n.67).

23 F. Sokolowski, *Lois sacrées des cités grecques, Supplément* (Ecole Française d'Athènes, Travaux et mémoires 11, Paris 1962) 206-7, no.123. See also pp.175-76, no.107, for a similar ruling from Rhodes, referring to "statues and other dedications". I do not know of an inscription from the Roman period making this kind of provision, but in some cases, at least, earlier regulations at these sites may have remained in force.

writing seems a marginal element.[24] Nevertheless, Harris' casual admission that "shrines and temples accumulated written material"[25] must be inadequate. Supported only by a brief reference to the temple of Clitumnus, it gives no hint of the widespread proliferation of writing in sanctuary sites across the Roman empire; it offers no avenue for exploring the significance of that writing within the broader context of Graeco-Roman paganism.

Signing up for paganism

Pliny was not a typical visitor to the sanctuary of Clitumnus. He probably wandered round the temple picking out texts for his own amusement in much the same way as, say, a sophisticated Parisian might now visit a shrine deep in southern Italy, with its crude offerings and naïve accounts (sometimes touching, sometimes laughable) of miracles worked by the local saint.[26] There is nothing the matter with this. Public writing cannot control its readership. Whoever the original addressee, once written it can be read and interpreted by the scholarly, the supercilious, or the downright hostile, just as easily as by the sympathetic or the faithful. Pliny (or our Parisian) has a right to his or her own view. Nevertheless, we should not let the simple accessibility of Pliny's text blind us to the fact that other visitors would have had other reactions, other 'readings'. We cannot know for certain what these would have been. But for the vast majority of the Roman population, illiterate or at best semi-literate, the overwhelming impression would have been simply of a mass of writing. Had they stopped to look more closely, they might (or might not) have been able to pick out the name of the god, or spot a text put up for, or by, a member of their own family. We can only guess. Their reactions and interpretations have left no trace.[27]

---

24 The general barrenness of the main temples of the Vesuvian cities is striking — even allowing for their valuables having been removed by the inhabitants or plundered later. It raises questions about the pattern of distribution of dedications, votives, and written material, not just across the empire, but also within the sanctuaries of particular towns and in local regions. What kind of shrines attracted such material, and why?

25 Harris 219.

26 I have in mind here Veyne's un-selfconsciously Plinian description of the church of Saint Michael the Archangel on the Gargano peninsula in south Italy ("Titulus Praelatus" supra n.9, 292).

27 The illiterate would no doubt often have been 'helped' by official or unofficial exegetes. For their rôle at sanctuaries, see Paus.1.13.8; 1.31.5;

We know almost as little about the circumstances of the *writing* of this kind of private religious text, as about the circumstances of the *reading*. It is true, of course, that many of the surviving examples imply a particular event lying behind their composition and inscription: it is on the occasion of the pilgrim's visit to a shrine that he (normally *he*) chooses to leave his name on its wall; it is in the worst throes of an illness that the invalid makes a written record of a prayer for recovery; it is following an act of sacrifice, in fulfilment of a vow, that a votive altar is inscribed, *VSLM*. But we know almost nothing else. We do not know who actually wrote or inscribed the text — even an apparently casual graffito could be the work of a professional inscriber, or of a literate friend writing on behalf of an illiterate companion. We do not know who chose the exact words to be used in the final version — how far, that is, even illiterate customers might impose their own idiosyncratic phrasing on the scribe who wrote out their prayer; or how far the professional writers took control. We do not know with what reverence or cynicism any particular text was written, inscribed, or affixed to the temple.

All of these uncertainties make a convincing interpretation of individual inscriptions very difficult. It is next to impossible to judge the religious background and significance of any one of these normally short, private texts that were present in such quantities in many of the sanctuaries of the Roman world. This does not mean, however, that we can reach no further understanding of this proliferation of writing; that its significance is irretrievably lost in that incoherent mass of personal readings and motivations to which I have referred. For *taken as a group* these private religious texts (at least, those that survive[28]) show certain common characteristics which allow them to be assigned a place — in my view a *central* place — in the broader context of Graeco-Roman paganism. As I hope to show, this type of *group* analysis manages to escape from the uncertainties that necessarily undermine the interpretation of single texts, or small series of texts.

1.35.8, etc., with further references in MacMullen, *Paganism* (supra n.10) 156, nn.54-55.

28   It would, of course, be wrong to pretend that the surviving inscriptions are a random sample of what once existed. It is highly likely that the flimsier, less permanent texts (those, for example, written on papyrus) had a different character, and would need to be understood in a rather different way. These probable variants indicate that the analysis I am presenting here is by no means complete; yet they do not, in my view, undermine my conclusions.

The most striking feature of these private religious inscriptions is their resolute insistence on *naming*. The scratched graffiti of 'pilgrims', like those at the fountain of Apollo at Cyrene, almost invariably *name* their subject.[29] The great mass of inscribed votive texts foreground the *name* of the dedicator and that of the deity. Modern studies may, admittedly, be more interested in those inscriptions which appear to offer some background information on the circumstances of the vow: the theft of a ring, sudden blindness, a dangerous journey by sea, and all the other narratives of personal disaster (or near disaster) that lie behind these religious dedications.[30] But the overwhelming majority of surviving votive texts are entirely silent on such narrative detail — recording only the names of the human and deity concerned, and the simple fact of the fulfilment of the vow (*VSLM*). Even where the presence of a worshipper at a shrine is recorded by some *bodily* trace (commonly the scratched outline or moulded impression of a foot), it is regularly supplemented by a *written name* alongside.[31] *Presence* is fully defined only by *naming*.

This habit of naming might seem, at first sight, unsurprising. After all, the favoured locations of modern graffiti (the telephone kiosk and the public lavatory) are usually plastered with names. Are not graffiti, and all those other forms of informal, individualistic public writing, primarily and simply *about naming* — about inscribing the distinguishing mark of one's own personal identity into the public, visible sphere? In part, no doubt, yes. But a religious sanctuary is not just 'any place', the ancient equivalent of a telephone booth or bus shelter. We still have to ask precisely what rôle that insistence on writing and naming played within the complex world of Graeco-Roman paganism. We still have to recognize that more might be at stake, in that context, than a simple, self-evident "Kilroy-was-here" type of habit. Naming, as it appears in pagan shrines, is not a universal religious practice. Compare, for example, one of the favoured formulae on Christian dedications of late antiquity — actively suppressing the

---

29 These graffiti are often very fragmentary. For relatively complete examples see Oliverio (supra n.15) nos.35-36, 40 (= *SEG* 9 [1944] nos.274-75 and 278).

30 See for example *ILS* 3135, 3280, 3847, 4730.

31 For the latest discussion (with bibliography) see K. M. D. Dunbabin, "*Ipsa deae vestigia* ... Footprints divine and human in Graeco-Roman monuments," *JRA* 3 (1990) 85-109.

name of the dedicant, with the phrase "this is a prayer for one whose name is known to God".[32] What underlies this difference?

This habit of naming played, in my view, a central rôle in defining the place of the individual within traditional paganism; in asserting his or her incorporation within the amalgam of rituals, practices and 'truths' that made up ancient civic cult. We tend to take the idea of 'membership' of Graeco-Roman paganism very much (perhaps too much) for granted. We assume that to be born into a pagan community was, at the same time, to be born into and become part of the pagan religious traditions of that community; we assume that 'membership' of paganism was somehow inevitable — only to be shelved by some clear, public and active display of rejection of traditional gods and rituals. At one level, those assumptions are obviously true. There was no particular ritual of initiation associated with traditional civic cults.[33] There was no special procedure for 'opting in'. Nevertheless, the absence of a defined process of initiation does not mean that there was no perceived need within pagan cult for an individual's incorporation into the religious system to be marked and demonstrated. A large part of that demonstration, of course, was found in *practice*: 'membership' of paganism was asserted in the performance of sacrifice, in the sponsor-ship of festivals, in the consultation of pagan oracles, in the uttering of prayers, and so forth. But practice, even if constantly repeated, was necessarily impermanent. It was in the indelible, inscribed definition of one's relations with the gods, it was in the fixed written record of one's engagement in ritual, that the idea of 'membership', of 'belonging' to the pagan community could most clearly and permanently be defined. It was, significantly, this permanence of definition that the emperor Decius used in his persecution of the Christians. For he demanded written, witnessed certificates attesting that individual men and women had carried out pagan sacrifice. This was not just a reflection of

---

32 See for example R. Cormack, *The Byzantine eye: studies in art and patronage* (London 1989) study 1, p.25 (= *BSA* 64 [1969] 25). I am conscious of having made the modern practice of graffiti seem rather too unproblematic. Of course, much is at stake in exactly what is written, by whom, and where — one classic case, for example, being Byron's inscription of himself onto the temple at Sounion, a graffito that has itself become a tourist attraction.

33 Perhaps the closest approximation to such rituals of initiation were the rituals associated with the attainment of manhood in many city-states; but even these are not a marker of membership in a religion, so much as the attainment of a particular age and a whole range of civic, political, social, and no doubt religious rights and obligations.

the Roman 'bureaucratic habit', in operation here as an arm of persecution. It was a recognition that pagan practice could only be authoritatively defined (and, for Decius' purposes, tested) when converted into the written word.[34]

The idea of a permanent assertion of 'membership' helps us to understand the character of the vast majority of Roman votive inscriptions, which are so surprisingly reticent on the particular circumstances of the vow fulfilled. The underlying point of these texts was not (like perhaps those inscriptions that made Pliny smile) to record that yesterday you had performed a sacrifice because this or that god or goddess had miraculously found your lost coat. It was rather to make a permanent statement of your own (enduring) position in relation to a deity — a relationship that went much further than the particular needs of a particular occasion. Inscribed votive texts enacted that crucial conversion of an *occasional* sacrifice into a *permanent* relationship.[35]

In these terms, the proliferation of private religious texts at Graeco-Roman sanctuaries can be understood as a central element in traditional paganism, not as an 'optional extra'. Written records, with their insistence on naming, served as a marker of the individual's permanent place in relation to the gods or a particular god, as a symbol of active 'membership' of the pagan community. I am not arguing that this was the only way that pagans could make that assertion of 'belonging'. Nor am I suggesting that those religions with a carefully defined, or 'initiated', membership-group never encouraged the display of the names of the faithful; of course they did, but for rather different reasons. I am simply arguing that writing could form a symbolic defining centre of the individual's place in pagan traditions. Much of this kind of writing may very rarely have been read; and much of it was no doubt written on behalf of illiterates who could not even decode the simple texts they had commissioned and paid for. In this context, the act of reading was of secondary importance — lying far behind the symbolic power of the written word, in its own (w)rite.

---

34   For texts and full discussion, see J. R. Knipfing, "The libelli of the Decian persecution," *HThR* 16 (1923) 345-90, and P. Keresztes, "The Decian libelli and contemporary literature," *Latomus* 34 (1975) 761-81, with (more briefly) W. H. C. Frend, *Martyrdom and persecution in the early Church* (Oxford 1965) 406-10, and Lane Fox (supra n.11) 455-57.

35   The 'fixing' of a particular deity is also at issue here; the written text served as a permanent mark not only of the position of the worshipper, but also of the identity of an individual god or goddess, out of the vast range of options represented by polytheism.

The written word of the gods

The identity, will, and nature of the pagan gods themselves could also be defined in writing. So far I have discussed only the problems of negotiating the rôle and engagement of *human* participants in the set of reciprocal relations between men and women, on the one hand, and the gods on the other; I have stressed the problems of establishing and defining a place for the individual within traditional paganism. The 'place' of the gods, those collectively-constructed representations of more-than-human power, was equally problematic, and was also protected by means of the written word.

Traditional pagan deities intervened directly in human life. They 'spoke' to men and women in dreams, or as mysterious disembodied voices audible (at least to the chosen few) at times of crisis, or, most notoriously, as spoken oracles. The utterances of the Pythia at Delphi are the best known — the priestess who became, in her religious trance, the very mouthpiece of the god Apollo, a vessel through which his words were transmitted to the world. But Apollo and other gods 'spoke' also at a variety of different oracular shrines — at Claros, for example, and Didyma and Dodona.[36] Modern analysis has tended to privilege these direct, 'spoken', oracular utterances as the most authentic form of communication from the divine. It is well recognized that such oracles were often committed to writing, and that it was often as written texts that they won widespread popular appeal. It is recognized also that there were some oracles that existed only in written form — such as the famous Sibylline books at Rome, "so authoritative" (Harris says) "that it was natural to use them, in 44, in a revolutionary attempt to make Caesar into a king".[37] But what counted most, it is generally assumed, was the immediate, direct *voice* of the god.

I hope to show that the written word played an equally important, sometimes more important, part in defining the gods' relations with individuals and communities in the pagan world. I am not denying the

---

36   The voice of the god was mediated in various ways. At Dodona (whose heyday was in the pre-Roman period) Zeus 'spoke' on different occasions and at different periods through a divine oak tree, sacred doves, even through the murmuring of a sacred fountain. For these various means, see H. W. Parke, *The oracles of Zeus* (Oxford 1967). More generally, see H. W. Parke, *The oracles of Apollo in Asia Minor* (London and Sydney 1985), and Lane Fox (supra n.11) 168-261.

37   Harris 219 (with 154).

obvious power of the *audible* word. But I am arguing that written oracles and oracular responses had a significance that went far beyond the generalized sense of 'solemnity' and 'awe' that Harris envisages. The word of the gods could be displayed, perceived, and understood in written terms. In some cases, communication between humans and the divine was conducted entirely in writing. Writing, in other words, *constituted* those relations between pagans and their gods.

An ancient city which had sent a group of ambassadors to consult an oracle on some matter of public business would often, on the embassy's return, inscribe a text of the oracular response. This practice is not, perhaps, surprising. It was, after all, a means of honouring the service of the ambassadors themselves, as well as providing evidence that the appointed task of consulting the god had been duly carried out — and displaying the result of that consultation. The oracular text, however, was more than a document of public information; it was more, even, than a permanent written validation of the spoken word of the god. For, among a community where few people would have the opportunity themselves to travel to distant oracular shrines, the text itself could *become* the word of god. No doubt it did not always gain that elevated status. In some cases, and for some people, we must imagine that such writing remained a secondary representation of the original divine voice. But in other cases it is clear that the text was effectively emancipated from the spoken utterance of the deity; it *was* the word of the god.[38]

One of the most striking examples of this emancipation of the written word is found in the Lycian city of Oenoanda, in a 3rd-c. inscription of an oracle of Apollo from Claros. As Louis Robert demonstrated, the relations of the various cities of Asia Minor with the Clarian oracle were publicly displayed in written form: the cities which consulted the god put up inscriptions all around the oracular shrine itself, giving details of their delegates' visits — the names of the chief

---

38 Harris 39 recognizes that "since early in the history of writing the gods have been imagined as expressing their authority by means of the written word"; but he hardly develops this observation. In fact, he implies that the most important aspect of the gods' writing is the (political and religious) authority of the gods' human intermediaries: "what this means is that men who claimed religious authority employed the reality or image of the written word to enhance their authority". I hope to show that (notwithstanding this important human element in the writing of the gods) writing and the identity of the divine itself could be crucially interlinked.

ambassadors, of the children who made up the accompanying choirs, and so forth — while the god's response to the embassy was later committed to stone back in their home city.[39] The text at Oenoanda is probably the result of a private (rather than an 'official', civic) enquiry put to the Clarian oracle: "what is the nature of god?". The response, or a version of it (six lines of [predictably] enigmatic hexameters), was inscribed high up on the city wall, on a block of masonry whose exposed face had been roughly reworked into the shape of an altar. The exact position of this text was crucial. It was sited so that the first rays of the morning sun brightly illuminated it. The written word of the god, that is, was seen as if under a natural spotlight, the object of brilliant display. It also appears to have become the object of cult. For about a metre below the inscribed text, again built into the city wall, a certain Chromastis dedicated an altar to the Most High God — and on the altar there stood, it seems, a lamp burning in honour of the deity.[40] It is inconceivable that this dedication was unrelated to the written text directly above it. What exactly was it that was being honoured? Writing and the nature of divinity itself had begun to merge.

Some oracles, in fact, had no spoken register at all; they replied only in writing. Harris refers to the written Sibylline books at Rome, a collection of Greek oracular texts kept in the charge of the *Quindecimviri sacris faciundis* (the priesthood of the Fifteen), and consulted (we do not know exactly how) after a prodigy or in times of crisis.[41] Even for the Romans, the ultimate origin of these books in the *oral* prophecy of a Sibyl was lost in the mists of prehistory; by the time of their (mythical) introduction to Rome, in the reign of Tarquin, they were already in written form.[42] Other written oracles had not even that

---

39 See J. and L. Robert, *Claros I. Décrets hellénistiques* (Paris 1989) 1-6 and, for an analysis of some individual texts, L. Robert, "Les inscriptions" in J. Des Gagniers *et al.*, *Laodicée du Lycos: le nymphée* (Quebec and Paris 1969) esp. 298-305. For an overview, see Parke, *The oracles of Apollo* (supra n.36) 112-70, and Lane Fox (supra n.11) 171-80.

40 A. S. Hall, "The Klarian oracle at Oenoanda," *ZPE* 32 (1978) 263-68, citing earlier material, notably L. Robert, "Un oracle gravé à Oenoanda," *CRAI* 1971, 597-619.

41 See above n.37, with H. W. Parke, *Sibyls and sibylline prophecy in classical antiquity* (London and New York 1988) 136-51, 190-215.

42 Dion.Hal., *AntRom* 4.62.1-6, for the story of the old woman who sold the books to Tarquin: after the king had refused her first offer of 9 books, she burnt 3 without changing the price; when she had burnt 3 more, Tarquin bought the last 3 for the price of the original 9.

faint trace of a spoken past. The oracles (*sortes*) of Fortuna at Praeneste existed only as written characters inscribed on pieces of wood. The story went, as reported by Cicero, that they had been discovered by a certain Numerius Suffustius: obeying instructions given to him in a dream, despite the disbelief of his fellow-citizens, he miraculously split open a solid flint rock and found the written texts inside. These were then hidden in a holy well; and when a query was put to the oracle, a young (illiterate) boy was sent down into the well to select a text at random and offer it as the oracular response.[43] Cicero, in the second book of his *De divinatione*, is highly sceptical of this procedure; and Harris seems to follow Cicero's view, that, by the late republic "only the *vulgus* was impressed — *sortes* had lost favour with the upper classes".[44] This may or may not have been the case. Cicero's paraded scepticism (and, in particular, its relation to the expressions of traditional piety in the first book of the same *De divinatione*) is very hard to evaluate.[45] The much more important point, however, is that these oracles consisted solely of writing: the goddess Fortuna at Praeneste 'uttered' only the written word.

There is a further stage in this tendency to define communication between humans and gods in written terms: some oracles cast not only the divine response in writing, but also the human query. So, for example, inscribed 'alphabetic oracles' demanded that the enquirer choose letters of the alphabet — and then match up those letters to a list of answers, each also identified by a letter of the alphabet.[46] And even more striking in their use of writing were the 'books' of oracular questions and answers, such as the so-called 'Fates of Astrampsychus', which are preserved in a number of papyrus copies. These books were probably in the hands of diviners, who would first make the enquirer

---

43   Cic., *De div.* 2.41.86-87. Note also O. Brendel, "Two Fortunae, Antium and Praeneste," *AJA* 64 (1960) esp.45-46.

44   Harris 171.

45   Compare the treatment of such oracles in the first book of the dialogue (*De div.* 1.18.34). For the general problem of 'reconciling' Cicero's piety and scepticism, see M. Beard, "Cicero and divination: the formation of a Latin discourse," *JRS* 76 (1986) 33-46, with M. Schofield, "Cicero for and against divination," *JRS* 76 (1986) 47-65.

46   See F. Zevi, "Oracoli alfabetici: Praeneste e Cumai," in M. C. Gualandi *et al.* (edd.), *Aparchai: nuove ricerche e studi sulla Magna Grecia e la Sicilia antica in honore di Paolo Enrico Arias* 2 (Pisa 1982) 605-9; C. Naour, *Tyriaion en Calabide: épigraphie et géographie historique* (Stud. Amst. ad epigraphicam, ius antiquum et papyrologicam pertinentia 20, Zutphen 1980) 22-36.

choose a written question out of a long list of possibilities. Each question was numbered; and, by an intricate system, the diviner would match up the numbered question to an appropriate numbered and written answer. Both human enquiry and divine response were defined in written form within a single 'book'.[47]

These forms of written oracles are normally treated by modern scholars as if they were some kind of 'second best' — a means of access to the divine for those who could not travel (at least, not regularly) to a major oracular shrine; or for those whose minor, domestic query did not justify a full-scale oracular consultation. "Like cash cards", as Lane Fox puts it, "they made the gods' resources swiftly available without priests or complex offerings."[48] This is, no doubt, part of the truth. Oracular books in the hands of private diviners could circulate widely, reaching where the spoken word of god was rarely or never heard. Any town could have its own alphabetic oracle, ready for the casual use of its citizens on whatever trivial, or not so trivial, matters were troubling them. But the widespread practice of these forms of divination still has important implications for our understanding of how human relations with the gods were defined. The enquirers themselves may well have been illiterate; they may have depended (even in these apparently 'popular' religious practices) on the skill of an expert, literate interpreter. The crucial fact remains that, for literate and illiterate alike, pagan communications with the divine could be seen as embedded in, or formed by, written texts.[49]

The written organisation of religion

The existence of a written tradition within a religious system can crucially determine the organisation of that religion — both politically, in terms of the definition and ranking of human religious power, and intellectually, in terms of the ordering and structure of religious knowledge. In this context, Harris alludes briefly to the importance of

---

47 See the Teubner text, edited by G. M. Browne (1983) with various studies by Browne, especially "The composition of the Sortes Astrampsychi," *BICS* 17 (1970) 95-100; "The origin and date of the Sortes Astrampsychi," *Illinois Classical Studies* 1 (1976) 53-58.

48 Lane Fox (supra n.11) 210.

49 There are, of course, other combinations of writing and oral communication in ancient oracles. At Dodona, for example, enquiries were sometimes submitted written on lead and the response given orally or by lot: see Parke, (supra n.36) 100-14. In *Alexander the false prophet* (19-23), Lucian pillories the fraudulence of one particular written oracle.

the Roman priestly books, which detailed (among other things, no doubt) the correct formulae for prayers and the correct procedure at rituals. He recognizes that such books represented power in the hands of the Roman political (and, at the same time, priestly) élite. The knowledge that they contained was inaccessible to the public; there was "nothing democratic about them". He even goes so far as to see such religious uses of writing as "a distinguishing mark of archaic Roman and Italic culture".[50] But, beyond this, he does not explore how far that written tradition might fundamentally affect the whole character of Roman religious organisation.

This final section will concentrate on the traditional civic religion of Rome itself — and argue that 'bureaucratic' forms of writing were centrally important within that religion, determining the character of religious thought and religious institutions. I shall be drawing here on a number of recent articles on the Roman calendar (most of which appeared too late for Harris to incorporate).[51] And I shall discuss, in particular, the work of Richard Gordon, who has analysed the political and social effects of *writing* within the Roman religious system. He has argued that the increasing use of writing played an important part in transforming that religion from its original form as a "common cognitive project" into "ideology" — into, in other words, "a means of maintaining the social domination of the élite".[52] This point needs developing in relation to Harris' claims that writing was little more than a marginal element in Roman religious traditions.

Numerous inscribed or painted calendars survive in Italy, dating from the 1st c. B.C. and A.D. They were once publicly displayed in the fora and temples of Italian towns — and no doubt also (though no example has survived) in those of Rome itself.[53] To the modern observer, these documents often appear curiously complex, presenting

---

50   Harris 154.

51   M. Beard, "A complex of times: no more sheep on Romulus' birthday," *PCPS* 213 (1987) 1-15; A. Wallace-Hadrill, "Time for Augustus: Ovid, Augustus and the *Fasti*," in M. Whitby, P. Hardie, M. Whitby (edd.), *Homo viator. Classical essays for John Bramble* (Bristol 1987) 221-30; J. Scheid, *PCPS* 217 (1991) forthcoming.

52   R. Gordon, "From republic to principate: priesthood, religion and ideology," in M. Beard and J. North (edd.), *Pagan priests* (London 1990) 179-98, esp. 184-91 (quotation on p.191).

53   Full publication in *InscItal* 13 (Roma 1963). For selections and explanation of the layout, see Gordon ibid., and M. Beard, J. North, S. Price, *Roman religion, a sourcebook* (Cambridge, forthcoming).

together and 'systematizing' various different types of religious and calendrical information: the months, and the days of the months; the sequence of religious festivals and games; market days; the 'civil' status of each day of the year (whether or not legal business was allowed to be conducted, or assemblies to meet); short explanations of the religious festivals listed; and so forth. Calendars of this type were not the pagan equivalent of Christian liturgical books: they provided no guidance on the performance of the rituals they included; and, in fact, some of the specifically *Roman* festivals mentioned (often with their location at a particular temple in the city) would have been in practical terms irrelevant to the inhabitants of the towns in which the calendars are found.[54] These documents acted rather as public, written representations of the Roman religious and civil year; they allowed that year to be seen as a whole and permanently displayed, rather than simply *experienced*, lived through by each individual, with a necessarily partial and piecemeal vision.[55]

The importance of the calendars is, as Gordon points out, very similar to the importance Goody has seen in the apparently simple idea of *the written list*.[56] By codifying large quantities of information that could not have been held in the head by any one individual, by juxtaposing different kinds of information within a single (written) framework, the calendars acted not just passively to *record* knowledge, but also actively to stimulate new questions about that material. What is the connection between this festival and the one that immediately follows it? Why is no public business allowed on this day? Why do some months have more religious festivals than others? To follow Harris' approach here,[57] one would presumably have to object that this

---

54   There was a partial overlap between the cults and rituals of Rome and those of colonies and *municipia* in Italy (see, briefly, J. Scheid, "Les cultes publics des colonies et municipes," in F. Jacques and J. Scheid, *Rome et l'intégration de l'empire* 1 [Paris 1990] 124-25); but it remained a distinguishing feature of much Roman state cult that it was tied to the city and to particular locations in the city. The Lupercalia, for example, was not, and could not be, celebrated in any place other than Rome.

55   The underlying point here is that no individual could experience the religious year as a totality; no individual could have been in all places at all times. Totality existed only in written display.

56   J. Goody, *The domestication of the savage mind* (Cambridge 1977) 52-111.

57   Harris refers to Roman calendars only once, and very briefly — in (ironically) his *list* of the functions of ancient writing. In talking of Harris' 'approach' here, I am extrapolating (I hope fairly) from his discussion of other, similar material.

type of questioning was a highly intellectual, élite activity — and so of little significance for the wider character of the religious system. It is certainly true that part of this calendrical exegesis took place in the scholarly, antiquarian writing of the Roman upper class — in, for example, Ovid's *Fasti*, Suetonius' *De anno*, or Varro's section on festivals in his *Antiquitates rerum divinarum*. But the habit of exegesis (in oral as well as written form), the circulation of explanatory stories for particular festivals, the sense that there were indeed questions to be asked about religious traditions, was not restricted to a tiny minority of the élite. Roman state religion was insistently exegetical; it was defined and explained by the stories that were told about it. The root of much of that exegesis (which often in the telling had no obvious link with a written text) lay in the cognitive possibilities opened up by writing, and in particular by the written calendar.[58]

The existence of the written calendar had other implications for the organisation of Roman religion. As a comprehensive, ordered representation of the religious year, the calendar could be seen as proof that there was a 'system' in Roman religion above and beyond the daily religious experience of any individual; it amounted to a claim to a higher order of theory, rule, and abstraction. Similar claims were no doubt implied also by the complex series of religious decisions and precedents contained in the priestly books of the pontifical and augural colleges. It was not just a matter, though, of rules and theory. The more crucial question was, Under whose authority and power did those rules lie? Harris rightly observes that the priestly books were very much under the control of the Roman élite.[59] Gordon goes beyond such a simple observation. He argues that the literate forms at the heart of the Roman civic cult became, at least by the late republic, a crucial weapon in the élite's appropriation of state cult for their own ends — that is, for the preservation of their own dominance.

This growing ideological dominance of the élite is particularly clear in the history of the various collections of priestly books. These books were not static or fixed. They came over time to incorporate more and more religious decisions and precedents — presumably often in conflict with one another. This proliferation of decision-making, in its turn, came to demand a whole set of higher-level rules and higher-level

---

58 See Beard (supra n.51), and Scheid, *PCPS* 1991.
59 Harris 154: "all these books were in varying degrees inaccessible to the public". For priestly books, note especially recent studies by J. Linderski, "The libri reconditi," *HSCP* 89 (1985) 207-34; "The Augural law," *ANRW* 2.16.3 (1986) 2146-312.

religious 'experts' to offer authoritative interpretation of the otherwise confusing mass of conflicting data, men of the élite who (unlike the majority) could assert their claim to 'understand the system'.[60]

Élite superiority is also an element in some of those cases of Roman religious 'literacy' that we generally find almost ludicrous — the preservation of antiquarian religious mumbo-jumbo. Writing, as Gordon argues, allowed the Romans to preserve ancient, apparently obsolete pieces of religious practice that within an oral culture would have either have fallen into complete oblivion or would have been updated. So, for example, the ancient hymn of the Salii (an élite priestly group, composed entirely of patricians) continued to be publicly sung on the basis of a written text, even though by the late republic it was almost completely unintelligible and had in fact become the subject of learned linguistic commentaries. Such obscurity was not, however, without its political point; the preservation of the unintelligible could be used (consciously or not) as a neat exercise in religious and social control. In the case of the Salian hymn, the general mass of Roman citizens were confronted not just with a sense of bafflement, but also with a sense that a group of priests possibly had access to privileged communication with the gods, in a language that was, in everyday terms, incomprehensible. An inability to understand what the priests were singing paradoxically served to legitimate the religious power of the priests, and the exclusion from that power of the general mass. The joke is, of course, that the priests were just following the written text; they did not 'understand' the hymn either. But the people did not know that. Writing, or the capacity of writing to preserve the redundant, could allow obscurantism to flourish — and, with it, the sense of an exclusive élite group privy to the arcane secrets of religion.[61]

---

60 This second order of discourse is evident in, for example, the ancient antiquarian writing cited by E. Rawson, *Intellectual life in the late Roman republic* (London 1985) esp. 302-3. But Rawson does not comment on the social, political, and intellectual processes implicated in this antiquarian tradition.

61 Gordon draws on the work of E. Gellner, especially his "Is belief really necessary" in I. C. Jarvie and J. Agassi (edd.), *The devil in modern philosophy* (London 1974) 52-64: "Unintelligibility leaves the disciple with a secret guilt of not understanding or not avowing it, or both, which binds him to the master who is both responsible for it and seems untainted by it. The belief that the naked emperor is clothed is better social cement than that a naked one is naked — or even that a clothed one is clothed" (p.55, quoted by Gordon [supra n.52] 189).

Writing is necessarily connected with power. At the same time as it opens up new intellectual possibilities, new ways of representing human (in our case religious) experience, it raises the problem of closure and control: who has the right to determine or interpret those written representations. Of course, in Rome there were many and various means by which the élite exercised their dominance over state cult; but writing was, as I have shown, central among them. Even for those who were completely illiterate, the existence of a written tradition — written representations of the religious 'system', its rules and rituals — determined the nature of their religious experience and their perception of religious power.

Harris has given us one side of the history of literacy — a history of numbers and levels, learning and schooling, messages and information. His achievement is, on any reckoning, impressive. But there is another history of ancient writing to be written — a history of the insinuating power of the written text, its capacity to define experience, to change perceptions, to display dominance. In this 'new' history, writing and ancient paganism will be seen to be inextricably intertwined: there will be no understanding of Graeco-Roman paganism without an understanding of its textual strategies.

Newnham College, Cambridge

Acknowledgements:

My thanks are due to Robin Cormack, John Henderson and Keith Hopkins, who listened to the first ideas and read various versions; and (especially) to Joyce Reynolds, who pointed me towards some important groups of texts, as well as improving the arguments.

Statistics or states of mind?
Nicholas Horsfall

Preamble

About 12 years ago, I began collecting, unsystematically, material towards a study of Roman literacy; doubtless, I should have been condemned for my "woolly and grandiose thoughts" (Harris p.41), but I became aware of the vastness of the topic, of the difficulties facing the young lecturer who did not yet merit the big grants which Harris' splendid record secured (Harris vii-viii), and of the conceptual modernity, alien to my own methods and so effortlessly displayed by some of those working in the field.[1] Worse, in the spring of 1981, I mislaid a crucial reference; the files were consigned to an old plastic shopping bag, which I pilfered for various articles over the next few years.[2]

JRA's kind invitation left me perplexed: I had no desire to seem to return to the topic as a grumpy outsider, an extraneous warthog chased from an intended waterhole by a large pedigree carnivore, and left to grub in the undergrowth. As I read Harris, it became clear that I had to find the missing reference (cf. Harris 199, n.123: but how many such inscriptions would Harris have to find to make him change his mind?). I did, eventually, and it was indeed, as I remembered, extraordinarily interesting: *Gallia* suppl.17 (1963) n° 533, from Montenach (Moselle) (2nd c. A.D. on clay): *cum Anaillo dies ... | cum Tertio dies I| inbricis dies III, inbricem baiolandam mortari VI dies III, | tegul(a)e in campo Rassure dies I | [P]atercli dies I.* This is a memo left by a bricklayer's labourer and in the countryside: it is not pretty Latin, but it is not diluted with Gaulish (Harris 270). On Harris' account (see below p.65), a rural labourer should not be able to write, though he knows some did (ibid.): "It is true that some artisans could write a kind of Latin".

---

1   Cf. M. Beard, "Writing and ritual," *PBSR* 53 (1985) 114-62, and R. Thomas, *Oral tradition and written record in classical Athens* (Cambridge 1989) 15-60 — an exemplary and engrossing study.

2   Elizabeth Rawson talked to me sagely while my interest in literacy was in its infancy, gave me excellent advice when it was put in the carrier bag (to which it has now been returned), did not let me forget what I'd done once I had stopped, and might have enjoyed some of what I have written: I offer these pages to her beloved and treasured memory. I also owe much to Callie Williamson, who helped keep my interest in problems of literacy alive during the carrier-bag years.

Harris supplies interesting statistics (pp.266-68) for inscription-densities over most of the Roman empire, but has not looked at every published graffito and underestimates (p.199; see below p.68) their utilitarian content.

The survival of archives or of substantial bodies of graffiti presupposes discovery, compatibility between material and environment, legibility, and editorial competence (on Egypt, see Harris 117). Should Harris have mastered the Palmyrene, Safaitic and Thamudic inscriptions he dangles before us (189, 202)? Perhaps not, but I suspect we might have learned a good deal from analysis site by site of our major collections of archives and graffiti: the Ostia graffiti are published only in part,[3] and when I taxed Russell Meiggs with the absence of any reference to schools or education in his *Ostia*, he smiled enigmatically and said he too found the silence eloquent. Bu Njem is still awaiting publication (132 ostraca, v. infra); the editors are busy with new finds from Vindolanda; now we have Masada, the Hebrew and Aramaic inscriptions edited by Yadin and Naveh (Jerusalem 1989), the Latin and Greek documents (30 papyri, 45 ostraca, 130-odd *tituli picti*, 18 graffiti and 6 amphora stamps) by Cotton and Geiger. Qasr Ibrim (not yet fully published) and Qumran are equally relevant. But, given Harris' dim view of the literacy of the provincial poor, it would also have been helpful to have a more explicit account of why Condatomagus and Magdalensberg (see below p.68) threw up so much written material. However, it does soon become clear (Harris 3-42) that, given Harris' general approach to the evidence, the discovery of such small, solid bodies of material, in however many provinces, is more or less irrelevant to him.

In the ancient world, writing materials were cumbrous or costly; the short-sighted had no spectacles, and Gutenberg (or the Chinese) had not yet revolutionised diffusion. Nor did mass-schooling exist (Harris 14-15). But general literacy has been shown (Harris 11) to depend largely on mass education, industrialisation, and modern urbanisation (p.19); ancient levels of literacy, in a fundamentally rural, economically-backward society, unblessed by Protestantism (p.20, 233) are therefore necessarily lower than any recent statistics (p.18, 22), with occasional exceptions in classical Greece. Harris will therefore argue *a fortiori* for an unprecedentedly precise (and minimalist) quantification (p.24, 141, 158, 259, 266f., 328) of ancient literacy. It was, moreover, wealth and power that entailed literacy (p.36) and Harris' illiterates and rustics are therefore necessarily disadvantaged both

---

3   R. Meiggs, *Roman Ostia* (2nd ed.) 230 n.4.

economically and politically (e.g. p.105, 134, 145, 190, 216, 335, 337). The neat and potent logic of this argument is not at all points convincing (though I know Harris calls people like me 'vague' or 'optimistic': p.8, 24, 36). I can only react to problem, approach and conclusion by expressing my doubts about Harris' methodology: on reaching the end of *Literacy*, I had, I hope, a clear and fair view of how the author thought and worked, but curiosity and obstinacy mean that Titius and Seius and *their* work and thoughts are more interesting to me. Let me begin and end with a favourite obsession: ancient means of training the memory.

Ancient means of training the memory

Harris is perfectly right to say that the strength of ancient memories mitigated the need for personal reading and writing (p.30), and right too to distinguish cautiously between the literate and the illiterate memory (p.30-33). But he has perhaps never seen Mezzofantic linguists or the owners of freak memories (contrast p.32-33, 301) at play: his scepticism is thus unnecessarily severe, and on the history of *Mnemotechnik* he should have consulted H. Blum's book:[4] whether Augustine used such methods is not certain;[5] Martianus' interest is clearer (Blum 142), though Harris' chronology (301) is badly awry.[6] Harris and I would certainly agree that formal mnemonic techniques and exceptional feats of retention are largely irrelevant to literacy. However, he seems to me to minimize the widespread use of active (and passive) memorisation in many branches of ancient education and life (cf. my note on Nep. *Att*.1.3). The rôle of memory in Roman education is given due weight in S. F. Bonner's manual,[7] and the scene in Horace, *AP* 326-29 (cf. Aug., *Conf*. 1.13.22) suggests strongly that fraction-tables (as known from Egypt; cf. *ILS* 7755) were simply memorised, at least in part.[8] For quick multiplications of fractions (duodecimal weights and money units; monthly interest), I would back the memory against the abacus.[9] Augustine's words *odiosa cantio* (*Conf*., supra) suggest a text

---

4   *Die antike Mnemotechnik, Spudasmata* 15 (Hildesheim 1969).

5   Blum ibid. 136-41, against F. A. Yates' *The art of memory* (London 1966).

6   Shanzer's date (ed. Mart. Cap. 1, University of California Press 1986) 1-28 is *c*.470-80.

7   S. F. Bonner, *Education in ancient Rome* (London 1977).

8   Bonner ibid. 180, R. MacMullen, *Roman government's response to crisis, AD 235-337* [New Haven 1976] 58, Horsfall, *GR* 36 (1989) 203-4, and for the serious reader, F. Hultsch, "Volkstümliches Rechnen bei den Römern," *NJhb* 139 (1889) 335-43.

9   Mart.10.62.4, Bonner 183-87.

chanted by teacher and class.[10] Even Cicero talks of learning the 12 Tables as a *carmen necessarium*.[11] The means of ensuring retention is, as we shall see (below pp.73-75), the Christians' own for religious texts, *mutatis mutandis*. Repetitive chanting sears text or figures into the brain. Literacy hardly enters into it. What text might commemorate such tedious, painful acquisitions of mastery over fractions and what teacher might have led the chant? This is learning at a truly modest level: the technique is clearly so simple that it can function in the slave-*familia*, in the school, at work, in church: mechanical memorisation sidesteps both literacy (as Harris admits) and (potentially) school, while imparting knowledge and thus (above all through numeracy, p.64 f.) the means towards an income.[12]

"A pervasive system of schools is a prerequisite for mass literacy" (p.233; cf. p.15, 16). But especially in the west the evidence for a network of schools is slender: "skeletal and anaemic" indeed (p.312), with clear implications, on Harris' argument, for the rate of literacy. However, he allows that in the late empire "as in earlier periods some people learned to read and write without going to school at all" (p.307): home-taught literacy is grudgingly admitted as a possibility (ibid.). Professional skills passed from father to son, among doctors,[13] vets,[14] and architects;[15] cf. the Theodosian Code — *artifices* in many (listed) categories shall transmit technical knowledge in the family.[16] It is not, I hope, unduly hazardous to suggest that, particularly where schools are wanting, overpriced, or otherwise unsatisfactory, parents (or other members of the family; cf. p.15, 129, 252, 307; index *s.v.* family, teaching within) took over, where they could (so *BGU* II 423). It would be rash to generalise (but compare the evidence collected at Harris 233, n.296) on the basis of the elder Cato.[17] The phrase *lapidarias litteras scio* (Petr.58.7) prompts me to suggest that public inscriptions in the Roman world provided a large-scale and abundant (if not richly amusing) reader for any child who learned his letters informally, in the way I have suggested: that is how I learned to read;

---

10   So too Virgil, SHA *Alb*. 5.2, Macr. 1.24.5, Horsfall, *Atti del convegno mondiale scientifico di studi su Virgilio* 2 [Milan 1984] 48).

11   *Leg*. 2.59; cf. Hier., *Ep*. 107.4, a little girl *non solum ordinem teneat litterarum ut memoria nominum in canticum transeat*.

12   Cf. Colum. 1.8.4; Cic., *Rep*. 5.5.

13   Galen 2.280K, V. Nutton, *JRS* 61 (1971) 55; *PBSR* 45 (1977) 200, 202.

14   *IG* 2.1953.

15   Vitr. 6 *praef*. 6, 10 *praef*. 4.

16   *Cod. Theod*. 13.4.2 (A.D. 337).

17   Plut., *Cat.mai*. 20.3, Bonner 10-12, Harris 160.

the method seems to work. Neither teaching[18] nor learning was necessarily a full-time activity, nor one carried on beyond the bare minimum. Other alternatives to orthodox schooling are easily identified, and I mention three.

a. The slave household

This is interestingly discussed by Harris (p.255-59), and indeed held up both as a rare source of education for slaves (p.256-57; but cf. p.64 below), and as a disincentive to education for the poor but free.

b. The army (p.166-67, 213, 217-18, 253-55).

Vegetius[19] points to a military bureaucracy so elaborate that literate recruits are positively welcome.[20] It is clear that clerical ranks enjoyed much easier conditions of service,[21] Cavallo denies the army undertook teaching; cf. however Tarruntenus Priscus:[22] *librarii quoque qui docere possunt* (literacy? clerical procedures?). The surviving duty-rosters suggest that the illiterate soldier was seriously disadvantaged and a positive encumbrance, to be taught urgently.[23]

c. At work.

If the ability to write makes you faster, more useful, better-paid or better-treated at work, then, if you cannot already, you surely learn quickly, somehow, if you possibly can. Literacy improves livelihood: that powerful stimulus is underplayed by Harris (197-98, 202-3). Compare my discussion of the evidence from Petronius:[24] literacy plus a specialised application (accountancy, the law[25]) is what the guests at the *Cena* plan for the younger generation. How will Trimalchio

---

18   Harris 308; cf. Petr.46, A. D. Booth, "The schooling of slaves in first-century Rome," *TAPA* 109 (1979) 18.

19   2.19.

20   Harris 294; cf. H. Teitler, *Notarii and exceptores* (Amsterdam 1985) 210-11; see A. Petrucci, *Gnomon* 51 (1979) 31 on Bu Njem.

21   *BGU* II 423; *P. Mich.* VIII 465, 466. Cf. G. R. Watson, *The Roman soldier* (London 1969) 75-77; R. W. Davies, *Service in the Roman army* (Edinburgh 1989) 43-46 = *ANRW* 2.1.312-14; cf. G. R. Watson, ibid. 493-507, E. E. Best, "The literate Roman soldier," *CJ* 62 (1966) 166-67, G. Cavallo in *Alfabetismo e cultura scritta* (Perugia 1978) 132-33.

22   *Dig.*50.6.7; Harris 218.

23   Discussion of these texts with Major Philip Powell-Jones (6th Gurkhas) elucidated much: I am grateful for his conclusions based on long experience of training illiterate recruits.

24   "'The uses of literacy' and the Cena Trimalchionis," *GR* 36 (1989) 202-6.

25   Cf. *ILS* 7741, Juv. 14.190.

himself[26] have learned accountancy?[27] From a manual?[28] Or from a teacher?[29] But most swifly, and economically, I surmise, within the *familia*. 'School' has acquired disproportionate importance within Harris' perceptions.

Numeracy

That the accuracy of the sums on Greek papyri is imperfect[30] is no argument against widespread ancient numeracy: indeed, it is impossible to conceive of a business transaction (beyond that of the client offering the shopkeeper the correct change for a single item) for which some numeracy was not required. Numeracy, not literacy, is the key to the world of small business (we have seen something of how it was learned). Harris' argument[31] that business above a certain level presupposes literacy, while below that level letters are rather unlikely, seems valid (but cf. p.73, Caesarius of Arles' analphabetic tycoons). The world of Petronius' freedmen acknowledges limited literacy:[32] essential, though, was the calculation of percentages.[33] Law could help too: letters alone are not esteemed in the world of the *Cena*, which covers a wide social range and whose social realism I have tried hard to defend.[34] I find it a source of bewilderment that Harris nowhere mentions numeracy: market stallholders in Russia, Ghana, Uganda (so I am told) handle figures with minimal education and without writing. They can hardly be less accurate than their peers <u>trained</u> at <u>school</u> in <u>mathematics</u> in Italy or England! In the ancient world, the illiterate was at risk in business, but not incapacitated.[35] Compare the law codes[36] for second-century attitudes to the successful businessman who *negabat*

---

26   Petr. 29.4.
27   Cf. Galen. 1.38K, logistike.
28   *ILS* 7755, *P. Oxy.* 4.724.
29   *Edict. Diocl.* 7.67, *ILS* 7754 *doctori artis calculatoriae*; hardly Mart.10.62.4, *pace* C. A. Forbes, "The education and training of slaves in antiquity," *TAPA* 86 (1955) 342-43.
30   MacMullen (supra n.8) 238, H. C. Youtie, *Scriptiunculae posteriores* 1, 123 ff.
31   Harris 200, 251-52, 262-63; cf. also his "Literacy and epigraphy 1," *ZPE* 52 (1983) 107-8.
32   *in domusionem tamen litteras didici* (48.4), *nam litteris satis inquinatus est* (46.7; cf. 56.1).
33   This is discussed in *GR* 1989, 203-5.
34   Ibid. p.74 ff.
35   H. C. Youtie, *Scriptiunculae* 2, 620; cf. Harris 205, n.156.
36   *Dig.*27.1.6.19; *Inst.* 1.25.8.

se litteras scire. The illiterate later receives some recognition and protection at law;[37] unfortunately, Harris' note (p.35 n.35) concerns primarily ignorance of law, not inability to write (compare though p.203-6 for a helpful discussion of the legal evidence).

The importance of literacy to the individual's career and prospects Harris tends to minimise (p.18, 19, 202-3). Some attention is paid to clerical jobs in the army bureaucracy (p.217-18), in the imperial household (p.248; contrast p.255-59 where private clerks and readers are played down), and to the importance of literacy in business (p.197-98, 202-3). But our evidence for ancient awareness of the importance of literacy is not limited to Petr. 46.7 (*habet haec res panem*).[38] And the patient and careful reader will discover in the technical manuals hints that architects (p.203), midwives (p.203), *dispensatores* (p.197), bailiffs (p.257), even head shepherds (p.256) are best literate. Doctors too.[39] Also surveyors.[40] The sum of this evidence suggests an altogether closer causal relation between literacy and employment than the casual reader of Harris might imagine.

Even some modern 'romantic' objections to literacy (cf. Harris p.37 ff.) can be found already in the technical manuals ('practical experience of herbs more important than education'[41]). Of course the lettered expert sneered at the uncouth pragmatist, often enough to suggest that the latter was not discouraged unduly.

If Harris finds urban literacy fragile and limited, then in the countryside, *a fortiori*, it is almost non-existent (cf. p.17, 53, 67f., 104 and notably 191). Let us not forget the hod-carrier from the Moselle; Harris himself scatters occasional examples pointing towards at least minimal rural literacy (p.256, 269f., 275) and collects both anecdotes (215, n.207) and references from the technical manuals (p.163, 256)[42] pointing in the same direction. This evidence is widely dispersed, nowhere correlated, and reduced to the barest minimum. One might therefore wish to contemplate the petitions delivered to the younger

---

37   *Novell. Theod.* 16.3, *Cod.Iust.* 6.23.29.1, 6.30.22.26, *Dig.* 48.2.3.2.

38   Cf. Galen 1.38K, *ILS* 7741, Juv.14.189 ff., Mart. 9.73.7; cf. also Cic., *Off.*1.151; Sen., *Ep.* 88.20.

39   For Greece see Harris 82; for Rome, F. Kühnert, *Allgemeinbildung und Fachbildung* (Berlin 1961) 22.

40   Agennius Urbicus, *Gromatici* 1, p.13.

41   Pliny 18.205, 25.16, Galen, 10.5K, Theod. Priscian 1.2, Scrib. Largus *praef.* p.1.9 Helmreich, etc.

42   Cf. E. Rawson, *Intellectual life in the late Roman republic* (London 1985) 50.

Pliny,[43] the quantity of references to instructions in writing left for overseers in the countryside[44] (Harris p.256 is not enough). We even know a little of the literary tastes of country people.[45] The literary standards of country towns we have learned were disconcertingly high,[46] and some variable too from town to town.[47] "Some artisans could write a kind of Latin" is Harris' verdict (p.270) on the few graffiti published from Roman Britain. One would be foolish to question the general principle that literacy diminishes with distance from major urban centres: it does not, however, disappear, and we need not only an explanation of this modest yet obstinate resistance, but, as I have suggested, a comprehensive survey of graffiti, etc., from rural areas,[48] of the texts which suggest ability to read and write in the countryside,[49] and a recognition that materials, conditions for survival, and standards of excavation, have tended to warp our conclusions.

Harris (p.199) writing of Pompeii remarks "Not many of the graffiti can be classed as utilitarian", though (p.200) exceptions exist (cf. p.260-64). One could have listed 'utilitarian' graffiti more fully; others have done so.[50] Particular groups of graffiti have been analysed usefully, in connection with similar material from elsewhere.[51] Not many

---

43　*Ep* 7.30.3, 9.15.1, 9.36.6.

44　Cat., *Agr.* 2.6, Varro, *RR* 1.17.4, 1.36.1, 2.1.23, 2.2.20, 2.5.17, 2.5.18, 2.10.10.

45　Quint. 5.11.19, fable; Plin., *NH praef.* 6: "I could have written for the *turba* of *agricolae* and *opifices;*" cf. ibid. 18.206; cf. Pliny, *Ep.* 8.8.7: rustic graffiti, 5.6.6, rustics' taste for historical reminiscence.

46　T. P. Wiseman, *Roman Studies* (Liverpool 1987) 297, Rawson (supra n.42) 34.

47　H. Solin, "Die herkulanensischen Wandinschriften. Ein soziologischer Versuch," *Cron.Erc.* 3 (1973) 9.

48　Cf. A. Petrucci, "Nuove osservazioni sulla b minuscola," *Arch.Pal.It.* 3.1 (1962) 118.

49　Cf. Harris 241, citing Ulpian, *Dig.* 50.5.2.8: elementary teachers in *vici*.

50　E. Diehl, *Pompeianische Wandinschriften* (Bonn 1910) 24-28, 37-38, W. Krenkel, *Pompeianische Inschriften* (Leipzig 1961) 56 ff., H. Geist, *Pompeianische Wandinschriften* 2nd ed. (München 1960) 56 ff., E. Magaldi, *Le iscrizioni parietali pompeiane* (Napoli 1931) 91 ff. From my own rapid excerpting, cf. *CIL* IV. 10520, 10566, 10575, 10645, 10664, 10674 (Herculaneum) and 10067, 10106, 10106a, 10117, 10150 (Pompeii) from the unsatisfactory fascicle of the graffiti found in 1951-56 (cf. H. Solin, *Gnomon* 45 [1973] 258 ff.), just to give an impression of the frequency or density of the material of 'business' content.

51　I refer particularly to T. Kleberg, *Hôtels, restaurants et cabarets* (Uppsala 1957) 118-20 on price-lists; cf. H. H. Tanzer, *The common people of*

utilitarian graffiti, perhaps, but clearly not as few as might appear
from Harris. And why so few? Harris is quite right to point to the
scarcity of the material, though grudgingly and with unfortunate
under-emphasis. We might wonder whether his reasons (illiteracy of
the working poor; transactions involving small sums go unrecorded) are
quite the full and true story. I mean no more — once again — than that
the nature and density of the epigraphic material from a given site is
determined not merely by its educational and economic level in
antiquity but by the skill of the excavators, the competence of the
editors, by the circumstances of destruction, where applicable, and by
the benevolence of geology and climate towards the survival of the
writing materials once in use. Our evidence for the entire Roman empire
has to be weighed up in such terms: Tyche has skewed our evidence
with malice and thoroughness. Harris dwells (p.95, 194-95, 239) on the
high cost of papyrus (but note the extreme scepticism of others.[52]
Writing tablets "in later Greece ... were the familiar recipient of
anything of an impermanent nature .. bills, accounts, ... memoranda".[53]
That refers to tablets of wood and wax or of plain wood (for full
bibliography, see Harris 193, n.96). As a writing material, the sherd
will hardly have been less fire-resistant than the wall, but at Pompeii
it seems not to have been used as it was in Egypt and at Bu Njem,[54]
though one supposes it could have been. The Jucundus tablets were found
inside a box on the first floor of his house.[55] The Murecine tablets were
preserved in mud, within a wicker box.[56] The Poppaea tablets were
wrapped in cloth and left in the corner of a bath-house.[57] Chance did
not favour wood/wax tablets during the eruption of 79, least of all those
of ephemeral importance., not in some way stored, hidden or protected.

Pompeii. A study of the graffiti (Baltimore 1939). For the procedure for
recovering lost goods or slaves, cf. Harris 200, J. Crook (infra n.75) 186.

52   C. H. Roberts and T. C. Skeat, *The birth of the codex* (Oxford 1983) 7.

53   Ibid. 11.

54   Cf. E. Posner, *Archives in the ancient world* (Cambridge, MA 1972) 158-59.
      Bu Njem: cf. Rebuffat, R. Marichal, *REL* 51 (1973) 281 n.1 for previous
      bibliography (notably in *CRAI* 1969, 1972); cf. further *Ann.Epig.* 1975, 242;
      1976, 221; 1985 n° 849; 1986 n° 709; 1987 n° 993; R. Marichal, *CRAI* 1979, 436
      ff.

55   J. Andreau, *Les affaires de Monsieur Jucundus* (*CollEFR* 19 [1974]) 14.

56   L. Bove, *Documenti processuali dalle Tabulae Pompeianae di Murecine*
      (Napoli 1979) 2 f.

57   *NSc* 1887, 415. On the Herculaneum tablets, cf. V. Arangio-Ruiz, *Epigrafia
      e papirologia* (Napoli 1974) 297, G. Pugliese-Caratelli in *Pompeiana*
      (Napoli 1950) 266.

That should go some way towards redressing the balance detected, exaggerated and exploited by Harris.

It is truly perplexing that Harris does not discuss (p.260, 269 n.1 are not enough) the rich documentation (over 300 graffiti in the main cellar[58] of the Magdalensberg,[59] revealing an extraordinarily complex and active commercial life, in import, export and local re-sale under the early Julio-Claudians. Business and its financing depend on a continuously maintained written record; *pari passu* the graffiti reveal the tradesman's passion for gladiators. The quantities involved perhaps fall into the category of "business matters of some importance" (p.201 on the Murecine tablets, as against the small shopkeepers of Pompeii and their customers whom (ibid.) "the evidence does not suggest ... wrote much or indeed at all in the course of business"). You can record 110 *cumbae* or *disci* in Carinthia, even a paltry 28 *scyphi*. At that rate, one wonders, how did the tableware-sellers of Pompeii manage to restock? If there was a line to be drawn, it should perhaps have been done more precisely. At Magdalensberg, five pounds of *defrutum* or of *olei flos* are recorded.[60]

Condatomagus (La Graufesenque) interests Harris no more (260, 269 n.473).[61] Indeed, Harris offers no generalisations or conclusion. The nature of the documentation has been amply studied.[62] They are lists of pottery from single workshops to be fired in the few large ovens. Harris may have concluded that only a single nimble and perspiring clerk need have been involved. Clearly that is not the only explanation possible.

Over the very familiar evidence of writing material exposed to public view at Rome and Pompeii,[63] discussed recently not only by Harris but by Mireille Corbier,[64] I pass rapidly, pausing only to consider, firstly, the public scribe, and secondly, the literacy level of a Roman crowd.

---

58   R. Noll, in *Princeton Encyclopedia of Classical Sites* (Princeton 1976) s.v.
59   Cf. G. Alföldy, *Noricum* (London 1974) 73-74, with bibliography p.363; A. Obermayer, *Kelten und Römer am Magdalensberg* (Wien 1971) 53 ff., 129 ff.
60   *Carinthia* 149 (1959) 132.38; ibid. 153 (1963) 97.34.
61   For bibliography cf. A. Petrucci, *Bull.Arch.Pal.Ital.* 3.1 (1962) 86 n.4.
62   R. Marichal, *Les graffiti de La Graufesenque* (Gallia Suppl.47 [1988]), with earlier literature.
63   Cf. Harris 261, n.451: Harris is not always quite reliable, and here minimises the evidence for the reading of Virgil in modest environments: see Horsfall (supra n.10) 50 n.50.
64   *L'Urbs* (Coll.EFR 98, Roma 1987) 27-60.

The public scribe

The public scribe plying for hire is not a secure indicator of limited literacy: there will have been those well able to write a bar-bill who will have jibbed at a delicate letter. The scribe is, however, an interesting figure (p.35, 265).[65] "This must have been a common scene in every town" (p.265). The artistic evidence cited by Harris is hotly debated and ultimately inconclusive.[66] ILS 7751, P. Cornelius Celadus, *librarius ab extra Porta Trigemina*, might be cited by way of comparison; his regular place of work seems to confirm his function as a 'public writer'. *Dizionario Epigrafico* s.v. *Librarius* 960 (R. F. Rossi) quotes nothing else really similar and the terms *scriptor, scriba, librarius* are too polyvalent to serve as reliable indicators. "*Scriba* is always a clerk" (p.159); that might have been phrased more cautiously in the light of recent work;[67] at least that derogatory monosyllable 'clerk' required full and nuanced explication. The evidence from the west stops here, at least until the early middle ages (p.316), so far as I know. Compare Isidore, *Etym.* 9.4.27: *scriba publicus*. Egypt is of course quite another story.[68] The street-lawyer is a well-attested phenomenon in the later empire in the west:[69] the evidence for the public scribe is by comparison so very scanty; this may be mere chance, or we may be confused by imprecise terminology. I would not wish to use the public scribe's rarity as an argument for greater literacy by comparison with Egypt! Certainly the more important a document — e.g. a will or a loan — the likelier the use of a semi-professional writer: subject matter

---

65   Cf. also Harris, ZPE 52 (1983) 111 n.113.

66   See the ed. princ., *Le pitture antiche di Ercolano* 3 (Napoli 1762) 210.

67   N. Purcell, "The *apparitores*: a study in social mobility," *PBSR* 51 (1983) 125 ff., and D. Armstrong, "*Horatius eques et scriba*," *TAPA* 116 (1986) 255 ff.

68   H. C. Youtie, *Scriptiunculae* 2. 611 ff. = "'Αγράμματος. An aspect of Greek society in Egypt," *HSCP* 75 (1971) 161 ff., E. G. Turner, *Greek papyri* (Oxford 1980) 83, R. Calderini, "Gli ἀγράμματοι dell'Egitto greco-romano," *Aegyptus* 30 (1950) 27 ff.

69   Crook (infra n.75) 92, TLL s.v. *Forensis* 1054.14 ff., J.-O. Tjäder, *Die nichtliterarischen lateinischen Papyri Italiens aus der Zeit 445-700* (Skr. Svensk. Inst. Rom 4° 19,1-2) p.148, Lauffer on *Edict. Diocl.* 7.41, L. Wenger, *Die Quellen des römischen Rechts* (Wien 1953) 740 ff., 754 f., F. Schulz, *History of Roman legal science* (Oxford 1946) 109, 277, A. Berger, *Encyclopedic dictionary of Roman law* (Philadelphia 1953) s.v. *Tabelliones*, W. Kunkel, *Herkunft und soziale Stellung der römischen Juristen* (Weimar 1952) 148.

again overrides writing capacity, and in turn warps the evidence (see below for fear of writing on important matters).

The literacy level of a Roman crowd

Descriptions (or representations) of crowds reading (or appearing to read) have long stood at the centre of the debate on literacy levels: for a 'minimalist' (notably Harris) such material is easy meat: a scene such as the painting of the group reading notices in the forum at Pompeii, or the various anecdotes of crowds gathering to read edicts or proscription-lists in Rome[70] have been contemplated from many angles: is it important that the notice be posted or that the public be informed? The man who posts a 'This is NOT a public urinal' notice relieves only his own ire.[71] Is it necessary that all the crowd be readers, or only the little fellow who has squeezed to the front and reads the text out to the rest? Is it enough (p.260) to dismiss the gladiatorial announcements at Pompeii with the remark that the poor do not have to be the primary audience for the games?[72] We still need a full analysis of the gladiatorial graffiti. So an unending and at times circular debate winds hotly on. There is another side to the question. Crowds gather round notices, as they do round the skilled shorthand writer or *calculator* (Mart.10.62), as they do indeed round the schoolmaster, often at work in a public place.[73] Much depends on the ratio of illiterates to semi-literates, to literates in a given crowd (compare the dramatic account in Dio fr. 109.14); much also upon the audibility of the street-teacher or the legibility of the public notice. The literary tradition refers to notices intended to frustrate their readers,[74] while the Lyon text of Claudius' speech is still a joy to the eye. Street-schools, I suggest, reached beyond paying pupils, and public notices helped spread a min-imal reading ability. Hearing, sight, and human curiosity are factors not much less important than money, status, and family tradition.

---

70 Harris 34-35, 207-8, Corbier (supra n.64) 43-46, with much further bibliography.
71 I cannot omit my favourite example, strangely neglected: a dog's collar, *CIL* XV.7199 *De ortum Olibri v.c. sum prefecti pretoris* (i.e. 378-79). *Noli me tenere. non tibi expedet.*
72 Cf. R. Etienne, *La vie quotidienne à Pompei* 437, G. Ville, *La gladiature* (Roma 1981) 334 ff., Obermayer (supra n.59) 53 ff., *Carinthia* 145 (1955) 58, 65-66.
73 Bonner (supra n.7) 116-17, Harris 236.
74 Cic., *Att.* 2.21.4; Suet., *Cal.* 41.1.

Fear engendered by writing

Harris, much to his credit, gives due space to the sinister quality of writing and to the fear it may engender, at least in the Greek section of *Literacy* (index, *s.v.* sinister ..). I have long wondered whether a similar fear may not be involved — alongside, undeniably, cases of total or partial illiteracy — in the use of the *scripsi rogatu* (e.g.) 'illiteracy formula' both on the Jucundus tablets from Pompeii and in Egypt (Harris 262, 276, 278; one could carry the discussion on to the Tjäder papyri). When writing is not a daily activity, when unfamiliar legal language is involved, when your livelihood, even your freedom is at stake, of course fear is engendered, and fear, or at least strong dislike of the law at a humble level, is amply attested.[75] Note *ILS* 7750, P. Pomponius Philadespotus of Venafrum, who wrote wills for 25 years *sine iuris consulto* (cf. ibid. 7749, 7763.7 *testamenta scripsit cum fide*), *ILS* 1896 *vixi iudicio sine iudice*, CIL 6. 10525 *HMDM et ICA*, 12133 *huic monumento dolus malus et iurisconsultus abesto.*[76] Law and thus perforce writing threatened your book-balance and your bones. At this point the discourse passes from palaeography, legal history, statistics to *mentalités*:[77] the best papyrologists have learned to view declarations of illiteracy with extreme circumspection.

Cultural implications

I am doubtful too about the cultural implications of illiteracy. Because there was no printing, there was no cheap reading-matter and that limited the social range of literacy (Harris p.14). There was no stimulus to advance beyond "a certain level of craftsman's literacy" (p.19). Though Harris refers (p.226) to the performance of poetry in the theatre and even in the street, he concludes (p.227) that "there was no such thing as "popular literature" in the Roman empire, if that means literature which became known to tens or hundreds of thousands of people by means of personal reading ... As for works written expressly for the masses, there were none." So in conclusion (p.335): "It would be quite unrealistic to suppose that literacy by itself led ordinary literate

---

75 Cf. R. MacMullen, "Social history in astrology," *AncSoc* 2 (1971) 107, on anxieties displayed in astrological texts; J. Crook, *Law and life* (London 1967) 35, citing *Dig.* 31.88.17, etc.

76 Cf. Crook (ibid.) 138, *Diz. Epigr.* s.v. *iuris studiosus* for further examples.

77 Cf. H. C. Youtie, *Scriptiunculae* 2 (Amsterdam 1973) 611 ff., 629 ff., 677 ff., *Scriptiunculae posteriores* (Bonn 1981) 179 ff., 255 f.

Greeks and Romans to a knowledge of the outside world or of novel
ideas, still more to think that it led them to critical modes of thinking.
Presumably most literate Greeks and Romans used their knowledge of
reading and writing for nothing more than practical or mundane
purposes". The Roman proletariat was therefore culturally deprived
and would necessarily remain so because no means towards its mental
improvement lay to hand. I have been over the same ground myself
recently, more than once,[78] and with very different conclusions.

Harris toys (p.226), as we have seen, with the oral performance of
the products of literary culture, but does not pursue this mode of
diffusion in its various branches. Let us not forget Cicero's regard for the
ear of his Roman audience,[79] or the history they learned from his
exempla, from painting, processions, and statues. Indeed, Cicero himself tells us (*Fin.*5.52) that *opifices delectantur historia*. Let us leave
out ambulatory story-tellers (though they cut across the full range of
socio-economic levels) and the popularity of the fable.[80] They are
perhaps not sufficiently improving. But Miss Rawson established the
importance of philosophical elements in the popular mime.[81] The
myths that Romans learned from the tragedians were delightfully
travestied by Plautus; the continuing popularity of second-century
drama in the first century requires no detailed justification.[82] Virgil
was a triumphant popular success in his lifetime, mobbed in the street,
honoured in the theatre, indeed performed there:[83] how so, if he did not
reach and was not in part understood by a very wide audience? In an
imminent Italian discussion (supra n.78) I discuss how this could have
happened, how such an audience could have coped with any of the
levels of his density of reference, and here I only summarise salient
points. What, after all, did Pliny (*Nat.Hist. praef.*6) think might
have been written for the *turba* of craftsmen? Hardly just fairy-stories
and porn;[84] Dionysius of Halicarnassus (*Thuc.*50) is of course right to say
that Thucydides is not for shopmen, but the debate is significant: he is

---

78   *GR* 36 (1989) 74 ff., 194 ff. (supra n.24), *Roman myth and mythography*
      (*BICS* Suppl.52, 1987) 3, chapt.3 of my *L'epopea in alambicco*, in press
      (Liguori, Naples).
79   *Orat.* 173, 168, A.-M. Guillemin, *Le public et la vie littéraire* (Paris 1937) 14.
80   Cf. M. Nøjgaard, *La fable antique* 1 (København 1964) 552, citing Quint.
      1.8.19, 1.9.1-2; compare Harris 228.
81   *Homo Viator* (Bristol 1987) 79 ff.
82   I do not repeat bibliography currently in the press elsewhere.
83   Horsfall (supra n.10) 47 ff.
84   Cf. Wiseman (supra n.46) 253, 255; C. Schulze in *Past perspectives* (ed. I.
      Moxon *et al.*, Cambridge 1986) 134-36.

not suitable only because he is too hard, not because they do not have historical interests. High culture, I agree, does not often reach the literate craftsmen undiluted (except in the tragic theatre), but it would be flying in the face of ample ancient evidence and much recent research to deny the *opifex haud inlitteratus* cultural interests, even curiosity, or the existence of occasions (or performances), if not of paperback editions, to satisfy him.

The Christians

Lastly, the Christians. Harris is quite right to observe that the scriptures were *heard* in the early church and that doctrine (orthodox or heretical) might be taught through the medium of a hymn (p.305). Neither observation is developed in detail, nor are the appropriate conclusions drawn. That the early church, though very much a religion of the book,[85] did nothing to encourage ordinary believers to read for themselves (p.326), is a polemic exaggeration (p. 305, 311-12, 319), sadly ornamented with relics of sectarian malice.[86] The case for Christianity as an instrument of a growing illiteracy (p.326) is likewise, I imagine, sketched out to provoke, not to convince. If you can, buy a Bible;[87] not 'if you can read it', but 'if you can afford it'. The evidence of Caesarius of Arles (p.316; here we are in the early 6th c.) seems to me booby-trapped: *Serm.*6.2 (Morin) urges the Christian unable to read to do what rich merchants do — get someone to read to you, for a fee; at least you thereby lay up treasure in Heaven, in contrast to the *negotiator*. In *Serm.*8.1, it usually happens (*et quia solet fieri*) that, in this same situation, there are rich Christian illiterates and poor potential readers; hire yourself a reader, hear the scriptures at home and spread your money around the right way. The Christians do not themselves educate, but, despite p.311, the evidence that they press continuously for reading of the scriptures at home by all believers is overwhelming. And we thus return to the mnemonic devices with which

---

85   C. H. Roberts, *Cambridge history of the Bible* 1 (Cambridge 1970) 66.

86   Harris 305 n.97: Catholic scholars defend the Fathers' insistence on private reading of the Bible with equal vigour: J. Rousse, *Dictionnaire de la Spiritualité* 9.472 ff., M. Todde, "Lettura e meditazione della scritura," *Servitium* 7 (1973) 515-26. "The other evidence cited is if anything even less relevant" (Harris 305); so sweeping a dismissal of so very large a body of evidence carries little or no conviction; certainly the texts that I have myself read on the topic suggest a quite different approach and conclusion.

87   Epiphanius, *Apophthegmata* 8 (PG 65.165a).

we began, mentioned (p.305), but not fully understood by Harris: the effect of repeated readings,[88] of repeated psalms,[89] of communally sung hymns of doctrinal content, both orthodox and heretical.[90] Such material carries a mixed literate/semi-literate/illiterate congregation regularly over a large but limited corpus of written material. What you hear, and, even more, what you sing frequently, you remember.[91] This is the method, more or less, that we have seen in use in the classroom for (e.g.) the fraction-tables. After ten years of a not specially intense Anglican education, my own memory is cluttered, twenty-five years later, with fragments of the Psalter and of the English Hymnal. The experience is in no way unique. An illiterate early Christian will hardly have needed to read texts he had so often heard or sung, though the Fathers repeatedly urged him to do so. The step from passive reception (by ear or by communal singing) to active reading will not

---

88   J. A. Lamb, *Cambridge History of the Bible* 1 (Cambridge 1970) 563 ff., *DACL* s.v. *Leçons*, V. Saxer in *Le monde latin antique et la Bible* (Paris 1985) 157 ff., with full bibliography.

89   J. Quasten, *Musik und Gesang* (Münster 1930) 142 ff., J. A. Jungmann, *The early liturgy* (Notre Dame 1959) 167-68, Lamb (supra n.88) 568-70, Wille (infra n.91) 371 ff., A. von Harnack, *Über den privaten Gebrauch* (Leipzig 1912) 86-89. The references missing from Father Jungmann's most interesting discussion are: John Chrys. on *Psalm* 140, 1,2 (Migne *PG* 55, 426, 427), Caes.Arel., *Serm.* 536.5, 903.13 (Morin). For the memorisation of psalms by baptismal candidates, cf. Ps.John Chrys., *Serm.* 30, *PL* Suppl.4, 825, 830. The attribution to Johannes II Mediocris, Bishop of Naples (6th c.) is now rejected (see W. Wenk, *Zur Sammlung der 38 Homilien des Chrysostomus Latinus*, WSt Beih.10 (1988) 8 with n.7); Jungmann (ibid), M. Righetti, *Storia liturgica* 4 (Milan 1953) 43 and D. Ambrasi in *Storia di Napoli* 1 (Cava dei Tirreni 1967) 690, are all therefore to be recast: authorship, place and date of this sermon are all in doubt. But it is not in doubt that the mnemonic effect of memorisation was perceived by contemporaries in the way I have suggested. Catherine Cooper (Princeton) has helped me clear up this bibliographical disaster area.

90   Cf. Aug., *Retr.* 1.18 *volens etiam causam Donatistarum ad ipsius humillimi vulgi et omnino imperitorum atque idiotarum notitiam pervenire*. Recent bibliography in J. Fontaine *s.vv. Inno/Innologia* in A. Di Bernardino, *Dizionario Patristico* 1 (Casale Monferrato 1983/84). M. Simonetti, "Storia dell'innodia cristiana," *Atti Lincei* 8.4 (1952) 341 ff., and very conveniently H. Leclercq in *DACL s.v. Hymnes* 2826-2928: see in particular 2859 ff. on heretical hymns; doctrinal battles, at popular level, were fought verse against verse, as W. H. C. Frend's unforgettable lectures, tutorials and books made plain.

91   So Cassian, *Conl.* 1.17.2, see Jungmann (supra n.89); G. Wille, *Musica romana* (Amsterdam 1967) 373.

have been, I suspect, all that difficult for many, once the substance of the texts in question was well-rooted in the memory.

Harris' discussion (pp.285-322) of Christian literacy raises numerous problems of interest; as elsewhere, his energy deserves our thanks. He is quite right, for example, to point out the existence of a strong anti-cultural streak in some writing of the patristic period, heir to the Gospels' attitude to the scribes, and product also of one Christian reaction to pagan cultural values and traditions (p.302).[92] Throughout this response to *Literacy*, I have sought to avoid detailed criticism but cannot pass by a very surprising account of the availability of books in the Christian west (p.298): Lactantius is driven to the short cuts charted by R. M. Ogilvie in consequence of the conditions of libraries and the book-trade in Trier and Nicomedia. The passage cited for Augustine's inability to find much of Cicero seems misunderstood (p.298 n.50),[93] and indeed it is clear that most of Cicero was in fact available to Augustine.[94] Harris should perhaps have concentrated not so much on Augustine[95] as on Jerome, on the difficulty of obtaining Christian texts in Palestine.[96] Availability had become a little more of a problem than it had been to Cicero or to Gellius.[97] If professional copyists became rarer (p.298), monks increased in number, and only exceptionally do the fathers copy *manu sua*.[98] It would also have been useful to have Harris' reactions to the intellectual and practical revolution wrought by the rapid spread of shorthand (composition of sermons, records of doctrinal debates and church councils).[99]

---

92   Cf. A.-J. Festugière, *Les moines d'Orient* 1 (Paris 1961) 77.

93   Cf. H. Hagendahl, *Augustine and the Latin classics* 2 (Göteborg 1967) 709 n.3.

94   Hagendahl 570.

95   Cf. J. Scheele, "Buch und Bibliothek bei Augustinus," *Bibliothek und Wissenschaft* 12 (1978) 73-75.

96   E. Arns, *La technique du livre d'après Saint Jérôme* (Paris 1953) 167-68, PL 22.622; the reader of Hier., *vir.ill.*, will note occasional complaints of unavailability.

97   Cf. chapt. 2 of my forthcoming book (supra n.78).

98   Cf. the first part of my "Two problems of late imperial literary history," *Tria Lustra* (ed. H. D. Jocelyn, forthcoming), *Essays in honour of John Pinsent*, with bibliography there listed. Both Arns (supra n.96) and Scheele (supra n.95) discuss the availability of copyists, scholars, professional scribes, and monks.

99   R. J. Deferrari, "St. Augustine's method of composing and delivering sermons," *AJP* 43 (1922) 97 ff., H. Hagendahl, "Die Bedeutung der Stenographie," *JAC* 14 (1971) 24 ff., Arns (supra n.96) 37 ff., Teitler (supra

And do my grubbings and grumblings lead to any general conclusions, or, better, to any statistics? That would be too much to hope for — except that, time and again, such understanding as I have of ancient attitudes to literacy and related topics leads me to the suspicion that Roman states of mind outwit modern statistical methods, leaving tables and results nicely warped, while alternative systems of learning and communication outwit the deficiencies, as perceived today, of Roman elementary education.

Rome, Italy

---

n.20), E. Tengström, *Die Protokollierung der Collatio Carthaginiensis* (Göteborg 1962). I should never have ventured back to the Fathers after so long but for the kind encouragement of Henry Chadwick and Emilio Rasco SJ, the strange chance which led me to lecture on Christian biography this year at the University of Messina, and the enthusiasm of Julia Budenz for, most conveniently, Caesarius of Arles.

Literacy and the parietal inscriptions of Pompeii

James L. Franklin, Jr.

Introduction: the study of written materials from Pompeii

Perhaps the greatest disappointment faced by students of Pompeii has been the absence of literary material in the discoveries. Despite the promise of the famous Epicurean scrolls found carbonized at the Villa dei Papiri near Herculaneum, no substantial continuous prose or poetry has ever been recovered at Pompeii. Yet over 11,000 pieces of writing have been recorded at this site, everything from shipping labels to scurrilous graffiti, from the famous campaign posters to lapidary inscriptions of the kinds common throughout the Roman world.[1] Even fragments of business records on wax tablets (the *apochae* of L. Caecilius Jucundus) survived the eruption.[2]

The material at hand for the student of daily life is stunning, but it remains largely neglected, at least in part because the key to understanding what has been recovered lies in a thorough knowledge of the topography of the site.[3] Few scholars have had the opportunity to pass the years necessary to acquire that knowledge by walking the ground and correlating the more than 200 years of excavation reports with their personal familiarity with the site.

---

1   The count is that of H. Mouritsen, *Elections, magistrates and municipal élite: studies in Pompeian epigraphy* (Analecta Romana Instituti Danici, Supplementum 15, Roma 1988) 9, and does not take into account conflated graffiti and election notices mistakenly counted as single inscriptions in the various publications.

2   The tablets recovered at nearby Agro Murecine in 1959 record matters relating to Puteoli rather than Pompeii: see F. Sbordone, "Preambolo per l'edizione critica delle tavolette cerate di Pompei," *RAAN* n.s. 51 (1976) 145-68.

3   *Pace* A. Mau, *Pompeii: its life and art* (2nd ed., transl. F. W. Kelsey, New York 1904) 491: "Taken as a whole, the graffiti are less fertile for our knowledge of Pompeian life than might have been expected". See H. Tanzer, *The common people of Pompeii* (Johns Hopkins University Studies in Archaeology 29, Baltimore 1939) 6, on Mau's non-egalitarian biases.

Over the years nearly all of the writing has crumbled from the walls, and the student must therefore turn to publications, especially to the *CIL*, the organization of which presents its own difficulties. The writing is catalogued there according to type, with parietal (i.e. everything written rather than carved) inscriptions placed in *CIL* IV and its three supplements, and lapidary inscriptions in *CIL* X. Unfortunately, neither volume is current, the final fascicule of the third supplement to *CIL* IV (which records inscriptions found only through 1956) having appeared in 1970 and without an index; while the last update of *CIL* X was in 1899.[4] Parietal inscriptions found after 1956 and lapidary inscriptions found after 1899 must be traced in Italian archaeological and learned publications.

The parietal material is further subdivided by type. There are professionally painted inscriptions (*pictae*), in turn subdivided into announcements of games (*edicta munerum*) and newer (*recentiora*), older (*antiquiora*), and very old (*antiquissima*) political posters (*programmata*). Graffiti scratched with stylus (*graphio exaratae*) form a separate category, as do alphabets and masons' marks, although this last category does not qualify as writing. Writing present on amphorae and other containers is subdivided into that written with brush, charcoal, or pen (likely to prove to be labels), that scratched with stylus (likely to prove casual), and that written in Greek. Since professional letterers, for example, sometimes painted graffiti which because painted were classified as *pictae* rather than graffiti, there is also some confusion among the types. Business records found on wax tablets are separately treated, and, of course, there are suspect or false inscriptions. Some entries have been mistakenly transcribed, and others contain two or more conflated readings.

Within their divisions, painted inscriptions, graffiti, alphabets, and lapidary inscriptions are catalogued by their locations at the site.

---

4   The initial issue of *CIL* IV was compiled from over 130 earlier sources by C. Zangemeister and contains many variant and often conflated readings. The first supplement to this collection, produced by Zangemeister in 1871, was the edition of the *apochae* of Caecilius Iucundus. The second supplement, again of written inscriptions in general, was prepared by A. Mau in 1909; it is the most magisterial and reliable of the volumes. The third supplement by M. Della Corte began appearing in fascicules in 1952; following his death, it was completed by Fulcher Weber in 1970. *CIL* X was updated by M. Ihm, "Addimenta ad corporis vol. IX et X," *EE* 8 (1899) 1-221; pp.86-90 pertain to Pompeii.

Amphorae were collected in *magazzini* prior to their publication, so that often an exact provenience is unknown, although as archaeological methods improved so did record-keeping.

The initial issue of *CIL* IV is keyed to the plan of Pompeii published therein. Later volumes are keyed to the masterplan of the site first drawn under the supervision of Giuseppe Fiorelli, in which the system of numbering by *regio, insula,* and *ianua* was developed. Between editions, however, the *regio* or *insula* numbers of 14 *insulae* were changed; 13 of these are correlated by Hans Eschebach in the introductory matter to the most recent plan of the site, but the change of the final supplement's *insula* I.11 to his I.19 escaped even his list.[5] Doorways, too, frequently had their numbers changed or regularized over time. Every entry in Zangemeister's volume, and many of those in subsequent supplements, must therefore be carefully correlated with the standard plan of Eschebach.

The problem of literacy

This mass of evidence obviously bears on the question of the level of literacy — or rather of writing and its corollary, reading — at Pompeii, and perhaps throughout early imperial Italy.[6] Yet the evidence is more complex than has been recognized. Even simple arithmetic inaccuracies bedevil the material and thus the student. Not only are the counts and categorizations of the inscriptions inexact, but estimates of the population that produced them vary widely, with current best guesses ranging from 8,000 to 20,000 persons — a very wide range.[7] Nor are the specific dates of most examples known. Further, they were produced over a considerable span of time.[8] One of the oldest datable graffiti,

---

5   H. Eschebach, *Die städtebauliche Entwicklung des antiken Pompeji* (Mitteilungen des DAI Rom, Ergänzungsheft 17, 1970) 115.

6   On the problems of defining literacy, see Harris 3-8; on extrapolating the Pompeian evidence to imperial Italy in general, see Harris 265. Note too that while reading is a corollary of writing, writing is not a corollary of reading: see R. Chartier, "Du livre au lire," *Pratiques de la lecture* (Paris 1985) 65: "dans toutes les sociétés d'ancien régime, et encore au XIXe siècle, existe en effet une alphabétisation féminine réduite à la seule lecture ...".

7   For the most recent discussion of the problem, see W. Jongman, *The economy and society of Pompeii* (Amsterdam 1988) 108-12.

8   Presumably however the damage from and repairs following the earthquake of 62 will have cleared a significant proportion of the walls.

scratched on the interior north wall of the basilica, records the date of
3 October 78 B.C., over 150 years before the destruction:
  C Pumidius Dipilus heic fuit
  a(nte) d(iem) v nonas octobreis M Lepid(o) Q Catul(o) co(n)s(ulibus)

(CIL IV.1842)

Moreover, the many varieties of types of writing must be kept in
mind. The business records of Caecilius Iucundus, for example, help
little in determining the general level of literacy; the ability to read
and write can be taken as a given in transactions of this sort.[9] Graffiti,
on the other hand, appear to have been written mostly by members of
the lower classes and therefore to offer the evidence of greatest value
in determining general literacy, which can safely be assumed for
businessmen and members of the local governing aristocracy.[10] Even so,
not all members of the lower classes wrote graffiti, and we lack the
perhaps more significant evidence of those who preferred to trust their
thoughts to less lasting media, or those who, like the literate but
hesitant elder Tom Joad, wrote only when necessary:
"No. Like I said, they wasn't people to write. Pa could write, but he wouldn'.
Didn't like to. It give him the shivers to write. He could work out a catalogue
order as good as the nex' fella, but he wouldn' write no letters just for ducks."[11]

To ask of this evidence a statistical evaluation of the level of
literacy, however literacy is defined at Pompeii, is to ask the wrong

---

9   The tablets have nevertheless been mistakenly interpreted as recording a
     number of persons unable to sign their names (so Harris 262, following T.
     Mommsen, "Die pompeianischen Quittungstafeln des L. Caecilius
     Jucundus," *Hermes* 12 [1877] 104-5, and G. Cavallo, *Alfabetismo e cultura
     scritta nella storia società italiana* [Perugia 1978] 121-22). The phrases
     justifying a second's signature for that of the principal involved in the
     transaction are variations on *se habere dixit* or *eum accepisse* by *rogatu*
     or *mandatu*. This language does not imply illiteracy, and more reasonably
     indicates that the transaction was considered so insignificant or
     customary, or the meeting so inconvenient to the principal, that a second
     was deputed out of preference (so V. Arangio-Ruiz, *FIRA* 3: *negotia* 408:
     manu ... alterius personae ab eo specialiter rogatae). The principal may
     have regularly employed such an agent. Or it may be that one's actual
     signature was not of overwhelming significance *per se*. Had it been, any
     mark from an illiterate principal's own hand would have been preferred to
     the second's signature.
10   So Harris 248: "within the elites of the established Graeco-Roman world a
     degree of written culture was a social necessity, and an illiterate male
     would have been regarded as bizarre".
11   J. Steinbeck, *The grapes of wrath* (New York 1941) 57.

question. Given such variables in the town's possible population and in the dates and counts of the inscriptions, meaningful statistics are beyond the evidence. In Pompeian society of the 1st c. A.D., literacy for the lower classes can be assumed to have lain somewhere beyond the craftsman's level, in which "the majority, or a near majority of skilled craftsmen, are literate, while women and unskilled labourers and peasants are mainly not" — but assessment of how far beyond the craftsman's level will result only from a close study of the evidence that has hardly begun.[12] Cruces of interpretation confront the student with nearly every example, and assumptions must always be guarded against, especially in the case of such apparently familiar formats as posters and graffiti. Indeed, perusal of this evidence in its mass has led scholars to estimate the level of literacy from "far, far lower than 65%" to "a high degree", a variation comparable to that displayed in the population estimates.[13]

Given the absence of those factors — industrialization, Protestantism, and the printing press — that Stone found significant in the growth of mass literacy in England, and the positive impediments — expensive materials, poorly organized schooling, predominantly rural living patterns, and limited economic bureaucracy — that Harris has identified in classical antiquity, high levels of literacy might not be expected at Pompeii.[14] On the other hand, the vivacity and sheer mass of the evidence suggests a widely literate population. To resolve such contradictory impressions into a solid picture of the reality will take sustained effort of the kind recently given to the *apochae* of Caecilius Iucundus, in which the evidence was approached with a variety of methodologies to produce new insights into the social structure of the town as well as the content of the tablets themselves.[15] For the present, a brief example of directions for further work — the content and the context of the writing — must suffice. But work cannot focus exclusively on the writing. Numerous paintings of reading and writing, their materials and instruments, have been recovered. The value of Pompeii has always lain in the entirety of the picture that it can provide, and the pictorial evidence must be included in any analysis. Unfortunately

---

12   I follow here the distinctions of Harris 7-8, between "scribal", "craftsman's" and "mass" literacy.

13   Harris 262-63 (and at 259 on Italy in general: "the level of male literacy was well below the 20-30% range"); and H. Tanzer (supra n.3) 6, respectively.

14   L. Stone, "Literacy and education in England 1640-1900," *Past and Present* 42 (1969) 69-139, esp. 69-98, and Harris 12-24.

15   J. Andreau, *Les affaires de Monsieur Jucundus* (Coll.EFR 19, 1974).

pictorial material can also be subject to widely differing interpretations. A section of the forum frieze from the Praedia Iuliae Felicis, for example, has always seemed to show citizens reading public announcements written on placards secured to the bases of the statues along the northwest corner of the forum. Yet it has recently been suggested that one of the figures could be reading aloud to an illiterate second.[16] However, it remains possible to observe the value and status of reading and writing in this and other representations, and to employ the observation in analysis.

The walls of Pompeii

One of the best known graffiti from Pompeii —

> admiror te paries non c(e)cidisse (ruinis)
> qui tot scriptorum taedia sustineas   (*CIL* IV. 2487)

— first found in the amphitheatre, has been found repeated once in the large theatre (*CIL* IV. 2461) and perhaps twice in the basilica (*CIL* IV. 1904, 1906). Examination of reproductions that have been preserved makes it clear that four different hands produced the graffiti (fig.1). This elegiac couplet was evidently a well known lament, and would seem to be a gnome of widespread application in Roman cities, just like the traveller's weary longing for Rome, found eight times at Pompeii, once at Herculaneum:[17]

> venimus huc cupidi, multo magis ire cupimus
> ut liceat nostros visere, Roma, Lares   (*CIL* IV. 8114).

So well known was this ditty that it was cleverly modified at the House of Fabius Rufus to comment on the beauty of one of its inhabitants:[18]

> venimus hoc cupidi, multo magis ire cupimus
> set retinet nostros illa puella pedes.

Both repeated couplets confirm that writing on walls was normal, if tiresome, not only at Pompeii but elsewhere, and that clever graffiti were remembered and repeated, sometimes even with personalizing

---

16   The suggestion is that of Harris 34-35, although he seems to abandon it at 264, n.464.

17   Copies of *CIL* IV. 8114 at Pompeii: *CIL* IV. 1227, 2995, 6697, 8231, 8891, 9849, 10065*a*; at Herculaneum: IV. 10640.

18   C. Giordano, "Le iscrizioni della Casa di M. Fabio Rufo," *RAAN* n.s. 41 (1966) 82.

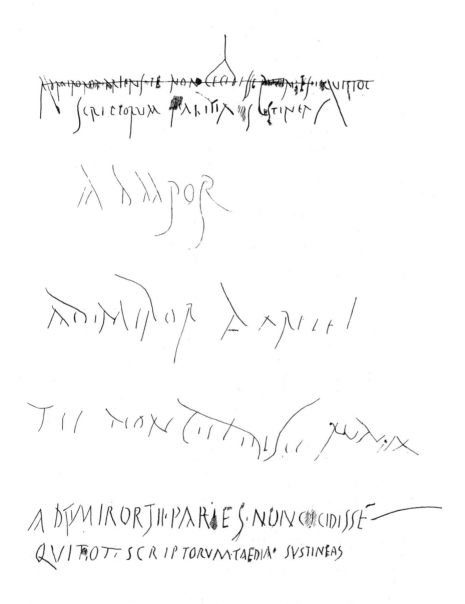

Fig.1. admiror te paries non cecidisse ruinis   from top to bottom
   qui tot scriptorum taedia sustineas *CIL* IV. 1904, 1906, 2461, 2487.

truths. At Rome, in fact, inscribed walls were referred to by Plautus, Cicero, Pliny, and Martial, and a Greek graffito echoed the sentiment of the famous Pompeian couplet:[19]

πολλοὶ πολλὰ ἐπέγραψαν
ἐγὼ μόνος οὔτι ἔγραψα.[20]

Programmata and edicta

The walls bordering the major streets of Pompeii were heavily inscribed not only with graffiti but also with painted political posters and announcements of public events. Typically the name of the candidate or the provider of the event was lettered far larger than the details of the election or the event, so that it could, presumably, be worried out even by the semi-literate. But in most posters and in all announcements details were carefully included by skilled professional letterers (scriptores) and appear to have been intended to be read and understood. The simple existence of the profession indicates the importance of legibility throughout.[21]

A typical political poster was also filled with abbreviations:

Valentem
filium aed v a s p p ovf   (CIL IV. 7557)

Whether abbreviations in contrived ligatures, such as ovf for oro vos faciatis, were in fact understood as more than symbols by some readers, the elections were warmly contested; thus, even complicated abbreviations for the various offices (such as aed v a s p p for aedilis viis aedibus sacris publicisque procurandis) must have been intelligible to the voters if only by virtue of their constant repetition.[22]

---

19   Plaut., Merc.409: impleantur elegeorum meae fores carbonis; Cic., Verr., 3.33.77: versus plurimi supra tribunal et supra praetoris caput scribebantur; Plin., Ep.8.7: leges multa omnibus columnis omnibus parietibus inscripta; Mart. 12.61.7-10: carbone et creta scribet carmina.

20   P. Castrén and H. Lilius, Graffiti del Palatino II: Domus Tiberiana (Acta Instituti Finlandiae 4, 1970) 145.

21   On scriptores and their modus operandi, see J. L. Franklin, Jr., "Notes on Pompeian prosopography: programmatum scriptores," CronPomp 4 (1978) 54-74.

22   Even names of candidates are sometimes reduced to initials in the campaign posters; on their ready intelligibility and the possibility that initials were what electors inscribed on their voting tablets, see J. L. Franklin, Jr., Pompeii: the electoral programmata, campaigns and politics

Presumably public notices, particularly *edicta munerum*, were meant to be thoroughly comprehended (fig.2):

D(ecimi) Lucreti / Satri Valentis flaminis Neronis
Caesaris Augusti fili / perpetui, gladiatorum paria XX et
D(ecimi) Lucreti{o} Valentis fili / glad(iatorum) paria X
pug(nabunt) Pompeis VI, V, IV, III, pr(idie) idus apr(iles),
venatio legitima / et vela erunt.[23]   (*CIL* IV. 3884)
"Twenty pairs of gladiators of Decimus Lucretius Satrius
Valens, perpetual flamen of Nero Caesar son of Augustus, and
ten pairs of gladiators of Decimus Lucretius Valens his son will
fight at Pompeii on the sixth, fifth, fourth, third and day
before the Ides of April. There will be a genuine hunt and
awnings."

Fig.2. *CIL* IV. 3884.

In these announcements, details of date and place were particularly important, while specific inducements — the supply of gladiators, an animal hunt, and the provision of awnings, in this case — enhanced the attraction, the anticipation, and the remembered enjoyment of the games after the fact.

But whether campaign poster or announcement of public event, advertizing the immediate was only a part of a notice's value and purpose. *Programmata* and *edicta* were left in place, often for several

---

A.D. 71-79 (Papers and Monographs of the American Academy in Rome 28, 1980) 27, n.3.

23   Text of P. Sabbatini Tumolesi, *Gladiatorum paria: annunci di spettacoli gladiatorii a Pompei* (Tituli 1, Roma 1980) 27, who notes that the excess "o" in line 3 must simply be due to error of the *scriptor*. On the comments of the *scriptor* Aemilius Celer added to this notice, see below.

years, until the space on which they were painted was needed for reuse. Hence the name of the candidate or generous patron — the element of posters that was regularly lettered in larger scale — in the end proved more important than the details. Over the course of time even the semi- or illiterate will have had occasion to absorb the powerful name and the type of poster with which it was associated. Decimus Lucretius Satrius Valens and his son will have become firmly fixed in the minds of all as generous statesmen from an established family.

The same principles apply to the honorary, dedicatory, and funerary inscriptions that cluttered this and all other Roman cities. Particularly those cut from the Augustan age were heavy with details of office-holding and honors that bore significance for the educated reader, whereas the name alone — again normally cut at a larger scale, and at least recorded first — was what signified to the less deft.[24]

M Holconio M f Rufo
trib(uno) mil(itum) a populo IIvir(o) i(ure) d(icundo) V
quinq(uennali) iter(um)
Augusti Caesaris sacerd(oti)
patrono coloniae   (*CIL* X. 830)
"To Marcus Holconius Rufus, son of Marcus, military tribune by (choice of) the people, five times *duovir iure dicundo*, twice *duovir quinquennalis*, priest of Caesar Augustus, patron of the colony."

Indeed, for all the major varieties of inscriptions, the most important reading was visual, not literate. Whether lapidary or parietal, the type of inscription was immediately clear to any passer-by from visual clues. For example, first one noted that it was an honorary inscription, for it was on an honorary gate and identified an impressive statue; secondly, a capable reader noted the name of the honoree, which could be read rapidly without stopping; finally, the interested (normally an educated preserver of or striver for social status) could pause to decipher the detailed and abbreviated *cursus*.[25] General cognition was not dependent upon reading ability.

---

24   On the change to detailed inscriptions in the Augustan age, see W. Eck, "Senatorial self-representation: developments in the Augustan period," in F. Millar and E. Segal, *Caesar Augustus: seven aspects* (Oxford 1984) 129-67.

25   On the significance of place in reading an inscription see Eck (ibid.) 132: "monument and inscription formed, for a Roman, a self-evident unity, to be sure; an inscription without an object to which it belonged was scarcely conceivable". And such continued to be the case according to J. Sparrow,

Pompeii's *programmata* and *edicta munerum* were similarly understood. Given their regularity of format, they could be categorized immediately by all passers-by; the large scale names of patron or candidate could be deciphered even by the semi-literate (and over time revealed to the illiterate); the details (largely of short-term importance) studied by those for whom they were of significance. And these readings were valuable in a descending scale — the first two available to most people over the course of time, the third of least value and available to the smallest number. What therefore at first glance appear to be easily analyzed posters of a rather modern kind, announcing an event or a candidate to a reading public, in fact served a second, equally important purpose at Pompeii, since they affirmed the prominence and solidity of the leading families over the long term. Ironically, this second purpose required few or no reading skills on the part of the passer-by, and the modern interpreter of these posters must beware of his too literate vision shackled by his tendency to focus on the text apart from its context. Yet despite this, notices are posted to be read, as the detailed information provided (some of it crucial) and careful lettering demonstrate.

Graffiti

Graffiti likewise must be studied on more than one level, and their contexts prove as important as their contents. The information they convey can explain the spaces in which they were found, their locations can illuminate patterns of traffic or of loitering. Written almost entirely by Pompeii's lower classes, and without ulterior purposes, they yet reveal far more when taken in context and in conjunction with other similar writing at the town.

Graffiti fall into 2 broad categories: those that are mainly self-indulgent, and those written primarily to convey information (although an element of self-indulgence is rarely lacking in any graffito).

1. Self-indulgent

Whether a self-indulgent graffito was read by another was irrelevant to its writer; one variety, the alphabet seemingly scratched

---

Visible words: a study of inscriptions in and as books and works of art (Cambridge 1969) 102: "By the beginning of the seventeenth century the inscription had come into its own; elaborate sculptured monuments were still of course produced ... but in most memorials the inscription was the dominant feature."

for practice, could have conveyed no overt message. Several alphabets, however, are Greek or Oscan, and apparently point to the acquisition of a second language, Latin presumably being the first in the case of Greek, and the second in the case of Oscan.[26] Ironically, quotations from literature — exactly those graffiti that seem to attest to education and literary knowledge — generally fall also into the category of self-indulgent. The most common quotation was the first line of the *Aeneid*, which was found in a variety of locations and fragments, including simply the first two words — even misquoted:[27]

arma viru(mque)   (*CIL* IV. 3198)

arma virus[28]   (*CIL* IV. 1282)

(a)rma virumque cano Troia(e) qui primus ab oris
                       (*CIL* IV. 4832)

So well known was this line that it was reworked outside the house of Fabius Ululitremulus at IX.13.5 to refer to the distinctive noise of fullers:

fullones ululamque cano non arma virumque   (*CIL* IV. 9131)

Fragments and reminiscences of several other poets, Greek as well as Latin, have been identified throughout the town, but overall appear to have been written for the pleasure of the individual writer, not the edification of (or, as in this last case, comment on) the public at large.[29] Most are short fragments of a word or two, and they raise the issue of the ability to quote accurately and at length at the same time that they attest a basic familiarity with the poets.

2. Informative

Given the lack of alternative media for exchanging messages, informative graffiti seem to have been used more seriously and readily than they are today. Thus, outside a secondary entrance (I.10.16) to the Casa del Menandro, Novellia Primigenia of Nuceria, apparently a visitor and a great beauty known also at Herculaneum, seems to have aroused sufficient interest that a graffito provided her forwarding

---

26   Greek at *CIL* IV. 5461-62, 9263, 9274-76, 9281, 9288, 9296-97, 9303, 10255, 10258*a*; Oscan at R. Conway, *The Italic dialects* (Cambridge 1897) 1: 79, nos. 81*a-d*. On the retention of Oscan at Pompeii, see Harris 178.

27   On Vergilian references in the graffiti, see M. Gigante, *Civiltà delle forme letterarie nell'antica Pompei* (Naples 1979) 163-83.

28   At *CIL* IV. 1282: "ultima, quae litterae S formam habet, nescio an M sit inchoata".

29   See the recent, although at times too enthusiastic, survey of Gigante (supra n.27).

address to fend off constant enquiry:[30]

> Nucerea [sic] quaeres ad Porta(m) Romana(m)
> in vico Venerio, Novelliam
> Primigeniam   (*CIL* IV. 8356)

Just outside the town on tomb 23OS near the Porta Nocera, her name was again traced in a graffito, along with a complimentary couplet that was repeated twice elsewhere in the town:[31]

> vellem essem gemma hora non amplius una
> ut tibi signanti oscula missa darem   (*CIL* IV. 10242a)

Normally, however, more physical allures were addressed, as in and around the famous *lupanar* at VII.12.18-20:[32]

> hic ego puellas multas
> futui   (*CIL* IV. 2175)

> Felix
> bene futuis   (*CIL* IV. 2176)

In fact, concerns for the brassier aspects of life, both in physical pleasures and entertainments, dominate the graffiti. References to gladiators, their *familiae*, and win-loss records, often with accompanying illustrations, are found scattered all around the town, even in elegant houses like that of the Ceii (I.6.11) (fig.3):

Oceanus l(ibertus) XIII v(icit)   Arancintus l(ibertus) IIII

                                                    pestiario[33]
figura gladiatoris   *figura gladiatoris*   (*CIL* IV. 8055)

Gladiators in turn deemed themselves great woman-killers, as the graffiti left by Celadus Crescens, a Traex-retiarius, in the training school at V.5.3 reveal:

---

30   The interpretation is that of M. Della Corte, *Loves and lovers in ancient Pompeii* (transl. A. W. Van Buren, Cava dei Tirreni 1960) 101-20.

31   Along the Via degli Augustali was *gemma velim fieri hora non* (*CIL* IV. 1698); in the Casa di Fabio Rufo, *velle(m) essem gemma hora non amplius una / ut tivi* [sic] *oscula missa dare(m)* (C. Giordano [supra n.18] 83). On the couplet, its antecedents, and importance, see Gigante (supra n.27) 88-99.

32   On the graffiti found in this *lupanar* and the neighborhood see J. L. Franklin, Jr., "Games and a *lupanar*: prosopography of a neighborhood in ancient Pompeii," *CJ* 81 (1985-86) 319-28.

33   In line 2 *pestario* must stand for *bestiarius*; on confusion of *p* for *b* in the inscriptions, see also *CIL* IV. 538: *Bompeiana* for *Pompeiana*. On the subdivision of gladiator graffiti, its special vocabulary and abbreviations, see A. Mau, "Iscrizioni gladiatorie di Pompei," *RömMitt* 5 (1890) 25-39.

90   Literacy and the parietal inscriptions of Pompeii

puellarum decus
Celadus tr(aex)   (CIL IV. 4345)

tr(aex)
Celadus reti(arius)
Cresce(n)s
pupar{r}u(m) dom(i)nus   (CIL IV. 4356)

Fig.3. *CIL* IV. 8066.

There were great enthusiasms for pantomimes: Actius Anicetus and his troupe have been shown on the basis of graffiti at both Pompeii and Herculaneum to have toured the Bay of Naples, and fan clubs for Anicetus and the famous Neronian Paris (the Anicetiani and Paridiani) were organized at Pompeii where they saluted performers and also recommended political candidates for election:[34]

ania

Acti Castrensis va(lete) Anicetiane[35]   (CIL IV. 2413*d*)

C Cuspius Pansa aed ovf
Purpurio cum Paridianis[36].   (CIL IV. 7919)

---

34   On Actius Anicetus see J. L. Franklin, Jr., "Pantomimists at Pompeii: Actius Anicetus and his troupe," *AJPh* 108 (1987) 95-107.

35   Line 1 appears to be an intended correction of the spelling of *Anicetiane* in line 2. On the Anicetiani see Gigante (supra n.27) 148, n.252, and Franklin ibid. 104.

36   On the Paridiani, see M. Della Corte, *Case ed abitanti di Pompei* (3rd ed., Napoli 1965) nos. 660-61.

This writing can be surprisingly informative for the scholar. As in the notice of the Anicetiani, spelling and grammatical errors and alternatives litter the graffiti, showing that its writers were not the best-trained students. Yet the errors themselves are valuable for reproducing the spellings of words as they were pronounced. "Co", for example, was regularly pronounced "qu" and so spelled, as in an election notice posted by the workers in a dye-shop (*coactiliarii*) at IX.7.5-7:[37]

Vettium Firmum quactiliari [*sic*] rog(ant)　　　　(*CIL* IV. 7838)

Frequent occurrences of adverbs ending in *-biliter* show that this suffix was popular in the town, although not elsewhere.[38] Aemilius Celer, a *scriptor* and frequent graffiti-writer, who was fond of writing his own name in backwards script (viz. 'suillimeA'), left one of the two attestations (both Pompeian) of *fratrabiliter* in the entire language:[39]

suillimeA Cissonio fratrabiliter sal(utem)　　　　(*CIL* IV. 659).

Aemilius Celer introduces another problematic aspect of the analysis – that of the inveterate graffiti-writer — for he was responsible for perhaps 35 inscriptions scattered all around the town.[40] Celer was fond of pattern as well as of backwards script — characteristics that help distinguish his work from that of other Celers — and he even added his name and working conditions to his major surviving commission, the *edictum munerum* of D. Lucretius Satrius Valens and his son (fig.2):

P Ae
　m
　il
　iu　　amicu [*sic*]　　　　(*CIL* IV. 5291)

scr(ipsit)
Aemilius
Celer sing(ularis)
ad luna(m)　　　　(*CIL* IV. 3884*b*)

37　On *qu* for *co*, see V. Väänänen, *Le latin vulgaire des inscriptions pompéiennes* (Abhandlungen der Deutschen Akademie der Wissenschaften zu Berlin, Klasse für Sprachen, Literatur und Kunst, 1958, 3, 2nd ed. Berlin 1959) 53 n.1.

38　On the suffix, ibid. 99.

39　See also *CIL* IV. 8227.

40　*CIL* IV. 659-60a, 1689, 1759, 2400d-e, 3456, 3775, 3790, 3792, 3794, 3806, 3812, 3820, 3884, 4557, 4729, 4737, 4741, 5093, 5288-89, 5291, 5294, 5309, 5325, 5328, 5331-32, 5350, 6844, 7494, 8409, and perhaps 1255a.

scr(ipsit)
Celer   (*CIL* IV. 3884*a*)[41]

With other individuals, however, it is not so easy to trace and separate out different graffiti, a necessary step for accurate analysis of them.

A case-study: Pompeii VII.7.2.4-5, 14-15

The tracing of Aemilius Celer's scattered graffiti leads us to one case study of a defined sample of graffiti. This group promises to yield some deeper insights into the question of the overall level of literacy than our general survey so far. Aemilius Celer's backwards salute to Cissonius was recovered near the Porta Marina at VII.*Ins.Occ.* 2-3, just down the street from the property to which Cissonius was somehow attached, the large complex at VII.7.2.4-5,14-15.[42] At the house itself, Celer left graffiti in which his name was lettered correctly, backwards, and signed to a salute to two other friends, Saturnia and Vitalis, apparently also residents of the house:[43]

Aemilius hic   (*CIL* IV. 4729)

Saturniae Vitalio va(le)
suilimeA   (*CIL* IV. 4737)

---

41   I have here and below adopted the convention of an additional letter to distinguish separate features of *CIL* entries.

42   Della Corte (supra n.36) nos. 434-40 identified this as the house of L. Calpurnius Diogenes on the basis of a *signaculum* he reports found in the house. At *CIL* X. 8058.14, however, the findspot of the *signaculum* was merely "*pone aedem Veneris*". The evidence, moreover, was greatly confused by Della Corte, who failed properly to understand the salutes of Aemilius Celer and so created an Aemilius Crescens, architect, to whom he was forced to assign the property down the street at VII. *Ins.Occ.*3 (Della Corte no.430a, followed by Eschebach [supra n.5] 144), since he had already identified the property in which Crescens was named as that of Calpurnius. The elements Aemilius and Crescens nowhere appear together as a name, but are frequently attested apart, and Crescens was besides apparently a slave (see below on *CIL* IV. 4752), and so would not have referred to himself as Aemilius but rather Aemilii Crescens. In fact, Aemilius Celer and Crescens were separate individuals known to each other as well as to Cissonius, either the agent of Calpurnius or the new owner of the property who instigated its remodelling (so G. De Petra, the original excavator, at *Giornale degli scavi di Pompei* n.s.2 [1870-73] 178-82, 225-31, 369-77).

43   Vitalis is known also from the graffito *CIL* IV. 4731 found in the house: *Vitalis | Vitalis | Vedius*.

suilimeA   (*CIL* IV. 4741)

Observations made at the time of excavation noted traces of walls recently demolished and others newly built: remodelling was in course here when Vesuvius erupted.[44] The architect Cresces, whom we must properly call Crescens, was in charge and twice left his name and title in the house, working them into the shape of a boat by extending the *hastae* of the upright letters downward to form oars, and tracing the lower bend of the final 's' back under the whole inscription to suggest a keel. The upward extension of the first 't' of *architectus* to form a mast completed the effect (fig.4):

Cresces architectus[45]   (*CIL* IV. 4716)

Cresces architectus   (*CIL* IV. 4755)

He was even able to carry out the same design in a salute to a Spatalus (fig.5):

Cresces Spatalo
sal(utem)   (*CIL* IV. 4742)

Like the *scriptor* Aemilius Celer who left salutes all around town, Crescens seems to have formed warm friendships and to have been fond of advertizing them. He twice saluted Cissonius and also wished well to a Hispanus, and, apparently, to all his fellow slaves:

Cresces
Cissonio
sal(utem)   (*CIL* IV. 4715)

Cresces Cissonio sal(utem)   (*CIL* IV. 4728)

Cresces
Hispano
salutem   (*CIL* IV. 4778)

Cresces conservis
universis sal(utem)   (*CIL* IV. 4752).

Indeed, his even temper seems to have been recorded in another graffito:

Cresces have anima
dulcis et suavis   (*CIL* IV. 4783).

---

44   De Petra (supra n.42) 178: " ... ha tutti i segni di essere stata posterior-mente aggiunta all'altra, e di trovarsi in via di transformazione quando soprovvenne la catastrofe di Pompei".

45   Only *CIL* IV. 4755 preserved the design in publication; at 4716: ... *scripta in similitudinem navis.*

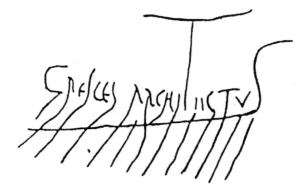

Fig.4. *CIL·*IV. 4755.

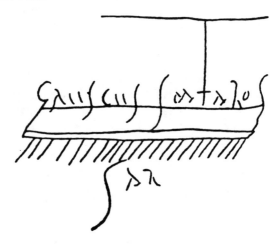

Fig.5. *CIL* IV. 4742.

In all 83 graffiti were found in the peristyle of VII.7.5 where Crescens seems to have set up his supervisory station:[46]

      Cresces hic situs   (*CIL* IV. 4734).

A Cypare was having a window installed on the north side of the peristyle and had marked and labeled its dimensions on the wall, and the imminent remodelling seems to have loosed the hands of the workmen:

      -----

      fenestra
      Cypares

---

46   *CIL* IV. 4706-85.

alta a terra
inter duo
hoc est   (*CIL* IV. 4713*a*)

------

lata fenestra
inter duo hoc est.[47]   (*CIL* IV. 4713*b*)

A Restitutus, perhaps by contrast to Perarius and Ladicula who were accused of theft, was stylized as a reliable slave:

Restitutus
servos [*sic*] bonus (*CIL* IV. 4719)

Perari
fur es   (*CIL* IV. 4764)

Ladicula
fur est   (*CIL* IV. 4776)

A Clymene was told to go hang herself:

(*restis in nodum*) habeat Clymene[48]   (*CIL* IV. 4756)

A unique adverb compounded with -*biliter*, of the sort favored by Aemilius Celer, seems to have urged on the work:

festinabiliter (*CIL* IV. 4758)

A Seubulio or Eubulio was named three times:

Seubuli Seubulio
          o   (*CIL* IV. 4727)

Eubulio   (*CIL* IV. 4773)

A Sabinio apparently considered himself an artist, for he twice (*CIL* IV. 4722, 4723) illustrated graffiti with drawings of animals, once adding a cryptic phrase about the art of the town (fig.6):

Sabinio ars
ars urbici ub(i)q(ue)
(*animal*)   (*CIL* IV. 4723)

An Aephebus saluted his father Successus, and was himself called a busybody, or *ardalio*:

Aephebus
Successo patri
suo salut(em) (*CIL* IV. 4753)

---

47   Mau at *CIL* IV. 4713: " ... fenestra alta et lata est inter duo quantum lineola, quae est supra utriusque inscriptionis principium, distat a terra."

48   For the correct interpretation of this graffito, see C. Huelsen, "Satura Pompeiana Romana," *Sumbolae litterariae in honorem Iulii De Petra* (Napoli 1911) 171-74; cf. Mau at *CIL* IV. 4756 "intellegas potius: *habeat Clymene* scil. phallum."

Aephebe
ardalio es   (*CIL* IV. 4765)

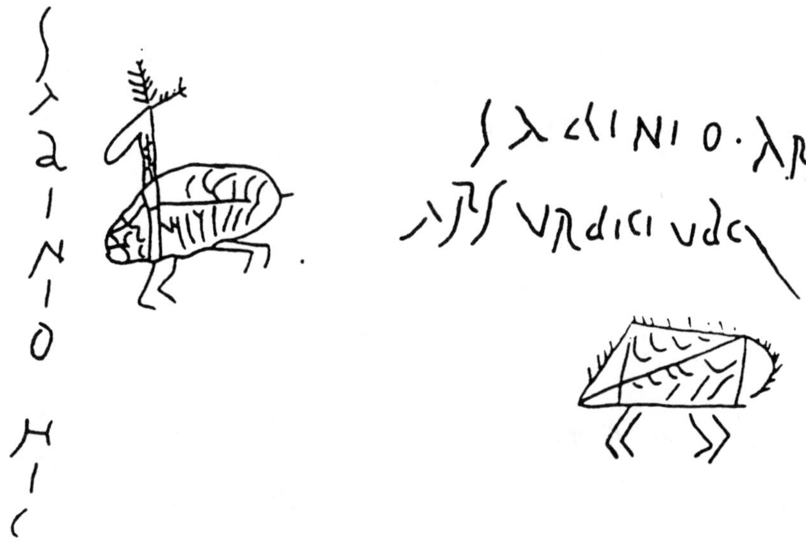

Fig.6. *CIL* IV. 4722 and 4723.

There were even traces of enthusiasms for the theatre:

comicus
hac [=hic]   (*CIL* IV. 4745)
chorus   (*CIL* IV. 4735)
Fumiolus
cum archimimo
a sipario
receptus[49]   (*CIL* IV. 4767)

Finally, there was a death notice:

Confirminus
L Otacilius moritur   (*CIL* IV. 4777).

Salutes, slanders, threats, building instructions, theatrical allusions, even a death notice: in all, it is a surprisingly vivacious picture, suggesting that nearly all of these workmen were capable of writing, given the impetus and the invitation by a stretch of

---

49   Just below was 4758, which may as well refer to a mime: Crome cum /
       noverca / tres pannosi / pater cum Agla(e?).

unrestricted wall. Of Crescens' literacy, requisite to the boss of the shop, few scholars would have had suspicion; but that his laborers also could read and write indicates literacy considerably higher than the 'craftsman's level'. The 83 graffiti that covered this peristyle, some eliciting others, confirm the ability to read and write among a class of laborers for whom literacy would not *a priori* have been assumed.

It is in fact the context of these graffiti — the unrestricted wall, a luxury normally unavailable, and the remodelling in progress — that allows their accurate interpretation. The knowledge of the situation in which and the laborers by whom they were written gives value to their content. Elsewhere in the town, too, studies of circumscribed, closely defined locales should offer the best possibilities of understanding our evidence. Thus at the famous brothel at VII.12.18-20, where too the walls appear to have been free for thoughts to be recorded, more than 120 graffiti were recovered — graffiti that had been written not only by clients but also by the whores, again a class probably below the 'craftsman's'. It is to such studies that analysis of literacy at Pompeii must turn, for they allow us to progress beyond the failure of statistics to characterize the evidence.

Writing at Pompeii

Whether professionally lettered poster, or quickly scrawled graffito, the parietal inscriptions of Pompeii present a complex picture. Only careful studies of both the context and content of the evidence, so as to identify its varieties, purposes, and writers, will clarify our vision. A number of approaches should underlie the various studies. Men like Aemilius Celer must be followed around town. Properties must be examined first individually, then generically. The details must first be clarified, then the larger issue of general literacy can be tackled. Yet even now some observations can be made. The laborers managed by Crescens *architectus* proved more literate and more prone to graffiti than one might have suspected; so too were the whores of the brothel at VII.12.18-20. Cypare, whose name suggests lowly status, was capable of writing instructions for the installation of a window. The admirers of Novellia Primigenia were at least assumed to be literate by the harried inhabitant in the rustic quarters of the Casa del Menandro. Not only could devotees of the theatre and games read and write: so could the gladiators themselves. Aemilius Celer enjoyed playing with his readers by lettering backwards. Even political posters and announcements of upcoming games were highly detailed, though also designed to be comprehended generically by the illiterate. All of that suggests widespread literacy.

The frequent appearance of elegiac couplets and quotations from the poets indicates education (though perhaps closer to the level of copybook, or a good ear in an oral society, than to true familiarity). Yet caution must be exercised. The very second word of the *Aeneid* was bungled. And only the last of the four writers of the famous lament on the heavily inscribed wall (fig.1) recognized that he was producing an elegiac couplet. Even Aemilius Celer, the professional letterer, produced an incorrect genitive in the important *edictum munerum* of the Decimi Lucretii Valentes (fig.2). But this does not negate the view that literacy was common among Pompeii's lower classes.

Why does our picture develop differently from that drawn by Harris? In his book he set out four classic impediments to widespread literacy: expensive writing materials, poorly organized schooling, predominantly rural living patterns, and limited economic bureaucracy.[50] At Pompeii, Tacitus' *celebre oppidum*, two at least of these impediments were lessened: urban living patterns prevailed, and a form of economic bureaucracy had penetrated even to the level of the *apochae* of L. Caecilius Iucundus.[51] Pompeii was an urban environment in which the populace had to earn its living — this was not an idle urban mass kept distracted by bread and circuses; for earning a living, even for construction laborers, literacy appears to have proved to be an advantage. Neither *rus* nor Roma, Pompeii may well be more illustrative of early imperial Italy than either.

Department of Classical Studies, Indiana University

---

50   Harris 12-24, and see above.
51   Tac., *Ann.* 15.22.4. The tablets actually refer to a slightly earlier period; Iucundus was in all likelihood dead before 79, and cannot be proved to have been active after 62 (Andreau [supra n.15] 29).

L'écriture en quête de lecteurs
Mireille Corbier

En adoptant le parti d'étudier le thème de l'alphabétisation sur la très longue durée — du VIIIᵉ siècle avant J.-C. au Vᵉ siècle après — William Harris a choisi, à juste titre et avec succès, la difficulté. Un tel parti, fondé sur une masse impressionnante de lectures, rend difficile la critique de la part de qui n'a pas la maîtrise d'une information portant sur plus d'un millénaire. Mais, dans la mesure même où la question posée est le degré d'alphabétisation, chaque spécialiste d'une période courte est fondé à relire dans ce contexte les propositions de l'auteur.

Je limiterai donc pour l'essentiel mes remarques à la période de l'histoire romaine traitée dans le chapitre 7 (The Late Republic and the High Empire), avec des aperçus sur quelques points traités par l'auteur dans les chapitres 6 (Archaic Italy and the Middle Republic) et 8 (Literacy in Late Antiquity).

Le sujet du livre est clairement défini: à la question liminaire "How many people could read, how many people could write in the Graeco-Roman World?", l'auteur veut fournir des réponses chiffrées qui s'inscrivent toutes à un niveau relativement bas, par comparaison avec ceux qui ont été atteints à d'autres époques plus récentes; ainsi (p.259) à propos de l'Italie tardo-républicaine et impériale: "All this evidence might lead us to conclude that the level of male literacy was well below the 20-30% range which prevailed in, say, England of the period 1580-1700. And the evidence we have so far encountered about Roman women suggests that their literacy was below, perhaps far below, 10%"; à nouveau (p.267) à propos de la seule Italie: "I conclude that the overall level of literacy is likely to have been below 15%"; et (p.272) à propos de l'Occident romain: "make it unlikely that the overall literacy of the western provinces rose into the range of 5-10%". Des arguments variés sont avancés à l'appui de la thèse, sans cesse réaffirmée, par réaction contre toutes les estimations optimistes antérieures, du "low level of literacy" de la cité romaine, puis de l'Empire.

L'alphabétisation: le comparatisme

Il n'est pas douteux que les recherches menées par les historiens médiévistes et modernistes sur l''alphabétisation' ont stimulé la réflexion des antiquisants: ceux-ci, il y a peu encore, s'interrogeaient

plutôt sur 'l'éducation' dans l'antiquité.[1] Pour l'Europe médiévale et
moderne, ce domaine de recherche s'est constitué dans les années 60 avec
le passage d'une histoire plus économique à une histoire plus culturelle.
En se tournant vers le domaine nouveau de la culture, les historiens ont
emprunté beaucoup de leurs méthodes aux économistes. Mais ils se sont
inspirés aussi des anthropologues.

La filiation directe avec l'histoire économique est patente: l'histoire de l'alphabétisation est, à ses débuts au moins, une histoire
sérielle, fondée sur des traitements statistiques, débouchant sur l'établ-
issement de tableaux, de graphiques, de cartes. Elle cherche en effet à
mesurer les signes de la capacité à lire et à écrire (l'un des indicateurs
privilégiés étant celle des conjoints à signer leur acte de mariage), de la
production et de la diffusion du livre, de la consommation du livre (à
défaut de chiffres relatifs aux ventes, des indices indirects sont tirés de
la composition des bibliothèques telle que la restituent les inventaires
après décès). Ce n'est que dans un second temps que les historiens
passeront à une approche plus qualitative sur les modes de la lecture et
les pratiques de l'écriture.

Vers les mêmes années 1960-1970, Jack Goody, étudiant les mêmes
problèmes avec le regard de l'anthropologue,[2] propose un modèle
distinguant dans l'évolution des sociétés trois stades de développement
quant à l'usage de l'écriture: des sociétés sans écriture, des sociétés à
alphabétisation restreinte, et des sociétés à alphabétisation de masse
— un fait contemporain correspondant à un choix politique et social de
la fin du XIXe siècle. Ce système de classement change cependant de
sens lorsqu'il est repris par les historiens. Car les sociétés sur lesquelles
ces derniers travaillent se situent pour la plupart dans le domaine de
l'alphabétisation restreinte: Rome ne fait pas exception, mais l'Europe
moderne et même médiévale rentrerait dans la même catégorie, et de
même bien d'autres sociétés correspondant à d'autres aires culturelles
comme l'Islam, l'Inde ou la Chine. Les historiens de l'Antiquité, comme
tous ceux qui s'intéressent à une époque et à une société données, ont donc
besoin d'une grille plus fine.

Or, c'est là que les difficultés commencent: par sa formulation même,
le modèle oriente en effet vers une évolution diachronique qui

---

1   Je pense au livre classique de H.-I. Marrou, *Histoire de l'éducation dans
       l'antiquité* (Paris 1948, maintes fois réédité), et à des ouvrages plus récents
       tels que celui de S. F. Bonner, *Education in ancient Rome from the elder
       Cato to the Younger Pliny* (London 1977).

2   J. Goody (éd.), *Literacy in traditional societies* (Cambridge 1968).

correspond à une théorie du développement, très à la mode à une époque où les historiens renonçaient au schéma des étapes de l''economic growth' chères à Walt Rostow pour se laisser tenter par l'idée du 'processus de la civilisation' (à la même époque — 1973 et 1975 — était traduit en français le livre de Norbert Elias).[3]

William Harris situe explicitement son étude dans une perspective comparatiste. Mais il n'échappe pas pour autant, à l'occasion, à la tentation d'une vision évolutionniste; on retrouve, implicite, sous certaines de ses démonstrations l'hypothèse que le moins doit précéder le plus, et non l'inverse, car l'alphabétisation est un phénomène cumulatif. Or, précisément, Rome fait l'expérience d'un premier type d'alphabétisation et d'usage de l'écriture dans la vie citadine, et l'alphabétisation de l'Europe médiévale et moderne se fera sur des bases différentes avant, puis après l'invention de l'imprimerie: une invention préparée et attendue, et correspondant à un besoin, socialement ressenti, que Rome ne semble pas avoir éprouvé.

Indépendamment même de cette rupture, qui m'apparaît essentielle, entre deux mondes agissant selon des logiques différentes dans l'usage et le contexte social de la lecture et de l'écriture, il serait de toute façon impossible de s'en tenir à une évolution linéaire même à l'intérieur d'une société donnée. Florence offre au Trecento et au Quattrocento le contre-exemple (non mentionné par Harris) d'un niveau d'alphabétisation masculine (estimé à environ 40%) élevé pour l'époque, et qui ne sera atteint que tardivement dans les campagnes de France étudiées par F. Furet et J. Ozouf.[4] "Au XVe siècle", précise C. Klapisch-Zuber,[5] "la capacité non seulement à souscrire son nom, mais à rédiger quelques lignes paraît assez largement répandue jusque dans les milieux populaires actifs de la ville [de Florence]. En revanche, qu'une fille lise et surtout écrive reste un sujet d'étonnement."

Or, précisément, les historiens de la culture nous invitent à passer d'une histoire des 'répartitions' à une histoire des pratiques: d'une histoire de la présence inégale du livre dans une société donnée à une histoire de la, ou plutôt des lectures; et de même à une histoire des

---

3   N. Elias, *La civilisation des moeurs* (Paris 1973); *La dynamique de l'Occident* (Paris 1975) (traductions de *Über den Prozess der Zivilisation* Bd.1 et 2).

4   F. Furet et J. Ozouf (sous la direction de), *Lire et écrire. L'alphabétisation des Français de Calvin à Jules Ferry* (Paris 1977) 2 vol.

5   C. Klapisch-Zuber, *La maison et le nom. Stratégies et rituels dans l'Italie de la Renaissance* (Paris 1990) 321.

emplois effectifs de la compétence scripturaire.[6] C'est la démarche que j'ai adoptée moi-même pour l'Antiquité romaine,[7] et dont d'autres travaux récents offrent aussi l'illustration (ainsi ceux de G. Cavallo[8]).

L'alphabétisation: le choix des indicateurs

Il serait bon au préalable de relativiser les critères auxquels les historiens de l'Antiquité ont l'habitude de se référer.

Le premier problème est un problème de sources. Pas question pour les historiens de l'Antiquité d'appuyer leur comptabilité sur une documentation de masse telle que les actes de mariage indiquant le nombre des personnes capables d'apposer leur signature. La partie ne peut être tentée que sur les papyrus d'Egypte, ou de rares tablettes campaniennes, auxquelles il serait hasardeux de demander une information de nature statistique; ces documents mettent précisément en évidence divers niveaux de l'illettrisme — avec notamment la définition de celui "qui écrit lentement". Dans les papyrus, la référence à celui qui ne connaît pas ses lettres concerne la capacité d'écrire en grec; certains sont capables d'écrire en démotique, c'est-à-dire en langue égyptienne.

L'école

Pour l'Europe moderne, il vaut la peine de le rappeler, les deux vecteurs principaux de l'alphabétisation — l'un et l'autre abondamment étudiés — ont été d'une part l'Eglise (ou les Eglises), d'autre part l'école. Rome n'ayant connu qu'à l'extrême fin de son histoire une religion du livre, pour pratiquer au contraire une religion du rite, le premier vecteur a fait défaut. Mais l'école — ou tout au moins la figure du maître d'école — étant présente à Rome, les antiquisants se trouvent amenés à lui reconnaître dans le processus d'alphabétisation une place excessive, et dans deux sens différents: tantôt pour lier un taux supposé élevé d'alphabétisation à un (tout aussi supposé) dense réseau scolaire dans les villes, tantôt au contraire pour évaluer à la baisse le nombre

6   R. Chartier (éd.), *Pratiques de la lecture* (Marseille 1985); *Les usages de l'imprimé (XVe - XIXe siècle)* (Paris 1987); *La correspondance. Les usages de la lettre au XIXe siècle* (Paris 1991); R. Chartier, *Lectures et lecteurs dans la France d'Ancien Régime* (Paris 1987).

7   M. Corbier, "L'écriture dans l'espace public romain," dans *L'Urbs. Espace urbain et histoire (Ier siècle avant J.-C. – IIIe siècle après J.-C.)* (Roma 1987) 27-60.

8   "Testo, libro, lettura," dans G. Cavallo, P. Fedeli, A. Giardina (éd.), *Lo spazio letterario di Roma antica 2. La circolazione del testo* (Roma 1989) 307-41.

des écoles et par là le nombre des alphabétisés potentiels. Harris a épinglé, non sans raisons, le premier travers, mais n'a peut-être pas su éviter le second. Après avoir introduit le sous-chapitre 'Schooling' par une prudente mise en garde rappelant qu'il existe d'autres formes d'acquisition de la capacité de lire et écrire, notamment à la maison (p.233), l'école est présentée comme le véhicule majeur de l'alphabétisation (p.234: "We have no reason to suppose that the Romans somehow transmitted literacy in great quantities without the help of formal schooling") avec la conclusion attendue: peu d'écoles, donc peu de lisants–écrivants.

Dans une étude classique,[9] M. Cole, J. Goody et S. Scribner développent le cas de l'écriture Vai au Libéria, dont l'apprentissage avait précisément lieu en dehors de toute éducation scolaire. Ce qui est sans doute un cas extrême. Mais, même pour des époques et des sociétés où l'école jouait un rôle important, les témoignages ne manquent pas d'autres formes d'apprentissage: le journal d'un célèbre autodidacte du début du XVIIIe siècle, Valentin Jamerey-Duval, édité par Jean-Marie Goulemot,[10] décrit les étapes d'"une alphabétisation latérale, par les pairs".[11] Laissons parler Jamerey-Duval: "... la fortune m'éleva au grade de berger en chef .... J'étais alors sur la fin de mon troisième lustre. Sans avoir la moindre notion de cet art divin qui apprend à fixer la parole et à peindre la pensée, pour donner du relief à ma nouvelle promotion, j'engageay mes confrères dans la vie bucolique à m'apprendre à lire, ce qu'ils firent volontiers au moyen de quelques repas champêtres que je leur promis." Plus près de nous, Marguerite Yourcenar n'a pas connu d'autres maîtres que son propre père et une succession de précepteurs appointés. Qu'une éducation aristocratique puisse se passer d'école va de soi — et, pour Rome, Harris l'a noté aussi. Mais, pour connaître les rudiments des lettres, comme l'affranchi Hermeros du Satiricon (*Sat.* 58.7), faut-il avoir fréquenté l'école? A la différence de Harris (p.248, n.391), je ne le tiendrai pas pour acquis. D'autant que le problème est posé par nos textes. Grégoire de Tours met ainsi en scène un

---

9   "Writing and formal operations: a case study among the Vai," *Africa* 47 (1977) 289-304 (repris dans J. Goody, *The interface between the written and the oral* [Cambridge 1987] 191-208).

10 *Mémoires. Enfance et éducation d'un paysan au XVIIIe siècle*, avant-propos, introduction, notes et annexes par J.-M. Goulemot (Paris 1981).

11 Cf. J. Hébrard, "Comment Valentin Jamerey-Duval apprit-il à lire? l'autodidaxie exemplaire," dans R. Chartier (éd.), *Pratiques de la lecture* p.45.

enfant surdoué qui aurait appris à lire seul grâce aux inscriptions accompagnant les images des saints dans un oratoire d'Auvergne.[12]

Le témoignage de l'épigraphie

"Graver un texte sur une pierre, ce n'est là qu'une des formes de l'écrit", nous rappelle le regretté Paul-Albert Février.[13] Et pourtant les historiens de l'Antiquité ne résistent pas à la tentation des repérages statistiques: combien d'inscriptions latines par milliers de km^2 selon la région d'Italie ou la province (Harris p.226 et 228)?

Appuyée sur une série de représentations graphiques, une recherche menée sur la Sardaigne[14] tente à partir de la *distribution* des inscriptions latines (et des marques sur les objets de l'*instrumentum domesticum*) sur le territoire d'étudier la diffusion de la culture écrite: pas de surprise à constater que la concentration de la documentation écrite dans les plaines et les zones côtières coïncide avec les principales cités de l'île, donc les lieux attendus d'une plus grande alphabétisation, et que l'écrit rencontré dans les régions montagneuses révèle essentiellement des décisions du pouvoir central, des bornes de confins implantées par l'autorité romaine, des diplômes militaires ramenés par les soldats sardes revenus au 'pays', des dédicaces religieuses officielles et des bornes milliaires. Mais, de façon paradoxale, le point fort de l'étude est moins de confirmer que les bergers sardes étaient analphabètes que de signaler, dans le premier groupe d'inscriptions, le caractère 'populaire' de l'épigraphie sarde, notamment sur les épitaphes: "un niveau archaïque évident, notamment dans l'onomastique et les formulaires, mais aussi dans le travail des officines lapidaires et dans la forme des lettres".

L'usage de l'écriture gravée est à la fois une pratique politique et une consommation de prestige des classes urbaines. Mais, en se diffusant du centre — Rome — vers les provinces, et des zones urbanisées, ou plus étroitement contrôlées par les villes, de chaque province vers les

---

12   Cf. L. Pietri, "Pagina in pariete reserata: épigraphie et architecture réligieuse," dans *La terza età dell'epigrafia* (Faenza 1988) p.149.

13   P.-A. Février, "Paroles et silences (à propos de l'épigraphie africaine)," dans *L'Africa romana. Atti del IV convegno di studio. Sassari, 12-14 dicembre 1986* (Sassari 1987) p.191.

14   A. Sechi, "Cultura scritta e territorio nella Sardegna romana," dans *L'Africa romana. Atti del VII convegno di studio. Sassari. 15-17 dicembre 1989* (Sassari 1990) 641-54; A. Mastino, "Analfabetismo e resistenza: geografia epigrafica della Sardegna (con informatizzazione dei dati a cura di A. Sechi)," sous presse dans les Actes du Colloque de Forli, *L'epigrafia del villaggio* (Forli 28-30 septembre 1990).

périphéries, cette consommation tend à se déformer. Les 'producteurs' (artisans) introduisent leur savoir-faire et leurs 'maladresses' et les commanditaires leurs goûts et leur style. Au IIIe siècle, certains commanditaires provinciaux d'épitaphes versifiées renoncent à l'écriture lapidaire traditionnelle et choisissent l'écriture 'commune' des manuscrits de leur temps (lire J. Mallon à propos du cippe d'une dame de Mactar nommée Beccut[15]).

Lire et écrire: divers niveaux de compétence

L'écriture et ses formes

A répertorier les fonctions de l'écriture dans la Rome antique (Harris p.196-233: Work and Business Affairs; Civic and Political Uses; Religious Uses; Commemoration; Literature; Letters), on court le risque de juxtaposer des usages, au lieu d'établir les rapports et les hiérarchies existant entre les différentes formes d'écriture. Telle ou telle forme ne peut pas être étudiée isolément; elle ne se comprend que par rapport à d'autres.

L'usage de la majuscule d'inscription — la *quadrata littera* ou les *lapidariae litterae* de Pétrone (*Sat.* 29.1; 58.7) — ne prend notamment son sens que si l'on se souvient que sa diffusion est contemporaine de la pratique — par ceux qui savent écrire — de la petite capitale et de plusieurs écritures cursives.[16]

A Rome, l'écriture n'est pas l'apanage de professionnels, libres ou esclaves, en d'autres termes une compétence reconnue à des inférieurs — même si, dans une société esclavagiste, il est aisé de disposer de spécialistes formés à cet effet. Pour des documents nécessitant le respect d'un strict formulaire tels que les testaments, on s'adresse volontiers à un homme de l'art.

L'écriture n'est pas non plus l'apanage d'une classe de clercs remplissant la fonction de la culture auprès de guerriers et de paysans illettrés.

On tient au contraire à montrer que l'on sait écrire. Pour ceux qui bénéficient d'une éducation — à la maison comme à l'école —,

---

15 J. Mallon, *De l'écriture. Recueil d'études publiées de 1937 à 1981* (Paris, 2e éd. 1988) 304-15.

16 J. Mallon, R. Marichal, C. Perrat, *L'écriture latine de la Capitale à la Minuscule* (Paris 1939); J. Mallon (supra n.15); R. Marichal, *Les graffites de La Graufesenque* (47e suppl. à Gallia, Paris 1988); B. Bischoff, *Latin palaeography: antiquity and the middle ages* (Cambridge 1990).

l'apprentissage de l'écriture est contemporain, en effet, de celui de la lecture, et même le précède, puisque les lettres sont préalablement dessinées et identifiées par leur nom dans l'ordre alphabétique. On apprend aux enfants à *bien* écrire à l'aide d'une technique d'apprentissage prônée par Quintilien (*Inst.* 1.1.27; 10.2.2), qui consiste non à imiter un modèle, mais à en parcourir le tracé incisé dans la cire ou le bois de la tablette.

L'écriture individuelle est même valorisée par des hommes qui dans la vie courante ont volontiers recours à la simple dictée à un esclave secrétaire: un correspondant de Pline le Jeune précise dans une de ses lettres qu'il est en train de rédiger un ouvrage, en partie dicté, en partie écrit de sa main (*Epist* 9.28.3: *multa te nunc dictare, nunc scribere*). Auguste, nous dit-on, aurait appris lui-même à écrire à ses petits-fils et fils adoptifs, Caius et Lucius Césars, ses successeurs potentiels, et surtout à imiter son écriture (Suétone, *Aug.* 64.5: *ut imitarentur chirographum suum*); Suétone (87.3) note une particularité de celle-ci: Auguste ne séparait pas les mots, ce qui était donc inhabituel. En tout cas, il était droitier: l'index de sa main droite était un peu faible, et il devait parfois l'entourer d'un anneau de corne pour écrire (80.3).

L'écriture personnelle est une procédure d'authentification du document. Elle tient lieu de signature quand la confection du texte est confiée à un tiers, comme l'attestent les tablettes récemment découvertes à *Vindolanda*. L'invitation envoyée par Claudia Seuera à Sulpicia Lepidina pour son anniversaire montre ainsi une écriture à deux mains; d'après les éditeurs, le corps de la lettre en caractères élégants serait le fait d'un professionnel, tandis que les dernières lignes, de facture plus rustique, mais plus 'personnelle', *sperabo te soror | uale soror anima | mea ita ualeam | karissima et haue*, auraient été écrites par Seuera elle-même, comme les quelques mots ajoutés à la main au bas d'une lettre tapée à la machine.[17] Inversement, la formule de politesse *bene ualeas frater* ajoutée par l'expéditeur à une liste de marchandises livrées présente une facture plus soignée que la liste des produits elle-même rédigée en cursive.[18]

La Table de Brigetio (*FIRA*[2], I n° 93) fait état d'une souscription écrite de la main même de l'empereur: *manu diuina*. Non sans exagération, le panégyriste Nazarius complimente le jeune fils de

---

17   A. K. Bowman and J. D. Thomas, "New texts from Vindolanda," *Britannia* 18 (1987) 137-40 n° 5.
18   Ibid. 140-42 n° 6.

Constantin âgé de cinq ans de savoir déjà écrire son nom et de pouvoir ainsi approuver des décisions généreuses (*Pan. Lat.* 10 (4) 37. 5-6).

L'écriture manuscrite jouit d'un réel prestige: les dévots de Sulis Minerva à Bath ont écrit leur requête maléfique sur lamelle de plomb; et ceux qui ne savaient pas écrire n'ont pas manqué de faire des gribouillages pour imiter l'écriture.[19]

Lire et écrire, lire où écrire

Apprentissage de la lecture et apprentissage de l'écriture vont-ils toujours de pair?

Hermeros fait référence explicitement à l'écriture lapidaire: "*Lapidarias litteras scio*"; mais il ne se vante pas de savoir écrire. Et surtout il ne se reconnaît qu'un niveau pauvre de la lecture. Il n'est donc pas capable de lire la cursive des lettres privées ou des documents d'affaires; mais il peut déchiffrer, outre les épitaphes, les inscriptions monumentales, les enseignes des boutiques, les affiches électorales, ou les annonces de spectacles ou de ventes aux enchères — toute cette écriture exposée au regard du passant à laquelle j'ai consacré une étude à l'occasion d'un colloque sur la Ville de Rome en 1985,[20] et dont un déchiffrement minimal est précisément accessible à ceux qui disposent d'un niveau réduit d'alphabétisation. Les autres convives de Trimalcion semblent connaître eux aussi les rudiments de la lecture: lorsqu'ils se voient servir du vin provenant d'amphores cachetées et étiquetées "Falerne Opimien de cent ans", ils donnent l'impression d'en déchiffrer laborieusement le texte — *dum titulos perlegimus* (34.6-7) — d'accès plus difficile peut-être s'il s'agissait de *tituli picti*.

Jean Mallon attire l'attention sur un document du Ier siècle qui nous est parvenu sous deux formes:[21] l'original serait la forme cursive (*PSI* X 1183 b); le papyrus en capitales (*PSI* X 1183a) serait "une copie qui au-rait été destinée à servir d'affiche ou à tout autre usage ostentatoire".

---

19 R. Tomlin, dans B. Cunliffe (éd.), *The Temple of Sulis Minerva at Bath* 2: *The Finds from the Sacred Spring* (Oxford 1988) 98-101, 247-52; J. Reynolds, "Gifts, curses, cult and society at Bath," *Britannia* 21 (1990) 380-82.

20 Supra n.7. Sur ce thème G. Susini vient de publier aussi deux études: "Compitare per via. Antropologia del lettore antico: meglio, del lettore romano — Spelling out along the road. Anthropology of the ancient reader," *Alma Mater Studiorum* 1,1 (1988) 105-24, et "Le scritture esposte," dans G. Cavallo, P. Fedeli, A. Giardina (éd.), *Lo spazio letterario di Roma antica* 2 (Roma 1989) 271-305.

21 Supra n.15, 180.

C'est à une analyse différenciée des niveaux de compétence que nous invite à son tour Robert Marichal[22] à propos des potiers de La Graufesenque auteurs des fameux graffites écrits avant cuisson: "Certes la plupart des potiers savaient, comme les vieux camarades de Trimalcion, lire les *litterae lapidariae* (...): ils en composaient leurs estampilles, il est même probable que beaucoup savaient lire la cursive, assez claire, des bordereaux [d'enfournement] (...), et étaient même capables d'écrire dans la même écriture leur nom sur des poinçons, des outils ou des vases" — ce qui ne fait pas pour autant d'eux des écrivants et des lisants cultivés.

La remarque de l'affranchi Hermeros toujours citée, on le voit, trouve un écho à plus de seize siècles de distance chez un personnage de Molière — le valet Lubin, personnage mineur de la pièce *Georges Dandin* (1668) — qui se flatte, lui, de lire "la lettre moulée". Le dialogue avec son maître, Clitandre, mérite d'être reproduit:

"Clitandre : Tu es curieux, Lubin.
Lubin : Oui. Si j'avais étudié, j'aurais été songer des choses où on n'a
          jamais songé.
Clitandre : Je le crois. Tu as la mine d'avoir l'esprit subtil et pénétrant.
Lubin : Cela est vrai. Tenez, j'explique du latin, quoique jamais je ne
          l'aie appris, et voyant l'autre jour écrit sur une grande
          porte collegium, je devinai que cela voulait dire collège.
Clitandre : Cela est admirable! Tu sais donc lire, Lubin?
Lubin : Oui, je sais *lire la lettre moulée*, mais je n'ai jamais su
          apprendre *lire l'écriture*." (Acte III, scène 1).

En matière de lecture, la compétence de Lubin — qui, pas plus qu'Hermeros, ne sait écrire — est limitée à une forme de graphie, qui s'identifie, selon Roger Chartier,[23] à la lettre d'imprimerie; il n'a pas accès à la cursive manuscrite. Dans la même perspective, Patricia Easterling m'a signalé, cette fois dans George Eliot, *Adam Bede,* ch. 52, la mention des maidservants "each holding ... a prayer-book in which she could read little beyond the large letters of the Amens".

Par référence à ces servantes, signalons que, dans la France d'époque moderne, l'Eglise catholique a veillé pendant longtemps, au moins dans certaines régions, à ce que les filles apprennent à lire (pour lire l'Ecriture sainte et en diffuser les enseignements dans leur famille), en évitant avec soin de leur apprendre à écrire (pour les empêcher, entre autres, d'écrire à leurs amoureux!).

---

22   Supra n.16 (1988), 55-56.
23   R. Chartier (éd.), *Pratiques de la lecture* (Marseille 1985) 68-69.

A Rome, les membres des hautes classes étaient certes plus habitués à se faire lire qu'à lire eux-mêmes: imaginant l'activité d'un prince idéal, l'auteur de l'Histoire Auguste (*Sev. Alex.* 31) mentionne la relecture — à haute voix donc — des lettres impériales au prince.

Mais ce trait n'est pas propre aux aristocrates romains: Pantagruel fera de même alors que Gargantua trace pour lui un programme d'éducation encyclopédique, à l'image des seigneurs des XVIe et XVIIe siècles, qui se font couramment lire des livres, de même qu'ils dictent à leurs secrétaires.

Pour les Anciens en tout cas, la lecture était un art difficile, et le déchiffrement spontané d'un texte inconnu n'allait pas de soi, comme en témoigne une anecdote rapportée par Aulu-Gelle (*Att. Noct.* 13.31.4): un fat qui prétendait connaître les *Satires ménippées* de Varron est invité à les lire (tout haut); il se ridiculise, "tant il coupait les phrases n'importe où et prononçait les mots de travers". Seule une solide formation chez le grammairien permet d'apprendre "où (...) retenir son souffle, à quel endroit couper la ligne, où finit la phrase, où elle commence, quand il faut élever ou abaisser la voix (...) quand il faut ralentir, accélérer, presser, radoucir" (Quintilien, *Inst.*1.8.1). L'esclave anagnoste préparait à loisir sa lecture.[24]

Mais, pas plus que Monsieur Jourdain ne savait qu'il faisait de la prose, les Romains ne se doutaient pas que leur compétence dans le domaine de la lecture se limitait bien souvent à l''alphabétisation phonétique', qui consiste à déchiffrer les textes syllabe par syllabe en oralisant, mais n'atteignait pas l''alphabétisation de compréhension', qui consiste à déchiffrer un texte mot à mot, et en silence, en le comprenant au fur et à mesure de la lecture.[25]

Quelques spécificités du monde romain

Sur la longue durée, le monde romain a connu des changements dans les usages de l'écrit. Il présente pourtant avec son organisation en cités et sa vie municipale un contexte très particulier.

Prestige de la culture

On n'imagine guère dans le petit monde citadin de l'Italie romaine, au dernier siècle de la République et aux premiers siècles de l'Empire,

---

24   F. Desbordes, *Idées romaines sur l'écriture* (Lille 1990) 229-30.
25   Sur cette distinction, cf. P. Saenger dans R. Chartier (éd.), *Les usages de l'imprimé* (1987) 192-93.

un notable qui aurait prétendu exercer une responsabilité civique sans savoir lire et écrire. Et, inversement, l'accès à la culture — et non à la simple alphabétisation — est une condition favorable pour devenir décurion dans sa cité, et accéder éventuellement au Sénat. André Chastagnol insiste volontiers sur le fait qu'à partir du règne de Constantin les empereurs sont moins sensibles aux critères censitaires, et plus portés à promouvoir des individus pour leur culture: l'historien Aurelius Victor serait ainsi devenu fonctionnaire, et finalement préfet du prétoire, grâce à la protection de Julien.

Les notables mettent leur point d'honneur à se faire représenter avec un livre (*uolumen* ou *codex* selon les époques) dans la main. Les souverains, les princes héritiers sont censés être des hommes de culture — au minimum des orateurs, voire des écrivains ou des poètes: comme César sur la guerre des Gaules, Trajan avait écrit des *Commentaires* sur ses guerres daciques. Une coupure sensible est intervenue au Moyen Age: à preuve, les exemples célèbres de Charlemagne[26] et de Guillaume le Conquérant (rappelés par Harris), souverains quasi illettrés. A cette époque, il est vrai, l'écriture était devenue le quasi-monopole d'une catégorie statutaire nouvelle, chargée de recopier et de lire les textes sacrés: les 'clercs' — un mot qui, en français, a gardé jusqu'à aujourd'hui ce sens particulier, et sert à désigner les 'intellectuels'. Rien de tel à Rome, où la culture écrite est d'abord l'apanage des classes dirigeantes ou aisées.

Primat de l'oral

L'écriture pour les Romains reste pourtant inférieure à la parole dont elle n'est en fait qu'une représentation. Dans sa version alphabétique, elle est une notation des sons. Sur ces 'idées romaines sur l'écriture' Françoise Desbordes vient d'apporter un nouvel éclairage.[27]

Evitons donc pour Rome la confusion tentante de l'oral avec la culture populaire et de l'écrit avec celle de l'élite. La forme oratoire correspond à un goût, à une éducation, à une culture, et la composition littéraire vise toujours à l'oralité. Si l'on en croit l'historien Cremutius

---

26   Eginhard, *Vita Karoli Magni imperatoris*, éd. Louis Halphen, Paris, Les Belles-Lettres, 1938, § 25 : "Il s'essaya aussi à écrire et il avait l'habitude de placer sous les coussins de son lit des tablettes et des feuillets de parchemin, afin de profiter de ses instants de loisir pour s'exercer à tracer des lettres; mais il s'y prit trop tard et le résultat fut médiocre". Sur ce point en tout cas, Eginhard ne s'est pas inspiré de Suétone: aucun des douze Césars n'était illettré, ni n'aurait pu l'être.

27   Supra n.24.

Cordus (Tacite, *Ann.* 4.34), le pamphlet *Anticato* de César, écrit en réponse à un livre dans lequel Cicéron avait couvert Caton d'éloges, affectait la forme d'un discours prononcé devant des juges: *Caesar ... rescripta oratione uelut apud iudices respondit.*

Des auteurs habitués à 'dicter', comme nous le précise Augustin (*Retract.* 2.93.2) pour lui-même, avaient un rapport particulier à l'écriture.

Importance de l'écriture affichée

Une page de Jules Renard, intitulée "La Chèvre",[28] exprime un certain pessimisme quant au nombre des lecteurs potentiels des nouvelles officielles, même fraîches.

> "Personne ne lit la feuille du journal officiel affichée au mur de la mairie.
>
> Si, la chèvre.
>
> Elle se dresse sur ses pattes de derrière, appuie celles de devant au bas de l'affiche, remue ses cornes et sa barbe, et agite la tête de droite et de gauche, comme une vieille dame qui lit.
>
> Sa lecture finie, ce papier sentant bon la colle fraîche, la chèvre le mange.
>
> Tout ne se perd pas dans la commune."

Le doute exprimé par Jules Renard dans cette histoire brève ne porte pas sur le niveau d'alphabétisation de ses contemporains; du moins nous rappelle-t-il que, même affiché, tout document officiel n'a pas vocation à être lu. Dans son livre sur la Galilée, Martin Goodman a noté l'observation contraire d'un rabbi du deuxième siècle:[29] "Quand un édit nouveau a été affiché, tout le monde se dépêche de le lire; mais quant aux plus vieux, on les néglige," qui concerne sans doute un affichage temporaire, mais prolongé.

Rome nous montre en ce domaine une remarquable complémentarité de l'oral et de l'écrit: diffusant la lettre de Claude aux Alexandrins (Edgar et Hunt, *Select Papyri*, n° 212), le préfet d'Egypte déclare que tous les habitants de la ville n'ayant pu être présents pour écouter la lecture publique de la lettre de l'empereur, le texte va être affiché pour qu'il soit loisible à chacun de le lire. La copie du discours du même

---

28   J. Renard, *Histoires naturelles*, textes établis et présentés par Léon Guichard (Paris, 1971) p. 121 (une référence dont je suis redevable à René Rebuffat).

29   *State and society in Roman Galilee, A.D. 132-212* (Totowa 1983) 141. Ce passage a attiré aussi l'attention de Fergus Millar ("L'empereur romain comme décideur," dans *Du pouvoir dans l'antiquité: mots et réalités*, sous la direction de Claude Nicolet [Genève 1990] 212).

empereur Claude au Sénat en faveur des notables de la province de Lyonnaise, gravée dans le bronze,[30] est toujours affichée à Lyon — mais au Musée de la Civilisation gallo-romaine —; par le soin apporté à la gravure de ses *litterae quadratae*, et à la mise en page facilitant le repérage des alinéas (grâce non à un retrait comme dans les textes contemporains, mais à un léger débordement sur la marge), les responsables de l'affichage ont manifesté un souci remarquable de *lisibilité*, qui caractérise d'autres documents officiels ainsi promus au statut de monuments de bronze destinés à l'éternité.[31]

L'écriture rend ainsi la parole durable.[32]

Une certitude: l'espace public de la ville romaine prévoit des parois consacrées à l'affichage durable ou temporaire d'informations destinées aux citoyens; celui du mur nord du 'forum' d'Assise vient de faire l'objet d'une publication exemplaire.[33] Mais quelle intention précise a présidé à la gravure et à l'exposition si longtemps après leur réception d'un choix de documents officiels témoignant de l'octroi de privilèges à Aphrodisias de Carie: le 'archive wall' dont Joyce Reynolds nous a offert une belle publication[34] reste encore énigmatique.

Le stockage

L'écrit est un puissant moyen de communication à distance et dans le temps. Il permet de stocker de l'information à l'extérieur de la mémoire. Mais il est aisé à falsifier. Même si les Anciens n'étaient pas toujours confiants dans la fidélité du lapicide à son modèle,[35] l'inscription une fois gravée est à l'abri de la négligence des copistes dont il était lieu commun de se plaindre:[36] son caractère inaltérable (sinon au prix d'un

---

30   Ph. Fabia, *La table claudienne de Lyon* (Lyon 1929).
31   Voir aussi C. Williamson, "Monuments of bronze: Roman legal documents on bronze tablets," *Classical Antiquity* 6 (1987) 160-83; M. Crawford, "The laws of the Romans: knowledge and diffusion," dans *Estudios sobre la Tabula Siarensis* (Anejos de Archivo Español de Arqueologia IX, Madrid 1988) 127-40.
32   Desbordes (supra n.24) 80.
33   P. Gros et D. Theodorescu, "Le mur nord du 'forum' d'Assise. Ornementation pariétale et spécialisation des espaces," *MEFRA* 97 (1985) 879-97.
34   J. Reynolds, *Aphrodisias and Rome* (London 1982) 33-37.
35   Cf. Sidoine Apollinaire, *Epist.* 3.12.5: *uide ut uitium non faciat in marmore lapicida* .
36   Quintilien, *Inst.* 1.3 (dédicace); 7.2.24 ; Symmaque, *Epist.* 1.24 ; Jérôme, *Epist.* 71.5.

martelage, qui ne passe pas inaperçu) et la pérennité de son support —
pierre, marbre, bronze — lui donnent tout son prix.

Par le choix du matériau, le support a aussi la charge de témoigner
du statut du document qu'il conserve pour la postérité: les sénatus-
consultes qui accordèrent à César le droit à un tombeau à l'intérieur du
pomerium furent gravés en lettres d'or sur des tables d'argent déposées
aux pieds de Jupiter Capitolin (Dion Cassius 44.7.1: en 44 av. J.-C.).

Les diptyques de bronze connus sous le nom de diplômes militaires
constituent à la fois des documents authentiques infalsifiables destinés
à servir de *preuve* des privilèges reçus, et de lourdes pièces de métal
aussi honorifiques pour leurs détenteurs que des décorations — ces
torques ou phalères, auxquelles il était permis de prétendre dans
l'armée romaine.

L'écriture est une mémoire: l'attachement des Romains à l'exercice
de la mémoire et aux procédés mnémotechniques ne les conduit pas à
déprécier cet instrument. Bien au contraire, les techniques de
mémorisation mises en oeuvre sont explicitement liées à une culture
écrite: si la mémoire des *choses* fait appel à l'image, l'agencement
spatial auquel elle se réfère a subi la marque de l'agencement
graphique;[37] quant à la mémoire des *mots*, elle consiste surtout à
apprendre par coeur un discours écrit: "on parle comme si l'on était en
train de lire" (Quintilien 11.2.32; lire F. Desbordes [supra n.24] 83-87).
Auguste pour sa part ne s'embarrassait pas de techniques de
mémorisation: il *lisait* tout simplement ses discours; il poussait l'aide
de l'écriture jusqu'à un point extrême, puisqu'il rédigeait à l'avance ses
conversations personnelles (Suétone, *Aug.* 85.4).

César, tentant d'analyser en ethnographe le refus des druides
gaulois de mettre leur doctrine par écrit (*Bell. Gall.* 6.14.3), n'envisage
que des explications 'laïques': le risque de divulgation, le moindre soin
mis à exercer la mémoire. Le possible conflit de la lettre et de l'esprit ne
semble pas l'effleurer.[38] Son attitude reflète celle des hommes de son
temps pour lesquels écrit et oral sont en fait la même chose. Cicéron et
Quintilien s'accordent sur ce point. "Pour moi, bien dire et bien écrire
sont une seule et même chose et un discours écrit n'est rien d'autre qu'un

---

37   J. Goody, *The interface between the written and the oral* (Cambridge 1987)
      180-82.
38   Lire l'analyse de ce passage proposée par G. Dumézil, "La tradition
      druidique et l'écriture: le vivant et le mort," dans *Georges Dumézil,*
      ouvrage collectif (Paris 1981) 325-27, ainsi que F. Desbordes, "Idées
      romaines sur l'écriture (Lille 1990) 82-83.

enregistrement du discours prononcé" (Quintilien 12.10.5). Inversement, écrire son discours est la meilleure des préparations à l'éloquence (Cicéron, *De orat.* 1.150-55).

La mémoire du nom

La part tenue par les épitaphes dans l'écriture 'lapidaire' est bien connue — de même que le soin porté aux affranchis à leur tombeau. D'où peut-être l'intérêt d'Hermeros pour "l'écriture lapidaire" déjà noté par Harris.

Mais faut-il cantonner le genre de l'inscription funéraire dans la commémoration? Paul Veyne[39] et Gabriel Sanders[40] nous rappellent au contraire que ces épitaphes visaient surtout à parler du mort au passant, invité à les *lire* — en dépit de l'ancien adage qui menaçait les lecteurs d'épitaphes de perte de la mémoire.[41] Trimalcion (*Sat.* 71.11) a prévu que son monument funéraire comporterait au milieu une horloge (un cadran solaire) — dont il perçoit donc la connotation funéraire[42] —, "pour que quiconque regardera l'heure soit, bon gré mal gré, forcé de lire [son] nom". En échange d'un geste de salut, d'un bref instant d'attention, le défunt offre au passant un moment de repos, un conseil de sagesse (*memento mori* comme *memento uiuere*) ou des voeux de bon voyage — voire, sur une épitaphe romaine: "Toi qui ne m'as pas salué, porte-toi bien toi aussi" (*AE* 1987, 125). Le constructeur d'un tombeau familial prévoit même le cas d'un passant qui se fera lire le texte de l'inscription (*AE* 1989, 247: *quicumque legerit, aut legentem auscultauerit*).

Mais, pas plus que les reliefs de la Colonne Trajane n'étaient nécessairement destinés à être 'vus',[43] le texte épigraphique ne prétendait toujours à être 'lu' en son entier. Il est en lui-même un monument. Ainsi l'épitaphe de cent dix vers dont T(itus) Flauius Secundus, de Cillium, en Byzacène, a orné le mausolée de son père,[44] *témoignait du*

---

39 P. Veyne, "Les saluts aux dieux, le voyage de cette vie et la 'réception' en iconographie," *RA* 1985.1, 47-61.

40 "Sauver le nom de l'oubli: le témoignage des *CLE* d'Afrique et *aliunde*," dans *L'Africa romana. Atti del VI convegno di studio. Sassari, 16-18 dicembre 1988* (Sassari 1989) 43-79.

41 Cicéron, *Senect.* 7.21, rapportant un propos de Caton l'Ancien: *nec, sepulcra legens, uereor, quod aiunt, ne memoriam perdam.*

42 Lire sur ce thème P. Veyne (supra n.39).

43 P. Veyne, *La société romaine* (Paris 1991) 311-42.

44 *CLE* 1552 = *CIL* VIII 212-13; les premières lignes de ce long *carmen* funéraire sont gravées à environ 5 m de hauteur. Cf. G. Sanders, "Texte et

statut social de la famille et, notamment, de la culture réelle ou supposée, en tout cas proclamée par le choix d'une inscription métrique, du fils.

Peu de Romains auraient repris à leur compte le mot prêté par Sénèque (*Epist.* 14.92.35) à Mécène: "de mon tombeau je ne me soucie pas" (*nec tumulum curo*). Et le coeur de ce *monumentum* reste le 'nom' du défunt. Les vers de Properce (2.1.71-72) *quandocumque ... breue in exiguo marmore nomen ero* ("Quand je ne serai plus qu'un tout petit nom sur une toute petite plaque de marbre") reflètent la sensibilité des contemporains.

Espace public, espace privé

Comme une ville romaine, la maison de Trimalcion est pleine d'inscriptions[45] — dont la présence et le contenu sont censés divertir le lecteur du roman de Pétrone comme déjà les protagonistes de l'histoire. Le motif de drôlerie n'est pas toujours le même.

Etre accueilli à la porte de la maison d'un ancien esclave par une pancarte (*libellus*) affichée sur le montant indiquant que "tout esclave qui sortira dehors sans l'ordre patronal recevra cent coups de verges" (28.6-7) relève du paradoxe: quant au "sortir dehors", il en dit long sur la langue du maître de maison. Trimalcion tient à annoncer l'entrée dans l'espace de sa juridiction domestique.

Rencontrer, non loin de la loge du portier, un énorme chien enchaîné peint sur le mur, accompagné de la légende en lettres capitales (*quadrata littera scriptum*) CAVE CANEM (29.1) — un usage attesté par des pavements de mosaïque à Pompéi — doit étiqueter par le goût excessif de l'illusion le maître de maison comme un homme du commun.

Un groupe de peintures évoque les étapes de la vie du maître de maison: le peintre n'a pas oublié les légendes explicatives. Sur la première scène les esclaves vendus au marché portent aussi leur écriteau — leur 'étiquette' — au cou (19.3-4). Trimalcion accueille ainsi ses invités par une gigantesque bande dessinée. Apparemment, on n'y voit pas Trimalcion apprendre à lire ni à écrire; en revanche un tableau le montre en train d'apprendre à compter: et, sur la scène suivante, il est devenu trésorier. Ce qui lui permettra de s'enrichir.

Les jambages de la porte du triclinium sont décorés des insignes des magistrats (faisceaux et haches) et d'un éperon de navire en bronze,

---

monument: l'arbitrage du musée épigraphique," dans *Il Museo epigrafico* (Faenza 1984) 104.

45   Comme me l'a rappelé P. A. Brunt; je reviens sur ce thème par ailleurs.

servant de support à la dédicace: "A Caius Pompeius Trimalcion, sévir augustal, Cinnamus son trésorier" (30.2). Trimalcion n'a pas perçu ici la frontière du public et du privé: en prenant sa maison pour le forum — ou un monument funéraire —, un modeste seuir (qui a droit aux seuls faisceaux) pour un magistrat supérieur et un simple armateur pour le vainqueur d'une victoire navale, il se ridiculise. Pour certains lecteurs du roman, l'association du nom et du décor devait suggérer un rapprochement entre la maison de "Pompée Trimalcion" et la *domus rostrata* de Pompée le Grand.

Sur l'un des battants de la porte, un tableau porte l'indication: "L'avant-veille et la veille des calendes de janvier notre maître Caius dîne en ville" (30.3); une information aussi individuelle et privée ne justifie pas un affichage à l'entrée de la salle à manger. Elle est aussi prosaïque que la formule "la marquise sortit à cinq heures", que Valéry se refusait à introduire dans ses écrits, et qui connotait à ses yeux de façon négative le genre même du roman.

N'en déduisons pas que l'écrit n'a pas sa place dans l'espace privé: bien au contraire. Mais il s'agit plutôt, au Ier siècle, d'écrits d'une autre nature: dans l'espace de la *domus* accessible au public sont peints les *stemmata* — de ceux qui en possèdent: "*Stemmata quid faciunt?*" (Juvénal, *Sat.* 8.1) —, sont affichées les tables de patronat. Plus tard, l'écrit se déploiera dans l'espace privé sur les mosaïques servant de pavement.

L'écriture et l'image

Dans la Rome des premiers siècles comme dans la maison de Trimalcion, l'écriture et l'image sont souvent associées, surtout sur les monnaies.

L'épigraphie monumentale chrétienne, que Luce Pietri[46] nous invite à découvrir, témoigne — du IVe au VIe siècle — de la persistance chez les élites d'une croyance dans la force du message écrit pour l'instruction des fidèles: le texte n'est pas simple légende de la représentation figurée; ce sont les images qui illustrent le texte — *picturae historiam illustrantes*. Cette conviction, exprimée en particulier par Paulin de Nole, marque certainement une césure entre ce qu'il est convenu d'appeler la fin du monde antique et le Moyen Age.

Plus surprenante encore — et bien digne d'un homme pétri de 'culture antique' —, la fin d'une homélie prononcée par Augustin (*Serm.* 319.8.7) dans les premières décennies du Ve siècle; mettant fin à l'office de la parole, il renvoie ses ouailles à la lecture des quatre vers qu'il a fait

---

46   Supra n.12.

graver dans la chapelle: le message épigraphique qu'il les invite à mémoriser leur tiendra lieu de livre (*codex*) sacré.[47]

Conclusion

Au fond, dans le souci légitime de réagir contre la tendance de certains historiens de Rome à surévaluer la signification de certains documents tels que les graffites, Harris me paraît avoir été conduit à des conclusions trop pessimistes, et ceci pour avoir voulu juger l'alphabétisation romaine à la mesure de celle qui l'a suivie en Europe. En fait, et même si les estimations chiffrées ont un sens, il convient de replacer d'abord les indices dont nous disposons dans le contexte des pratiques culturelles, sociales et politiques du monde romain. Or, celles-ci invitent à nuancer la vision d'une alphabétisation qui serait perçue comme un 'bloc', ayant la même fonction et la même signification dans des sociétés différentes, pour tenir compte des rapports spécifiques de l'oral et de l'écrit, et de la place elle aussi spécifique de l'écrit à Rome.

Si les degrés d'alphabétisation respectifs de l'Italie et des provinces, des villes et des campagnes, peuvent susciter l'interrogation, bien d'autres questions sur les diverses *pratiques* de la lecture et de l'écriture restent en suspens, plus importantes pour la compréhension de la société antique, mais aussi pour l'avenir de la civilisation occidentale: les étapes du passage de la capitale à la minuscule, qui reste un fait majeur de l'évolution de l'écriture latine — d'où sont issus nos caractères d'imprimerie —, l'abandon du *uolumen* pour le *codex*, plus maniable, et surtout plus favorable à la consultation (mais pourquoi penser seulement [Harris 294-97] à celle des textes sacrés?) — d'où nous vient notre 'livre'.[48].

Plus que jamais dans ce contexte la distinction que j'ai proposée en 1985 me paraît opératoire. Pour la population masculine d'une ville comme Rome, aux premiers siècles de l'Empire, l'hypothèse d'une alphabétisation *pauvre*, largement répandue — celle dont témoignent l'Hermeros du Satiricon, les potiers de La Graufesenque, les dédicants

---

47   G. Sanders, "Augustin et le message épigraphique: le tétrastique en l'honneur de Saint-Etienne," *Collectanea Augustiniana. Mélanges T. J. Van Bavel* (Institut Historique Augustinien 1990) 95-124.

48   Voir les actes des colloques sur "le codex" et sur "l'écriture": A. Blanchard éd., *Les débuts du codex. Actes de la journée d'étude organisée à Paris les 3 et 4 juillet 1985* (Turnhout 1989); C. Sirat, J. Irigoin, E. Poulle, *L'écriture: le cerveau, l'oeil et la main* (Turnhout 1990). Les actes d'un colloque sur les Tablettes à écrire qui s'est tenu à Paris à l'automne 1990 sont sous presse.

des lamelles de plomb de Bath —, paraît pertinente pour la société concernée: une alphabétisation pauvre par le contenu des textes qu'elle peut reconnaître et assimiler, par la maîtrise tâtonnante de l'écriture, par la place importante faite à la mémoire, par le rapport permanent qu'elle implique entre l'oral et l'écrit. La pauvreté syntaxique (absence de subordonnées, ellipses, etc.) caractérise les textes affichés, lorsqu'ils ne visent pas à divulguer la parole du Prince ou la loi.

Directeur de Recherche au C.N.R.S., 1, place Paul-Painlevé, Paris

Literacy in the Roman empire: mass and mode

Alan K. Bowman

Mass literacy

"The written culture of antiquity was in the main restricted to a privileged minority — though in some places it was quite a large minority — and it co-existed with elements of an oral culture." The minority envisaged was such that in the Roman imperial period it is "unlikely that the overall literacy of the western provinces even rose into the range of 5-10%."[1] After reading Harris's book, few will feel that there is much to be said for arguing the opposite case. The argument that mass literacy, as it is understood in modern times, cannot have existed in the ancient world because that world lacked the institutions by which it could have been achieved, is coherent and forceful. Perhaps more: given the nature and quantity of our evidence, the argument is all but impregnable. How, in principle, could we hope to undermine it? By examining the contents of a record-office in the Fayum village of Tebtunis during the Julio-Claudian period, by showing a high number of literates (at least, so-called signature literates) amongst cavalrymen in the Roman army, by a count of graffiti coming from the potteries of La Graufesenque?[2] None of these will suffice and, in fact, Harris has good reasons for dismissing these and many similar phenomena as indications of any degree of mass literacy. It might be thought, however, that this non-existent mass literacy is a modern anachronism and that his emphasis on this aspect of his subject comes at the expense of detailed discussion of other more significant features, many of which are mentioned only briefly or in passing. Quantification is, of course, a delicate matter and can easily yield a *reductio ad absurdum*. If we believe that there was more documentation and more literacy in Egypt than elsewhere, that is not simply because there are more documents from Egypt. By that criterion, if every fort in

---

1   Harris 337, 272. I am grateful to Dr. G. D. Woolf for his helpful suggestions and comments on a draft of this article.

2   *P. Mich.* II 121-28; cf. Harris 210-11, R. H. Pierce, "Grapheion, catalogue and library in the Roman empire," *Symbolae Osloenses* 43 (1968) 68-83; R. O. Fink, *Roman military records on papyrus* (Philological Monographs of the American Philological Association 26, Cleveland 1971) no. 76; R. Marichal, *Les Graffites de La Graufesenque* (Gallia, Suppl. 47, Paris 1988).

Britain produced 800 pieces of written material dating to the quarter-century between A.D. 90 and 115, we would reckon Britain more literate than any province except Egypt. Few would accept this as a legitimate argument. Nevertheless, 20 years ago the prediction that such material might be found in quantity would have seemed very far-fetched, and its discovery at Vindolanda surely does lead us to believe in a greater degree of literacy in this part of the empire than once we did.[3] By the same token, the chronological distribution of documents can hardly be used as a secure indicator of an increase or decline in levels of literacy.[4]

Other sources of distortion are less capricious than the archaeologist's trowel. Given the ratio of published Greek to demotic papyri from Ptolemaic and Roman Egypt, one might be forgiven for thinking that Greek was overwhelmingly preponderant as the language of the literate, that demotic was much more restricted in use and spread. In fact, the degree of preponderance we envisage must be affected by the many hundreds of demotic papyri in the museums of Europe and North America, unpublished because they are very difficult to read and there are too few suitably qualified scholars.[5] As the following remarks (largely based on material from Egypt and Vindolanda in the Roman imperial period) may show, those engaged with papyrology and documentary history tend to be optimistic about the centrality of literacy in the ancient world, and wary of the assumption that what we have is all there can be.

Harris allows that there was, despite the absence of mass literacy, "a vast diffusion of reading and writing ability", but takes issue with scholars such as C. H. Roberts who thought that in the Near East in the 1st c. A.D. literacy was widespread "at almost all social levels".[6] Since Roberts and many of the other scholars who took an optimistic view were neither stupid nor ignorant, it is tempting to ask why they took

---

3   For a general account of the discoveries in the second phase of excavation at Vindolanda see A. K. Bowman and J. D. Thomas, "Vindolanda 1985: the new writing-tablets," *JRS* 76 (1986) 120-23; "New texts from Vindolanda," *Britannia* 18 (1987) 125-42. By the end of the 1989 season the inventory numbers had reached 997. The figure of 800 is only a rough estimate of the number of tablets (including fragments) which have remains of writing. There is good reason to expect further, similar discoveries at other sites (see *Britannia* 18 [1987] 127).

4   Cf. Harris 288.

5   Some idea of the quantity and range can be gained from the bibliographies published by H.-J. Thissen in the journal *Enchoria*.

6   Harris 8-9.

this view. Part of the answer may be that, on the whole, their scholarly interests centred on written material. But another whose familiarity with written documents was of the highest order was not so optimistic.[7] Nevertheless, the classical ancient world has a literate 'feel' to it, perhaps largely because so much of the evidence through which we interpret it is written evidence. And it may be that there are enough superficial similarities between literacy in the ancient and the modern worlds to tempt us to analyse the one entirely in terms appropriate to the other. Scholars may thus have been influenced by evidence which seems, on a superficial interpretation, to assume mass literacy. Ταύτης μου τῆς ἐπιστο[λῆς] ἀ(ντίγραφα) ὡς περιέχει δημοσιωθῆναι εὐδήλοις γράμμασιν ἔν τε τῇ μητροπόλει καὶ τ[οῖς ἐπι]σήμοις τοῦ νομοῦ τόποις προνοήσασθε, ὡς μηδένα ἀγν[ο]ῆ[σ]αι τὰ διηγορευμέν[α] ("Take care that copies of this letter of mine, exactly as it stands, are published in plain letters in the metropoleis and in the well-known places of the nome so that no one may be unaware of my pronouncements,") or τῆς ἐ[π]ιστολῆς ταύτης τὸ ἀντίγραφον δημοσίᾳ ἔν τε τοῖς μητροπ[ό]λεσιν καὶ κατὰ κώμην φανεροῖς καὶ εὐαναγνώστοις τοῖς γράμμασιν ἕκαστος ὑμῶν [εἰς λε]ύκωμ[α] προθῖ[ν]αι προνοησάτο ... ("Let each of you take care that a copy of this letter is displayed publicly in the district-capitals and in every village in clear and easily legible writing on a whitened board ...").[8] Egypt may be a special case, but not, of course, to the extent that all its villagers were literate. We know of a village scribe who was only literate to the extent of a subscription painfully learned by rote. There is evidence of 11 writers at work in the documents coming from his office, and an almost contemporary text from Karanis shows evidence of a scribe with a degree of recherché learning. The crucial thing is to decide what weight to give to these different phenomena.[9] As for a general degree of literacy in the villages, it simply cannot be the case that the officials responsible for the texts quoted above did not know what they were talking about. If publication of a written text could be supposed to ensure that everyone was informed about something, whether they could read or not, it follows that inability to read would not have been

---

7   H. C. Youtie, "ΥΠΟΓΡΑΦΕΥΣ: the social impact of illiteracy in Graeco-Roman Egypt," *Scriptiunculae posteriores* (Bonn 1981) I, 179-99 at 180.

8   *P. Oxy.* XXXIV 2705. 10-12; J. R. Rea, "A new version of *P. Yale* inv. 299," *ZPE* 27 (1977) 151-56 ll. 12-15; cf. *FIRA* I, 13. 13-6 (the 'Lex Julia Municipalis').

9   H. C. Youtie, "ΑΓΡΑΜΜΑΤΟΣ: an aspect of Greek society in Egypt," *Scriptiunculae* II (Amsterdam 1973) 611-26 at 621; id., "Callimachus in the tax-rolls," ibid. 1035-43.

accepted as a legitimate excuse for ignorance. This has important implications for literacy because it can only mean that those who could not read (or write) participated in literacy in some significant way. Therefore the interesting thing is not that there was no mass literacy in the ancient world but that ancient society could be profoundly literate with a reading-and-writing population of, let us say, less (perhaps much less) than 20%, the precise figure being insignificant.[10] What is surprising, then, is not that there are so many illiterates appearing in documents, but the phenomenon of illiterates appearing in documents at all, participating in literacy, as did (in a slightly different sense) the huge number of illiterates all over the empire who were commemorated by written epitaphs.[11] Its significance is highlighted by contrast in the fact that the autograph signature certainly was regarded as important. On some occasions a mere list of witnesses' names might serve to authenticate (as it does in the *Tabula Banasitana*), on others an actual signature is clearly significant, as in a papyrus text which is probably a list of subscriptions to a bouleutic decree.[12] In the first case, we might think, the list of names authenticates the act of granting citizenship; in the second, the signatures might authenticate the document as well as the act. The normal formula employed by illiterates seems to be guaranteeing the link between the individual and the document — it might be paraphrased: 'I have submitted this document despite the fact that it is written not by my own hand, but by that of X.' The argument is, then, that a large proportion of the 80%+ illiterate population was thoroughly familiar with literate modes. Egypt, of course, may be exceptional and the argument that it was accustomed to a higher level of bureaucracy than other parts of the ancient world is duly put forward. But so may anything or everything else; regional differences need to be and are weighed carefully.[13] But this is hardly compatible with the belief that literacy in Latin and Greek is in some sense a single phenomenon, sustained by a continuous cultural tradition,

---

10 It is interesting to compare the deductions from capitularies in R. McKitterick, *The Carolingians and the written word* (Cambridge 1989) 36-37: "deeply committed to the written word", "enormous implications for the degree and scale of written skills", "deep penetration of literacy in Carolingian society".

11 Cf. M. T. Clanchy, *From memory to written record* (London 1979), A. E. Hanson in the present volume.

12 In general H. C. Youtie (supra n. 7) 188-90; *Tabula Banasitana*, A. N. Sherwin-White, "The Tabula of Banasa and the constitutio Antoniniana," *JRS* 63 (1973) 86-98; decree, *P. Oxy.* XLIV 3171.

13 Harris 329-30.

and that a line can be drawn between the literate and the illiterate population.[14] It is, in fact, a serious error to obscure the fundamental differences between literacy and orality and the relationship between them, and equally misleading to argue that mass literacy and widespread literacy are the same thing. There is good reason to believe in a very wide spread of literate skills in the ancient world.

Literate skills and social context

The belief that literacy was restricted to a small percentage of the population of the ancient world inevitably implies that it was a preserve of the élite, directly antithetical to the view that it was, at least in the Roman east, widespread "at almost all social levels". Along with this go the arguments, *inter alia*, that writing materials were too expensive and difficult to obtain for the lower strata of society, and that schooling was available only for the privileged. In reality, the scenario is much more complex.

First, we have to consider the social composition of this literate minority. One difficulty in assessing this is the broad spread and diversity of written material which, in itself, approached in the way that Harris approaches it, presents two related methodological problems. First, in attempting to describe, analyse and quantify ancient literacy for most periods, this approach tends to confine itself to the material relevant to and emanating from those who could read and write, ignoring the participation of the non-literate majority, and treating the lives and activities of the majority as if they were not part of the record. Second, there is the range of activity over which literacy is attested — it does not easily fit a scenario in which it is restricted to the conventional modern notion of the élite. We should be wary of applying an anachronistic concept of 'class-structure' and identifying the literate as the small percentage in the highest social stratum.[15] This is likely to be particularly problematical in multi-cultural societies. The notion of special 'kinds' of literacy ('craftsman's', 'scribal', etc.) is a device which attempts to circumvent this in order to explain phenomena such as graffiti, but it is liable to appear too mechanistic, to create too many special cases, and to invent labels which are inadequate as descriptions of what was written. The symbolic and practical importance of written material is implied in the

---

14 Harris 3.
15 See Youtie (supra n. 7) 180 ("lower middle class"), though Harris (277, n. 502) thinks he pays too little attention to the class element in the distribution of literacy.

context of the 'workshop', for example, by magical papyri — written texts whose antecedents clearly lie in the area of oral incantation and the like.[16] The illiteracy of a member of the gymnasial class in Egypt is viewed as mildly surprising, and we are then told that because he was a fisherman he was fortunate to be a member of that class — the relationship between class and occupation is here interpreted entirely in modern terms, as it is, by implication, in Roberts' translation of a papyrus text in which there is a dispute over the liability to liturgy of a person who is alternatively described as a 'foreman weaver' (ἐργαστεριάρχης λινόυφων) and a 'well-to-do-perfumer' (μυροπώλης εὐσχήμων ἄνθρωπος).[17] There are similar difficulties in interpreting the status and position of the γεωργός, "a term which generally conjures up the image of an Egyptian peasant struggling to eke out a bare subsistence", but may in fact designate someone like Dionysios, son of Kephalas, a man with three rôles in life (soldier, priest and farmer) and literacy in two languages.[18]

From the same context, there is evidence for a privileged Egyptian family whose members did not adopt Greek names (as Dionysios did); their archive of 72 papyri, dating from 145-88 B.C., consists of 51 Greek, 19 demotic and 2 bilingual texts.[19] Ptolemaic Egypt, then, provides excellent, but far from unique, illustration of another factor which complicates the analysis — bilingualism or multilingualism. Harris's decision to deal with literacy in Latin and Greek as a "single phenomenon" and "sustained by a continuous cultural tradition" creates serious difficulties for the multi-cultural Mediterranean in the Hellenistic and Roman periods, and fails to deal fully with the common assumption that the main significance of 'native' cultures and languages is at a level below that of the Greek- or Latin-speaking élite.[20] In fact, merely the Syriac deed of sale from Dura-Europos or the Archive of Babatha from the Judaean Desert suffice to show that there is more to it. The relationship between Greek, demotic and Coptic in Egypt is

---

16   *PGM* VIII. 1063 = H. D. Betz, *The Greek magical papyri in translation* (Chicago 1986) 146-47.
17   Harris 276-77. *P. Oxy.* XXII 2340.
18   N. Lewis, *Greeks in Ptolemaic Egypt* (Oxford 1986) 127, J. L. Rowlandson, "Freedom and subordination in ancient agriculture: the case of the *Basilikoi Georgoi* of Ptolemaic Egypt," *Crux. Essays presented to G. E. M. de Ste Croix on his 75th Birthday. History of Political Thought* 6. 1-2 (Exeter 1986) 327-47.
19   Lewis (supra n. 18) 139-52.
20   Against which see F. Millar, "Local cultures in the Roman empire: Libyan, Punic and Latin in Roman Africa," *JRS* 58 (1968) 126-34.

better attested than any other multi-lingual context. It is striking that in early 4th-c. Panopolis we find members of a highly cultured and literate, Greek-speaking family, which belonged to the 'international elite', holding religious offices in Egyptian cult.[21] In Roman Egypt there was a Greek-speaking readership for translations or adaptations of Egyptian literary works, and there is evidence for demotic poetry which seems to owe more than a little to Greek antecedents.[22] The development of Coptic testifies to the need for a different, written medium and its consequences are important, not merely in the Christian context.[23] It emphasises two important issues. First, the need to consider the complex relationship between orality and literacy. As the writings of Pinter or Hemingway should suggest to the modern reader, ancient texts cannot simply be written versions of what was spoken. The ancient perception of the relationship between a skill possessed by comparatively few, but affecting many, and the oral mode should be of great interest; what are the psychological implications, for instance, of the expression in a Latin letter, *illum a me salutabis verbis meis*?[24] The second issue is the importance of identifying particular purposes which may be associated with specific different literacies and different *kinds* of writing systems in the same cultural context, and of considering how they may affect each other.[25] The results may differ in different cases. Written Greek in Egypt was resistant to the influence of demotic, whereas the language of the Archive of Babatha displays semitisms which show the effect of Aramaic.[26] On the other hand, it can be argued that the development and spread of written demotic owed much to a bureaucratic or administrative need which was created by Greek. Again, the advent of a literate culture to an area where none, or a

---

21 Syriac sale: *P. Dura* 28; Babatha, N. Lewis, *Documents from the Bar-Kokhba period in the Cave of the Letters* (Jerusalem 1989); Panopolite family, *P. XV Congr.* 22.

22 S. West, "The Greek version of the legend of Tefnut," *JEA* 55 (1969) 161-83; H.-J. Thissen, "Der verkommene Harfenspieler," *ZPE* 77 (1989) 227-40.

23 J. G. Keenan, "On languages and literacy in Byzantine Aphrodito," *Proceedings of the XVIII International Congress of Papyrology* 2 (Athens 1988) 161-67.

24 A. K. Bowman, J. D. Thomas, 'Two letters from Vindolanda,' *Britannia* 21 (1990) 33-52, no. 1, lines 9-10.

25 See C. J. Eyre, J. R. Baines, "Interactions between orality and literacy in ancient Egypt," in K. Schousboe, M. T. Larsen (edd.), *Literacy and society* (Copenhagen 1989) 91-119 and cf. N. Mercer (ed.), *Language and literacy from an educational perspective* 1 (Milton Keynes 1988), especially the articles by D. R. Olson (221-30) and S. Scribner and M. Cole (241-55).

26 Lewis (supra n. 21) 13-21. For Britain see below p.128.

different one, existed before may actually change the social structure, as it certainly did in Ptolemaic Egypt.

The rôle of the army was, of course, crucial to social change in many regions of the Roman empire and, as Harris shows, literacy in the army is a striking phenomenon of this period, more striking since the discoveries at Vindolanda than before them. It should lead us to question the wisdom of treating the army merely as having a restricted and specifically technological rôle which allows its literacy, again, to be confined as a special case, developing in response to a particular need. Some of the complex implications of its rôle are vividly illustrated by Adams' analysis of the letters of Claudius Terentianus. Here we have an auxiliary soldier writing to his family in Karanis, early in the 2nd c. A.D., in both Latin and Greek (five letters in each language). Terentianus' letters are all written by other hands, but the one letter he receives from his father Tiberianus shows the father concluding in his own hand. Is it likely, then, that the son was incapable of writing? Did he draft or dictate his letters? Terentianus' Latin, which was fluent, shows linguistic unity and signs of Greek interference. Adams suggests that the legionary father, Tiberianus, was an immigrant from Italy who settled in Egypt, where his son acquired a spoken form of Latin with Grecising elements. Military service then introduced Latin literacy into the context of a Fayum village, where it can be documented because of an accident of climate.[27] This cannot be a unique case. It remains notoriously difficult, however, to demonstrate with any conviction a significant *depth* of literacy in the army. At Vindolanda, as elsewhere, it is difficult to show literacy among the ordinary soldiers, or to be certain that the army's economic and social needs created a literate, non-servile, population in its penumbra. Nevertheless, there are hints of the Romanised Gauls, Germans, or Britons participating in literacy — a subject of *litterae commendaticiae* named Brigionus, or the Germanic names of an *equisio consularis* and his circle.[28]

It is the movement from assessment of the literate individual (or particular group) in isolation to a more general notion of his place in the larger context which time and again causes difficulties. Slaves offer another example. It will not do, clearly, simply to treat them as if they occupied the bottom rung of the social ladder. This will lead to literate slaves appearing anomalous in a context where there are also

27   J. N. Adams, *The vulgar Latin of the letters of Claudius Terentianus* (Manchester 1977) 1-6, 85-86.

28   *Tab. Vindol.* 22, A. K. Bowman and J. D. Thomas (supra n.24) 33-52 and note the comments on p. 43.

illiterate free persons. It may be less so if the social universe of the slave and freedman is treated as a complex with its own rules and hierarchies which adapt, copy or concede to the rules of the universe of the free. That slaves supply the technology (hence, for example, the contracts which bind them to apprenticeships as writers of shorthand) is not simply a functional response to a need created by the illiterate free. Nor does it develop simply as a means of relieving the slave-owning free of the need to be literate.

Flavius Cerialis, the prefect of the Ninth Cohort of Batavians, who may very well have been a native Batavian, generates more texts at Vindolanda than any other identifiable individual. He was almost certainly capable of writing a very passable Latin cursive and could certainly compose good Latin. A few of his letters are drafted or written in what is probably his own hand, the majority by others, no individual hand appearing more than once.[29] This is, then, not so much a question of literate capability as of habits of writing. Careful examination and classification of handwriting is essential, as well as an appreciation of the technicalities which affect the 'look' of a hand. It is very dangerous indeed to make superficial judgements of the sort produced by Harris on the will of the Tiberii Julii Theones — that the two sons and the grandson wrote very negligently because, having slave scribes, they had no pressing need to write neatly. In fact, the palaeographical judgement is superficial and misleading: they all write a very passable Greek cursive, of a different character from the main hand of the document — it has simply been judged by the wrong criteria.[30]

Habits of Literacy

The advent of new evidence may change the picture in significant respects. The writing tablets from Vindolanda will receive detailed discussion elsewhere, but attention may here be drawn to some of their

---

29   *Tab. Vindol.* 21-29. It is now clear that *Tab. Vindol.* 37 is part of his archive, being written in the same hand as some of the more recent finds from the archive. This is likely to be Cerialis' own hand, see A. K. Bowman, J. D. Thomas, *Britannia* 18 (1987) 126.

30   See, for example, W. J. Tait, "Rush and reed: the pens of Egyptian and Greek scribes," *Proceedings of the XVIII Congress* (supra n.23) 479-81. Theones: Harris 249, *P. Oxy.* XLIV 3197 with pl. VIII. Compare the penetrating remarks of E. G. Turner, *Greek manuscripts of the ancient world* (2nd ed., rev. P. J. Parsons, BICS Suppl. 46, 1987) 4.

implications.[31] One feature of the writing tablets discovered at Vindolanda was the unexpected fact that the majority were of a type almost entirely unknown — thin leaves of wood, written in ink with a pen, as opposed to wax tablets, incised with metal stylus. Although the proportion of stylus tablets has increased in the recent discoveries of 1985-89, the proportion of leaf tablets is still more than 85%. The presence of these objects at Vindolanda cannot be a unique phenomenon. In fact, they have begun to appear at other sites now that archaeologists know what to look for. In any case, the presence among the Vindolanda finds of a very great number of letters which must have originated elsewhere (in Britain certainly, perhaps Gaul also) shows that the leaf tablet was in widespread use in the late 1st and early 2nd c.

The discovery underlines the crucial importance of establishing a typology of writing materials and their uses.[32] These leaf tablets must have been cheap (or free) and easy to make. They completely undermine the argument that writing materials were available only to the well-to-do; that may be true of stylus tablets, which were traded as manufactured objects, and of papyrus, for which there may just possibly be evidence in Britain.[33] Leaf tablets may, of course, be confined to military contexts, although it is likely that, if they originated there, their use will soon have spread. Context and content make it clear that they record matters which go beyond the strictly military, and the evidence of *peullawr* and *greiff(t)* as early loan-words in Celtic (deriving from *pugillar* and *graphium*) reinforces the impression. This, by implication, raises the whole question of the relationship between the two languages: there are hints that the traffic was not all one-way.[34]

---

31   A. K. Bowman, J. D. Thomas, *Vindolanda: the Latin writing-tablets* (Britannia Monograph 4, 1983) (= *Tab. Vindol.*), and the articles cited supra nn. 3 and 24.

32   See, for example, E. G. Turner, *The typology of the early codex* (Philadelphia 1977); id. (supra n.30); id., "The terms recto and verso and the anatomy of the papyrus roll," *Actes du XVe Congrès international de Papyrologie* (Brussels 1978) 1-71; Bowman & Thomas, *Tab. Vindol.* pp. 32-45.

33   D. Ellis Evans, "Language contact in pre-Roman and Roman Britain," *ANRW* 2. 29. 2 (1983) 968.

34   Evans ibid. 977, 967; J. P. Wild, "Borrowed names for borrowed things," *Antiquity* 44 (1970) 125-30; C. Smith, "Vulgar Latin in Roman Britain," *ANRW* 2. 29. 2 (1983) 936-38. On language mixture in Gaul see W. Meid, "Zu popularen gallo-lateinischen Inschriften," *ANRW* 2. 29. 2 (1983) 1019-44. For what followed see now J. Stevenson, "Literacy in Ireland: the evidence of the Patrick dossier in the Book of Armagh," in R. McKitterick

Second, format — a subject which has much wider relevance — on which the leaf tablets emphasise that it is not merely a matter of classifying literary manuscripts, important though that is. Although there is now evidence for more variation than we originally allowed, almost all the leaves are broadly comparable in dimension and method of use. For correspondence, what we described as the 'letter format' is dominant: the text is written in two columns commencing on the left-hand side, the leaf is folded between the columns (though the first, left-hand column often overruns the fold), the address is written on the back of the right-hand half of the leaf. But there are notable exceptions and they are interesting. Above all, perhaps, the letter of Octavius in which the columns proceed from right to left; the obvious explanation is that the writer — clearly in this case the entrepreneur Octavius himself — was left-handed.[35] Elsewhere, the authors of letters commonly write the closing greeting in their own hand, as does Claudia Severa, the literate wife of the officer Aelius Brocchus, who writes interesting Latin but in a hesitant, unpractised hand.[36] We should not assume, however, that they found it difficult to write, and it is fundamentally misleading to argue that those who wrote only a brief closing formula at the end of a letter were capable of no more.

The broadly similar practices of letter-writers underline an important consideration — the development of literate habits influenced by the need for a consistency which would present people with what they expected to see. Variation in the formulae and other signs of individuality will repay further investigation, as will, conversely, the evidence for *renuntia* — many examples of individually written chits bearing a repeated and curiously idiosyncratic formula.[37] It seems obvious that the development of literate habits in this context owes much to the need for military documentation. Thus the military documents will also offer important evidence, not least because of the very large number of individual hands (there are very few examples of more than one text in the same hand), but also for the opportunity to

---

(ed.), *The uses of literacy in early mediaeval Europe* (Cambridge 1990) 11-35 at 20-21.

35 Bowman and Thomas, *Tab. Vindol.* pp. 37-38, and *Britannia* 21 (1990) no.2.

36 Bowman and Thomas, *Britannia* 18 (1987) no. 5.

37 Bowman and Thomas, *Britannia* 18 (1987) no.2, probably related to the practices described by Polybius 6.34.7-36.9; Harris 166-67. Contrast A. E. Hanson in this volume.

compare Vindolanda practices — such as the *rotulus* or folded wooden notebook — and types of document with those from other places.[38]

Whatever conclusions we might reach about such subjects, it is undeniable that they need to take serious account of the palaeographical technicalities. What is, above all, remarkable about the several hundred different individual hands recorded at Vindolanda is the fact that they all fall within the broad palaeographical classifications which have been established almost entirely on the basis of material from the other end of the Roman empire. On the one hand, this would appear to support belief in a numerically-restricted literate élite. On the other, it is a remarkable demonstration of the discipline of the medium that both scribes and other writers in Britain (probably natives of northwest Gaul, Batavians and Germans) were writing a Latin script so very close to that being written in the Roman east.[39]

How and why do changes occur? The orthographic conventions and the criteria according to which palaeographers classify texts are of the utmost importance in determining the development and nature of literacy. Occasionally we have explicit evidence for the official imposition of a particular practice or change,[40] more often we rely on inference. Interpunct and word division at Vindolanda follow the patterns observed elsewhere; it is not characteristic of Greek texts — why did it gradually disappear from Latin texts after the mid 1st c?[41]

The difficult questions surrounding Old Roman Cursive in the period around A.D. 100 offer a different kind of case study. Texts from the military sphere are very interesting for their employment of capital and cursive hands in the same text, and Vindolanda offers examples which are not merely pay records. The letter forms, only a few of which are surprising, perhaps suggest a slightly less rigid distinction between the forms familiar in Old Roman Cursive and those of the later New Roman Cursive. It may not be possible definitively to establish the links between the earlier and later forms of cursive, but it is

---

38   Bowman and Thomas, *Tab. Vindol.* pp. 38-44; cf. the review by Jan-Olof Tjäder, *Scriptorium* 1986. 2, 297-301. For a pertinent note on the uses of the papyrus roll see T. C. Skeat, "Roll versus Codex — a new approach," *ZPE* 84 (1990) 297-98.

39   Cf. Tjäder's review of *Tab. Vindol.*

40   *P. Oxy.* I 34 verso; see W. E. H. Cockle, "State archives in Graeco-Roman Egypt," *JEA* 70 (1984) 116-20; erasures or insertions in documents are to be noted in the margins (a practice extended from the Arsinoite Nome), and the notes are to be compiled and sent to the central archives.

41   See Turner (supra n. 30) 7-8.

nevertheless important to consider the possible lines of development, in particular the relationship between capital and cursive and the question of whether the New Roman Cursive developed from bookhand or from an unofficial or 'popular' form of cursive which is not represented in texts from the military sphere. The nature and characteristics of such 'branches' of script are, of course, central to any analysis of the development and spread of ancient writing and literacy; some of these developments may be hypothetical, but they are propounded by scholars whose views need to be taken seriously.[42] They affect not merely our views about the relationship between two different types of Latin cursive script, but the ways in which we see the characteristics of 'chancery hands', for example, spreading from institutional uses. That the debate about the significance of a particular letter-form in graffiti or papyri can be conducted in terms of 'semi-literacy' is a clear indication both of the need to appreciate the significance of the minutiae and of the need to refine our terminology and the implicit conceptual framework.[43] There remains a rich harvest to be reaped.

Christ Church, Oxford

---

42   Bowman and Thomas, *Tab. Vindol.* pp. 51-71, R. S. O. Tomlin in B. Cunliffe
      (ed.), *The Temple of Sulis Minerva at Bath* 2 (Oxford 1988) 84-94, Tjäder
      (supra n.38).
43   Bowman and Thomas, *Tab. Vindol.* p. 59.

Conquest by book
Keith Hopkins

Introduction: detail, density, and growth

I start with three scraps of papyrus. One, the size of a credit card, records the payment of customs dues at 3% of the value of 6 measures of lentils carried by 2 donkeys out of the gate of a minor Egyptian village along a road into the desert in A.D. 190. The second is a similar customs receipt from the same village dated to "the 20th year of the reign of Aurelius Antoninus and Commodus" (A.D. 179). This papyrus still has a brownish-grey clay seal attached, stamped with the portraits of the emperor and his son Commodus, and with the words 'imperial' and 'gate' still just legible. The third scrap, not much larger (16 x 10 cm.), records that a peasant has duly performed his annual labour by working 5 days to maintain the field irrigation system. It is certified by 4 different villagers, each writing in his own hand.[1]

Several hundred similarly-trivial receipts and certificates have survived from Roman Egypt, a small fraction of the hundreds of thousands once written.[2] What sense, I wonder, did Egyptian donkey-drivers

---

1   These two customs receipts are both now in Oxford: *P. Grenf.* II 50 h and f2 = Bodleian MS Gr class g 27 (P). The labour tax certificate is *SB* VI 9567, on which in general see P. J. Sijpesteijn, "Penthemeros certificates in Roman Egypt," *P.Lugd.Bat* XII (Leiden 1964) 46-69: only about one-third of surviving complete labour certificates were signed, and usually by only one person. On clay seals attached to papyrus receipts, see A. E. R. Boak, *Soknopaiou Nesos* (Ann Arbor 1935) 23 ff.

2   The survival ratio, the ratio of texts surviving to those ever produced, is clearly a critical dimension of our historical understanding. It is risky to ignore it. Harris 218 deduced that prophecies were not written in great numbers, to judge from the 3 surviving copies of the *Oracle of the potter* (*P. Oxy.* XXII 2332). But the survival ratio could be lower than 1: 10,000. Consider the following: the Romans conducted 17 censuses of the Egyptian population by households at 14-year intervals between A.D. 19 and 257. If the average household size was 5 persons, and the population is deliberately estimated low at 3.5 million, and we have less than 1,000 surviving census returns, the survival ratio is *c.* 1: 12,000. Of course, this is only a rough estimate, a cautionary tale — adjustments would have to be made for documents of different value; but 3 surviving copies of the *Oracle of the potter* could mean anywhere between 3 and 35,000+ originals.

and taxpayers make of their tiny hand-written notes? Why did the Roman government insist on having these trivial and transient actions formally recorded? What sense can we make of them? And where do they fit in to the picture of classical literacy, or illiteracy, which William Harris has so vividly portrayed? Was Harris right or wrong in arguing that, even in bureaucratic Egypt, ordinary farmers and artisans probably made little use of writing? And if he was wrong, does it matter?

Harris has written an interesting, important, and path-breaking book on a large and important subject. He deals with literacy in the whole of the ancient classical world, covering a large area and well over 1000 years of history, from archaic Greece to the late Roman empire. His main hypothesis is clear, and completely convincing: in all periods of classical antiquity, only a minority of adult males (and a tiny minority of adult females) could read and write. These rates include both sophisticated élite litterateurs and barely functional, semi-illiterate artisans. Given the fragmentary state of the surviving evidence, Harris' statistical estimates can be only very rough orders of magnitude; but even so, they are useful as sighting shots. They centre on less than 10% adult male literates, both in the heyday of democracy in Athens in the 5th c. B.C. (p.61) and in Rome in the 2nd c. B.C. (p.173), and much less in the western provinces of the Roman empire in the first centuries A.D. (p.272); Harris estimates adult male literacy in the city of Rome and in Italy during the same period at well below 20-30% (p.259). If Harris' figures are anywhere near right, then his minimalist case defeats — even routs — the idealists who apparently believed in mass adult literacy, whether in democratic Athens or in pre-Christian Rome.

About proportions, in my view, Harris is right. But each victory has its costs.[3] And in securing his victory, Harris underplays the impact of absolute number and density. For example, if adult male literacy was about 10% across the Roman empire, then there were roughly 2 million adult males who *could* read and write to some extent in the empire as a

---

3   Harris' arguments are diverse and sophisticated. In several single sentences, he touches on or covers many of the arguments which I put forward in this essay. But the general impression which I gained from his book was that his minimalist drive led him sometimes to be overstrictly positivist. No surviving evidence for literacy, schools, popular reading, etc., becomes proxy for their non-existence. But then, as here, a single exculpatory footnote (e.g. n.376 on p.245) reminds the reader that the author may not be doing full justice in his text.

whole. In world history, this was an unprecedented number of literates for a single state. The sheer mass of people who could read and write, living in Roman towns (and, as I shall show, in some villages), made a political, economic, social, and cultural difference in the experience of living in Roman society. Over time, these literates increased the stored reserves of recorded knowledge, and thereby allowed both state and religion unprecedented control over the lives of the illiterate.

Let me reinforce my argument by expanding Harris' long time frame even further, in order to reinterpret his findings. In Pharaonic Egypt, in the 3rd millennium B.C., according to one estimate, only $1/2$ to 1% of the population could write, in hieroglyphs or hieratic; according to the same estimate, the proportion was similar even in the beginning of the last millennium B.C. By the first two centuries A.D., if the adult male literacy level in Roman Egypt was, say, 10-20%, then the proportion of literates had risen 20 times. And since the ability to read or write was predominantly in Greek rather than, or as well as, in native Egyptian (the ratio of surviving published papyri is 15 to 1 in favour of Greek over demotic), most of that important increase had occurred since the 3rd c. B.C.[4]

Literacy as product and producer of changes in the Roman state

The striking growth of literacy in the classical period throughout the Mediterranean basin was not self-generating. It did not have a single identifiable cause. Instead, it was part and parcel of a series of inter-linked developments, which reinforced each other. Literacy was not just an inert technical skill, whose level and dispersion can be analysed or measured. Its growth was a product of changes in the political, economic and social culture of the Roman empire. The growth of literacy was a response to a growth of demand for literacy. And its increased use itself then generated further increases in the supply and demand for writing. The mass of writing in existence and the density of its use were, I think, categorically different from what they had ever been before in the Mediterranean basin.[5]

---

[4] J. Baines, "Literacy and Egyptian society," *Man* 81 (1983) 572-99, esp. at 584. The basis of the calculations seems shaky. See also id. and C. G. Eyre, "Four notes on literacy," *Göttinger Miszellen* 61 (1983) 65 ff. The ratio of published documents in Greek and demotic can be only a rough guide to the proportions ever existing, since different modern factors affect publication rates.

[5] My arguments are deductive, hypothetical, and impressionistic. For example, I suspect that the growth in literacy induced by Roman rule was

Let us begin our analysis of these interlinked changes with the growth of states, and the corresponding growth of state power. The Roman empire was merely one in a long series of even larger conquest states. Its power was based on an expanded economy, and on sophisticated instruments of coercion. By 'expanded economy', I mean here both that the economy of the Roman empire was very large, and that under Roman rule relatively-backward provinces gradually incorporated superior agricultural practices from more advanced regions. Britain, for example, in Roman times imported the practice of growing peas and cabbage, which improved the British diet, even if it ruined British cooking.[6] The productivity of labour grew, as did total population and aggregate product. The surplus grew. There was a greater division of labour, and more and bigger towns. The growth in literacy was both a consumption good — a way of integrating more people within a larger society — and a necessity. A larger-scale economy needed (or operated better with) more writing.

A larger economy needed money. One symptom of these changes was coinage. Coinage was a Greek invention of the 7th c. B.C., used in significant quantities by Romans and Egyptians, perhaps only from the 3rd c. B.C. And yet at the end of the 1st c. A.D., the Roman government was irregularly minting some 20-30 million denarii per year; and in Egypt, it looks as though one emperor refinanced the Egyptian coinage-system in a 5-year period with a massive injection of 600 million new but debased silver coins. The implications of this huge volume of coinage for the network of taxes and trade, however difficult to interpret, leave us in no doubt that the economy of the Roman empire in the 1st c. A.D. was on a very different scale from the Mediterranean economy of the 8th or 4th c. B.C.[7]

---

greater in the western provinces than in the east, which had previously been governed by centralising monarchies.

6   So S. Applebaum, "Roman Britain," in H. P. R. Finsberg (ed.), *The agrarian history of England and Wales* 1 (Cambridge 1972) 108 ff. On improvements in Roman chickens and Danubian horses under Roman rule, *inter* much *alia*, see J. R. Sallares, *The ecology of the ancient Greek world* (London 1991) 398.

7   On the irregularities of Roman minting, see I. Carradice, *Coinage and finance in the reign of Domitian A.D. 81-96* (Oxford 1983) 88-89. On the reform of the Egyptian billon coinage, see E. Christiansen, *The Roman coins of Alexandria* 1 (Aarhus 1988) 96 ff. Christiansen's figures are not exact, but they provide rough orders of magnitude. I once produced a model hypothesizing a strong relationship between the volume of taxes in so far as they were levied in money and the volume of inter-regional trade:

The Roman government supplemented taxation with coercion and persuasion. The instruments of coercion, which helped maintain the Roman government and élite in power were, for example, written laws, courts of justice, bureaucratic administration, and the army. Once again, the Roman system of laws was not much more sophisticated than its predecessors in the Mediterranean basin (at least until the official codification of Roman laws in the 6th c. A.D.). Nor was the practice of Roman law courts, at least in the conquered provinces, particularly admirable. But the system of justice, the adherence to written law, to the precedents of previous decisions, and the reliance on written petitions, all symptomised the spread of the Roman legal system, over the whole of the Mediterranean basin.[8] One reason for the growth of literacy was the confrontation of Roman subjects with Roman power. Subjects wrote petitions, and did so in amazing numbers.[9] They learnt the language of the conquerors in order to borrow the conqueror's power, and to help protect themselves from exploitation. I am not claiming here that the number of literates exceeded Harris' estimates, but I am trying to explain why the Roman conquest state helped produce more literates than ever before.

"Taxes and trade," *JRS* 70 (1980) 101-25. I still think it broadly right. But see the recent criticisms of R. P. Duncan-Jones, *Structure and scale in the Roman economy* (Cambridge 1990) 30-58, 187 ff. He scores a few good points, but, given a little flexibility on both sides, the evidence which he adduces could easily be accommodated in the Hopkins model.

8   On the development of Roman law, see B. W. Frier, *The rise of the Roman jurists: studies in Cicero's Pro Caecina* (Princeton 1985), a book much broader in scope than the title implies. Too little has been written on the practice of Roman law in the provinces, but for complicated legal cases see *P. Oxy.* II 237, and *P. Fam. Tebt.* 24, with associated texts and commentary. See also R. Katzoff, "Precedents in the courts of Roman Egypt," *ZSav* 89 (1972) 256-92.

9   The 1804 petitions received by a governor on tour in 2 1/2 days (*P. Yale* I 61) are not as exceptional as Harris implies: see, for example, *P. Oxy.* XVII 2131, which is about petition number 1007 received by the same governor on tour in a different town. Perhaps he was an exceptional governor? But then, a Chinese description of the Roman empire singles out Roman governors' willingness to receive petitions and to read them as a noteworthy distinguishing feature of Roman government: see F. Hirth, *China and the Roman orient* (Shanghai 1885) 71. The governor of Egypt read and answered all 1804 petitions and publicly posted the replies, as law required, within 2 months.

The Roman army in the first two centuries A.D., with about 300,000 soldiers, was the largest formal organization in the Roman empire. Harris, with unusual idealism, noted the high rate of literacy among legionaries, implied by the surviving evidence; and he suggested that this may have been due to soldiers' recruitment from the propertied and educated classes (p.254). Soldiers serving in legions were paid an annual salary (before deductions for food, uniform, etc.) roughly equal to twice the subsistence of a peasant family.[10] Education was probably one factor which helped promotion, because the army by its procedures of written rosters, written orders, and book-keeping, fostered the use of writing. It was not simply that some or many Roman soldiers could write; they were repeatedly asked, ordered, or required to write; the Roman army's organization presupposed that many soldiers could write. We can see this by reconsidering a document of A.D. 179 which Harris mentions briefly (p.254: *P. Hamb.* II 39 = Fink 34). It is a roll (4.33 m. long) containing receipts for hay-money paid to 86 auxiliary (i.e. non-legionary) cavalry soldiers. To judge by their names, they were mostly native Egyptians; auxiliaries' pay was less than that of legionaries, and no one has seriously suggested that auxiliaries were recruited from among the well-to-do. And yet almost one third of them could write a receipt, which was a paragraph long (and a significant test of literacy), and they could write it in Greek. The sheer variety of their handwriting, quite visible in the surviving texts, suggests that they learnt how to write not in the army but prior to joining the army, in a variety of schools.[11]

Roman provincial administration was a powerful force in fostering and inculcating literate practice. This may seem surprising, because the

10   This can only be a rough calculation. I am assuming pay in the early 1st c. A.D. at 900 HS per year, wheat at 3 HS per *modius* of 6.55 kg = roughly 2 tonnes of wheat equivalent per year. In fact, wheat prices varied unpredictably, and probably systematically increased as one got nearer Rome. Those who believe that a large proportion of legionaries' pay was deducted to pay for food and uniform have to explain why large numbers of educated men voluntarily entered for service in the army. I suspect it was not only the glitter of uniforms but also because net pay was relatively high — but then, that is to privilege deductive thought over fragmentary evidence. See R. O. Fink, *Roman military records on papyrus* (Cleveland 1971) nos.68-73, and M. Speidel, *Roman army studies* 1 (Amsterdam 1984) 83-89.

11   This was pointed out to me by several palaeographers in a mediaeval history seminar at Berkeley. I would not have spotted it, or thought of it, by myself.

Roman bureaucracy was never very large. Even in the 4th c. A.D., when Roman officialdom had apparently expanded considerably, it numbered only 30,000 regular officials, a small number for such a large empire.[12] And so, compared with the army, the professional bureaucracy was in itself only a minor consumer of literates. Even so, the small size of the bureaucracy and the formality of its procedures induced tax-paying subjects to pay attention to writing, and helped persuade at least some of them to write for themselves.

Let me illustrate what I mean. In the Egyptian village of Karanis, male villagers were visited by the local tax-inspector on average 6 times per year to pay installments of the poll-tax. At each visit, they received a receipt of payment, written on either papyrus or sherd.[13] Many receipts survive, as do extracts from the registers in the village tax-office. From these and others, we can see how the village tax-office organized its files: there were alphabetically-arranged files of tax-payers, so that each villager's payment was entered against his or her name; there was a file for each tax: poll-tax, beer tax, weaver's tax, tax on grain; and there was a day-book, which listed each payment in order of receipt or entry, and kept running totals of receipts. Summary accounts, submitted at monthly intervals, had to be sent in multiple copies to the local district capital.[14] All this is well enough known, although the grinding quality of the details and their variations often obscure the significance of the system.

Three implications stand out. First, the system of written tax-receipts acquainted many simple villagers with the importance of writing. The ignorant ran the risk of being excessively charged. They needed the help of friendly literates to ensure that they received and knew the meaning of the written receipts. We shall return to this subject in a moment. Their dependence implies that there was public knowledge in the village about exactly who could read or write, and with what degree of proficiency. Social prestige attached to literacy

12   A. H. M. Jones, *The later Roman empire* (Oxford 1964) 1057.

13   *P. Mich.* IV 224 is a tax register from Karanis complete for over 11 months of A.D. 172. For small tax receipts, see L. Amundsen, *Ostraca from Karanis* (Ann Arbor 1935) 487; and see similarly C. Gallazzi, *Ostraka da Tebtynis* (Milano 1979).

14   For alphabetically-ordered tax-lists, see conveniently H. Kornbeutel, *Steuerlisten römischer Zeit aus Theadelphia* (Berlin 1937) 2-3 = *BGU* IX 1891. For day books, see for example *P. Mich.* IV 223-25 and *P. Cair. Mich.* 359, with the valuable commentary and bibliography by J. C. Shelton, *A tax list from Karanis (P. Cair. Mich. 359)* II (Bonn 1977) 2.

(Harris deals with this very well against the well-known arguments of Youtie); social stigma, however varied, attached to illiteracy.[15] I am not arguing that huge numbers of villagers learnt to read and write as a self-protective measure against Roman taxation. Once again, I agree with Harris' rough orders of magnitude. I am arguing, rather, that significant numbers of villagers learnt how to read and write, in either Greek or demotic or both — and that one of the reasons for learning was self-protection or prestige.[16] In the village of Tebtunis, for example, as I shall show in detail elsewhere, in the middle of the 1st c. A.D., certainly over 100 villagers — and perhaps over 200 — could write.[17] There was a village school-master and a significant temple library, each of them an index of the production and consumption of knowledge in Roman Egypt.[18] They indicate the density of village literacy and the store of recorded knowledge, which was quite remarkable and unprecedented in human history.

Secondly, because the regular Roman administration was so small, it supplemented its staff by a system of employing temporary adminis-

---

15   Harris 144-45, against H. Youtie, "ΥΠΟΓΡΑΦΕΥΣ, the social impact of illiteracy in Graeco-Roman Egypt," *Scriptiunculae posteriores* 1 (Bonn 1981) 179-99, and "'ΑΓΡΑΜΜΑΤΟΣ: an aspect of Greek society in Egypt," *Scriptiunculae* 2 (Amsterdam 1973) 611-28. Youtie argued for casual indifference to illiteracy in Graeco-Roman Egypt. This formulation assumes a dominant or unified view of literacy, instead of a diverse range of attitudes to it, depending on, say, social class or style.

16   Why else would many principals in contracts write their own authentication in painfully slow writing, only to be described, derogatively, as slow writers by an attendant literate? This description and their efforts betray ambivalence: the slow writer's pride, the literate's impatience. For much testimony, enlightening discussion, and another conclusion — "illiteracy carried no stigma in ... middle class life in Graeco-Roman Egypt", see Youtie, "Βραδεως γραφων, between literacy and illiteracy," *Scriptiunculae* 2 (Amsterdam 1973) 629-51.

17   See my forthcoming book, tentatively entitled *Crocodile mummy*, which will review the evidence and the thoughts in this essay in much more detail.

18   Many of the papyri from the temple library at Tebtunis have not yet been published. For the list of demotic papyri which have been published, see best W. Herck (ed.), *Lexikon fuer Aegyptologie* 4 (Wiesbaden 1982) 732. For the circumstances of the temple library discovery, see G. Botti, "I papiri ieratici e demotici degli scavi italiani di Tebtynis," *Atti del IV congresso internazionale di papirologia* (Firenze 1935) 217-23. On Egyptian temple libraries in the Roman period, see E. A. E. Reymond, *A medical book from Crocodilopolis* (Wien 1976) 23 ff.

trators drawn from the community. Over time, Roman administration gradually shifted from a system of selling minor administrative offices (such as local tax-collectorships) by competitive tender, to a much more far-reaching system of compulsory community service — the so-called liturgy system which allocated a wide variety of posts temporarily, according to importance, and according to taxpayers' declared wealth.[19] One of its functions was to rotate local administrative offices (for example, village secretary, high priest [prophet] of the local temple, village policeman) around a wide circle of villagers and townsmen. Of course, this meant that from time to time, perhaps often, men in putatively literate positions (for example, as village secretary) were barely literate. From a system point of view, that did not matter much (although scholars have occasionally made much of it), since the illiterate boss could always employ a literate subordinate.[20] What did matter was that the system of office-rotation encouraged what I shall call a literate consciousness in village circles. I stress that I am not concerned here with proportions, but simply with consciousness of, and openness to, learning literate forms. Villagers and townsmen had repeatedly to concern themselves with writing.[21]

Thirdly, Roman administrative practice massively increased the stock of information recorded and kept in archives. The very words, library (bibliotheke), archive, and catalogue, so influential in the later history of literacy, were composite results of Hellenistic intellectualism and Roman administration. Knowledge had to be stored in such a way that it could be effectively recalled. Hence the use of

19   On Roman innovations with the liturgical system, see N. Lewis, "Greco-Roman Egypt: fact or fiction," *American studies in papyrology* 7 (1979) 3-14; and U. Wilcken, *Grundzüge und Chrestomathie der Papyruskunde* 1 (Leipzig 1912) 319 ff. For liturgical obligations and liability at the village level, see, for example, *P. Oxy.* XVII 2121 of A.D. 209/10. For tendering, see for example *P. Tebt.* II 295-96, *P. Oxy.* XIV 1633.

20   See H. C. Youtie's justly celebrated article about a semi-illiterate village tax-collector (*Komogrammateus*), "Pétaus ... ou le scribe qui ne savait pas écrire," *Scriptiunculae* 2 (Amsterdam 1973) 677-95.

21   In Tebtunis, in a single year (A.D. 45-46) 377 men and 84 women acted as principals in a contract, affidavit, memorandum, or petition. The number of contracts, affidavits, etc. officially registered in the village scribal office (*grapheion*) totalled about 700 per year, an enormous number for a village. These figures are derived from *P. Mich.* II 123 and V 238, cf. 121V of A.D. 42. In the 20 months covered by these contract registers, almost half of all of the adult male villagers were formally involved in making a written contract. See further Hopkins, *Crocodile mummy* (forthcoming).

alphabetical files, file numbers, page numbers; to be sure, all of them are dull administrative details, but it was details like these which, for example, enabled Roman tax officials to examine back files for consistency of taxpayer's reporting, and which enabled litigants to search for legal precedents.[22] Writing was used as an instrument of power, by extending the collective memory.[23] My argument is not only that the proportion of literates grew, but also that the density of use by literates of writings also grew. And these developments had surprising pay-offs or imitations in other fields. For example, in the magnificent 4th-c. Manichaean Psalm Book, each psalm was numbered, each page had a title with the psalm number and first line, and the book was finished with a 5-page, 2-column index, listing each of the 289 psalms.[24] Religious knowledge, like tax knowledge, had to be ordered so that believers could find their place.

Literary culture was both unifying and differentiating. It was unifying in the sense that it provided a set of skills, symbols, and values, of which many Romans were aware, even those who could not deploy those skills well. Orators, for example, gave rather long public performances for entertainment, not only at the emperor's court, but also in town theatres, and in front of large audiences.[25] And they exercised their talents in welcoming a visiting emperor, governor, or grandee, or at simpler social venues such as wedding feasts or funerals.[26] Rhetoricians, poets, grammarians, and teachers were the high-priests, priests and door-keepers of this cultural system. Literary culture provided a common framework of communications for an upper class which was dispersed over a wide area and several status sets (senators, knights, town-councillors of large cities and small towns). Members of the élite quoted snippets of poetry and philosophy to each other at dinner parties (or so the litterateurs tell us), and if they could not they sometimes hired learned slaves to feed them with apposite quotations (or so the

---

22	For the constructive use of back-files for checking consistency of reporting, see *P. Panop. Beatty* 2. 128 ff., with further discussion in Hopkins (supra n.17).

23	Literacy undermines memory — a view discussed by Harris 30-33. But libraries and files increased the collective memory.

24	See C. R. C. Allberry, *A Manichaean psalm-book* (Stuttgart 1938).

25	Heroic lives of professors of rhetoric are celebrated by Philostratus and Eunapius in their *Lives of the sophists*. For an amusing example see Eunap. 488 ff.

26	See the guide for composing speeches by Menander Rhetor (ed. D. A. Russell and N. G. Wilson) (Oxford 1981).

satirists tell us).[27] The elaboration of this shared literary culture, in Greek or Latin or both, predated and certainly reinforced the unification of the political élite across the Mediterranean basin.[28] Literary culture provided a thin varnish of community (but not uniformity) among the educated classes, without forging a perceived community of interest. For a monarchy, that was politically advantageous.

Literary culture was differentiating, in that it provided a single set of criteria by which people's performances, and therefore their membership in different social strata, could be judged. The diversity of educational attainment ranged from the sophisticated to the superficial, from the economically functional to the marginal, sub-literate, and to the illiterate. This diversity of judgement and attainment was important, because it symptomised the permeability of Roman stratification, and underlined the possibility of using education as an effective ladder of social mobility.[29] Becoming educated disguised humble origins. Education was an attainment which could pay off, at many levels of society: among soldiers, as we have seen, or among traders, and, at a higher level of society, among minor landowners or intellectuals, who wanted to gain sinecures in the Roman bureaucracy. Education was the currency of a literary culture, which acted as a symbolic glue for a depoliticised upper class.[30] To be sure, there were

---

27 An idealised style of intellectual, sophisticated conversation is illustrated in Aul. Gell., *NA*; Macrob., *Sat.*; Ath., *Deipn*. The position of the intellectual hired for show by the vulgar but pretentious rich man is satirised by Lucian, *De mercede conductis potentium familiaribus*, and in Petronius' *Satyricon*.

28 One index of élite integration is the influx of provincials into the senate of Rome; by the end of the 2nd c. A.D., just over half of all senators whose origins are known came from the provinces. See K. Hopkins, *Death and renewal* (Cambridge 1983) 144 ff. On cultural integration, see best G. Bowersock, *Greek sophists in the Roman empire* (Oxford 1969); id., *Augustus and the Greek world* (Oxford 1965).

29 For a whole array of upwardly-mobile teachers, see Suet., *Gram*. and *Rhet.*, or Auson., *Prof.* in the 4th c.

30 The sheer formal difficulty of many ancient literary products is an indicator of their usefulness as social differentiators. Some authors wrote, still write, not just to be understood but to be appreciated as sophisticated by élite *cognoscenti*. Horace was not meant to be easy; the complex acrostic poems of Optatian Porfyry were presumably meant to be impressively amusing. See W. Levitan, "Dancing at the end of the rope," *TAPA* 115 (1985) 262. In the school-texts published by G. Goetz (ed.), *Corpus glossariorum latinorum* 3 (repr. Amsterdam 1965), and A. C. Dionisotti, "From Ausonius' schooldays?" *JRS* 72 (1982) 83 ff.,

many other criteria of status and attainment. Modern academics, in particular, have to be wary of exaggerating the importance of bookish knowledge. It also mattered in Rome how you dressed, walked, loved, rode, or hunted.[31] But it mattered to a surprising degree *how* you showed, and how much you showed, that you knew something of what was written in books.

The Roman empire was bound together by writing. Literacy was both a social symbol and an integrative by-product of Roman government, economy, and culture. The whole experience of living in the Roman empire, of being ruled by Romans, was overdetermined by the existence of texts. I need hardly stress again that I am not arguing for near-universal literacy; only a minority of Roman men could read and write. But the mass of literates, the density of their communications, and the volumes of their stored knowledge, significantly affected the experience of living in the Roman empire. Literacy and writing were active ingredients in promoting cultural and ideological change.

The birth and growth of Coptic

This process of cultural change, engineered via the accomplished literacy of provincial sub-élites, can conveniently be illustrated by the birth of Coptic.[32] Towards the end of the 1st c. A.D., some Egyptians began to write Egyptian using Greek letters supplemented with a few letters from demotic. The invention of Coptic and its widespread adoption over the next few centuries constituted an intellectually simple, but socially remarkable, technical innovation. Coptic was easier to learn than demotic; it had fewer characters, and gave clearer phonetic instructions. Its anonymous inventors succeeded without governmental aid. Contrast the reforms of the Turkish script in the early 20th c.; and of the Korean script in the 15th c., both executed by

---

conversations turn repeatedly on status-differences and on the social advantages of education.

31   Ancient historians' professional tendency to underrate what many Romans must have rated highly is only partly a function of surviving evidence and of what literate Romans either took for granted or deliberately obscured, by taking their pleasures without describing them. For the importance of pleasures in history, see for example the brilliant biography by J. Spence, *Emperor of China: self-portrait of K'ang Hsi* (London 1974), or T. Zeldin, *France 1848-1945* vol.1: *Love, ambition and politics* (Oxford 1973).

32   The best introduction to the growth of Coptic which I have found is P. E. Kahle, *Bala'izah* 1 (Oxford 1954) 193 ff.

central governmental decree against considerable opposition. In Roman Egypt, groups of nameless men somehow managed to cooperate in creating a new, simplified phonetic script for writing Egyptian. All by themselves they succeeded, without official support or interference, in creating an unofficial script for the Egyptian underclass.[33]

We really do not know how or why they did it. The earliest surviving old Coptic texts are magical spells. But the magical origins of Coptic (if these are not merely a matter of chance survival) do not get us very far in explaining its gradual diffusion, acceptance, and standardization. We know that somewhat later Coptic was in some way tied up with the spread of new religious ideologies (Gnostic, Christian, Hermetic, and Manichaean) by sub-élite sectarians. But two points are worth stressing: first, Coptic had developed into a weakly standardized way of writing Egyptian by the middle of the 3rd c., that is, well before the triumph of Christianity. Even then there were different dialects (Fayumic, Achmimic, Bohairic, Sahidic) which in turn probably reflected the pluralist, informal origins of the Coptic script, as well as local phonetic variations. Secondly, Coptic was eventually used for a whole range of writing purposes (just as Greek was) for farm accounts, contracts, tax receipts, private letters, medicine, and, of course, magic.

And yet, to judge from surviving manuscripts, Coptic was used particularly to disseminate and to preserve anti-authoritarian ideologies.[34] For example, the famous Nag Hammadi library, discovered in 1945, was a set of a dozen leather-bound codices, containing 50 tracts, mostly Gnostic in character.[35] They are Coptic translations of earlier

---

33   I use the terms 'underclass' and 'sub-élites' in a woefully loose way. As sub-élites, I have in mind local town-councillors and their village equivalents, or leading temple priests, with highish local status, enough land to avoid working with their own hands, and diverse educational achievements. By underclass, I mean the broad stratum of peasants, artisans and traders, also diverse, below the sub-élites. Note that sub-élites are plural.

34   I take early Christianity and Manichaeism and probably most forms of Gnosticism as in some sense radical breaks with élite traditions. It is difficult to know how consciously writers used Coptic as a 'religious' script, just as Christians in Egypt apparently used the codex or book form preferentially for religious writings, while the papyrus roll long continued to be used preferentially for traditional pagan literature. See the list of codices and rolls by date compiled by C. H. Roberts and T. C. Skeat, *The birth of the codex* (London 1983) 37 ff.

35   J. M. Robinson (ed.), *The Nag Hammadi library in English* (Leiden 1977).

Greek texts, buried in a jar perhaps by Christian monks, to preserve
them from destruction by orthodox book-burning Christians. The
Chester Beatty Library in Dublin has almost as large a collection of
Coptic Manichaean texts, many still unpublished, also dating from the
4th c. and found in a Fayum village, Medinet Medi.[36] Writing
penetrated even villages. Christians, too, used Coptic to help in the
conversion and education of the lower-class faithful. The Bible was
translated into Coptic by the 3rd c., when Christianity was still a
persecuted sect. And when Christianity triumphed, we know of two
inter-related developments.

First, monks in Pachomius' monasteries were taught to read, so that
they could study the Holy Scriptures for themselves. And they were
taught how to read Coptic, not Greek.[37] However imperfectly executed
this general policy was, it serves to remind us that evangelical
Christianity was an important stimulus to maintaining and spreading
literacy in Coptic among the underprivileged. Secondly, Coptic
Christianity helped preserve the sense of struggle by native Egyptian
believers against the Roman government, against Greek pagans, and
Greek-speaking upper-class Christians.[38]

Coptic originated as a script of protest. It was obviously first developed by Egyptians who already knew Greek (hence the Greek letters),
but who also wanted to write in Egyptian in order to communicate with
Egyptians, who did not know Greek. If both parties had known Greek,
it presumably would not have been worthwhile inventing the new
script. To be sure, at one level the new script represented a cultural
fusion between Greek and Egyptian. But on another level Coptic represents a cultural resistance of native Egyptian against the dominance of

---

36   See S. Giversen, *The Manichaean Coptic papyri in the Chester Beatty
      Library* (Geneva 1986-88) (4 vols. containing over 1000 pages of text).
37   Pachomius, *Regulae* 139-40 = *PL* 23.78, translated into English by A.
      Veilleux, *Pachomian Koinonia* 2 (Kalamazoo 1981). For context, see P.
      Rousseau, *Pachomius* (Berkeley, CA 1985) 70 ff. For a good balanced
      survey of later Roman literacy, see E. Wipzycka, "L'alphabétisation en
      Egypte byzantine," *RevEtAug* 30 (1984) 279-96.
38   See for example the equation repeatedly made by Shenute, abbot of the
      White Monastery in the 5th c., between Greek (speaker) = rich = pagan: J.
      Barns, "Shenute as a historical source," *Actes du Xe Congrès
      international de papyrologie* (Wroclaw 1964) 152-59; and J. Leipoldt,
      *Schenute von Atripe und die Entstehung des national ägyptischen
      Christentums* (Leipzig 1903) 166-91; Leipoldt's attribution of nationalism
      seems dated and exaggerated, but Shenute's Christianity is Egyptian
      rather than Greek.

Greek speakers and writers; by proxy it was, presumably, also aimed against the dominance of Roman rule. It was a development mirrored in other parts of the empire, in the apparent growth of Syriac literature. Coptic was used as a medium of communication among native sub-élites, who knew both Greek and Egyptian but preferred to write in Egyptian; and between them and those Egyptians who did not know Greek.[39] The invention and diffusion of a new script gives us a general insight into the educational level and ideological aspirations of lower social strata in a Roman province, of which we are usually ignorant, and which therefore we often choose either to underestimate or to ignore.

The growth of Coptic was complementary in an interesting way with the development of Christianity. Both were social movements which involved interaction, even cooperation, between sub-élites and the underprivileged. Both were movements of protest against Roman-dominated conventions. In popular Christian martyr acts, for example, the martyr always wins out, at least spiritually and symbolically, against a repressive representative of Roman power. It is both interesting and revealing that this confrontation between martyr and governor continued to be portrayed in martyr hagiographies written, elaborated, and circulated even after the triumph of Christianity.[40] And early Christian writers in their theological treatises repeatedly stressed the primacy of divine power over secular laws and mortal rulers.[41] Christian leaders wanted to subordinate Roman emperors to their own interpretation of God's law.

Christianity, like its competitor-religion Manichaeism, was a religion of the written word.[42] It was a religion of the book. To be sure,

---

39 On Syriac see the model article by S. Brock, "Introduction to Syriac studies," in J. Eaton (ed.), *Horizons in Semitic studies* (Birmingham 1980) 1-33. There seems no similar easy synoptic introduction to Coptic. In general see R. MacMullen, "Provincial languages in the Roman empire" in his *Changes in the Roman empire* (Princeton 1990) 32-40.

40 In addition to the well-known martyr acts edited by H. Musurillo, *The acts of the Christian martyrs* (Oxford 1972), see E. A. E. Reymond and J. W. B. Barns (edd.), *Four martyrdoms from the Pierpont Morgan Coptic codices* (Oxford 1973).

41 See for example *The martyrdom of Polycarp* 9; Justin, *Apol.* 1, 13; Athenag., *Apol.* 18; Tert., *Apol.* 33: "Caesar is appointed by our God"; Origen, *Cels.* 8.73-75.

42 Mani himself put enormous stress on the importance of the written word: see *Kephalaia* 154, cited by C. Schmidt and H. J. Polotsky, "Ein Mani-Fund in Aegypten," *Sitzungsberichte der königlichen preussischen Akademie der Wissenschaften* Phil.-hist. Klasse 1933, 41-43: "The writings and the

much religious experience was spiritual, psychic, and induced by ritual or the spoken word (cf. Harris 220). The oral and the written were complementary, and in dynamic interaction with each other. But the establishment of Christian orthodoxy and its associated heresies, and their maintenance over centuries and over the whole Mediterranean basin and beyond, were made easier (if not indeed possible) by the existence and repeated use of writings. Sacred texts, exegetical commentaries, letters, written prayers, hymns, sermons, and decrees of church councils, all helped to integrate Christianity into a coherent if sub-divided body; it had a recognisable identity, forged and continually reforged by an argumentative network of writers and readers. The existence of Christian books and readers, emerging from a differentiated set of sub-cultures, and disseminated all over the Roman empire, deeply affected the nature of Christian religious teaching and experience.[43] Literacy was not simply a passive technical skill; it was itself a cultural creation and a creator of culture. After all, the Roman empire was conquered by the religious coherence of Christians a century before the western empire was conquered by invading barbarians.

More details: literacy in village and town

In this final section, I want to analyse some minor texts which illustrate the operation of literacy at the level of village and town. Inevitably, these detailed texts come from Roman Egypt, where almost alone have such texts been preserved in dry sand. I leave aside the question as to how far Romano-Egyptian practice can be used as a valid basis for envisaging customs and attitudes outside Egypt: my own opinion is that, once proper allowance is made for cultural variation and differences in the level of economic development between provinces, much of what we find of governmental practice in Egypt was reflected elsewhere in the Roman empire. I would cite in support the limited number of surviving administrative papyri which originated outside Egypt but were kept there, and the rare papyri surviving

---

wisdom ... of earlier religions were gathered from everywhere and came to my religion ... As water will be added to water ..., so were the ancient books added to my writings and became a mighty wisdom ..." On context, see S. N. C. Lieu, *Manichaeism* (Manchester 1985).

43   The existence of heresies and of orthodoxy itself, as well as of attacks against heresies, rotated around a core of writings. It is interesting to wonder how many pagans, or Christians, in the persecutions of Decius in 250 were issued with written certificates of sacrifice (e.g. *P. Ryl.* 12).

outside Egypt.[44] They show some striking similarities with Egyptian practice. Those who wish to dismiss Egypt as an idiosyncratic exception at least need to answer that.

I shall look at 5 topics: 1. bi-partite receipts, 2. authenticators and signatories, 3. village schools, 4. guild rules and secretaries, and 5. tax-statistics in the village. Admittedly they are an odd assortment, reflecting adventitious survival and the accidents of my reading. But taken together, they illustrate, I hope, the pervasiveness of writing at levels well below the literary élite, and the uses to which writing was put as an instrument of social control and negotiation at several different levels of society.

1. Bi-partite receipts, and 2. Authenticators and signatories

My first data-set illustrates both surprising concentrations of literates, and a generalised expectation that illiterates would have a literate friend or patron readily available. I begin with a single papyrus (*P. Oslo* III 111), which records part of a house-to-house census, carried out mostly on a single day in A.D. 235 in the substantial administrative centre and market-town of Oxyrhynchus. As the census officials moved along the streets, they noted the location of each house. They extracted from each house-owner a spoken oath and a written statement that his or her census declaration was complete. The written statement varied; the most common type went along the following lines:

> I, Aurelius Isidorus, also called Harpokration, son of Pausiris and Sarapias, inhabit the aforementioned house with my son who is a minor, and (confirm) that we are registered in the Cavalry Camp district, or may I be liable under my oath. Year 14, 18th Mecheir (A.D. 235, February 12) (*P. Oslo* III 111.155 ff. — 17th hand).

Admittedly a few written statements were more cursory:

> I, Aurelius Ploutarchos, town councillor, have sworn the oath.

---

44   For the most recent discovery of papyri outside Egypt, with a list of previous discoveries, see D. Feissel and J. Gascou, "Documents d'archives romains inédits du moyen Euphrate," *CRAI* 1989, 536 ff. The petition included in this archive, dated to A.D. 245, seems very like those commonly found in Egypt. See similarly the case presented in A.D. 216 before Caracalla in Syria: a group of farmers against a tax-collector. The Syrian court report is structured just like so many court reports from Egypt. The text is in P. Roussel and F. de Visscher, "Les inscriptions du temple de Dmeir," *Syria* 23 (1943) 173 ff. For a now rather old list of papyri surviving in Egypt, but originating outside, see P. Taubenschlag, *Opera minora* 2 (Warsaw 1959) 29-43.

But by and large, these written declarations serve as a reasonable test of literacy.

The readable section of the text covers 31 occupied households; of these, 26 had at least one literate male in the household. Only 5 out of the 31 households used a literate outsider to write the declaration on their behalf, and each of these households used a different literate subscriber. The proportion of literate householders (84%) is amazingly high. It may simply be a matter of chance — the census tract may derive from a very prosperous sector of the town; but then several houses in the quarter were unoccupied, barred up, or confiscated by the Roman government. And several of the declarants wrote in awkward capitals or wrote in a handwriting which reflected a lack of practice, certainly not an educated fluency. In no sense do I wish to generalize from this chance find to the general population of Oxyrhynchus, or of Egypt. But we should note that the very procedure of the census officials presupposed that each householder would either be literate or would have a literate person available to help.

This expectation of pervasive literacy is found elsewhere, and surprisingly even among poor farmers in the Egyptian village of Karanis. I deduce this from a set of 135 tiny receipts for wheat seed borrowed from a state granary in November A.D. 158. In antiquity, these receipts had been stored together, presumably by an official at the granary, since when they were rediscovered at the end of the 19th c. several of them were still tied together with brown thread; still others had a hole in them for the thread to pass through. A typical receipt reads:

> To the grain collectors of Karanis. I have received an advance of seed, contractually acknowledged, in year 22 of the Lord Antoninus Caesar, 44th allotment, Horus, son of Akroes, Karanis, state land, $5^{1}/2$ arourai (= $1^{1}/2$ ha) (*P. Kar. Goodsp.* 44 = *SB* Bh. II 44).

These modest receipts for modest loans of wheat allow us to glimpse the percolation of literacy among small farmers in an Egyptian village. Each receipt was normally written by two people. The first part was written by an official in a practised hand. But the second part, beginning in the example quoted above at "44th allotment", was written by someone else. It is not at all easy now to analyse who these writers were, partly because the documents were published almost a century ago by excellent editors neither of whom was interested in statistics on literacy. One of them, Goodspeed, did draw attention to the "surprising number" of different handwritings visible in the second part of the receipts, some fine, some crude, many of them apparently written in haste and with abbreviations which were not standardised. We can supplement these editorial impressions with some figures: we can identify 24 different writers of the second part of these receipts by name. To be sure, 24 literates from a village with over 700 adult male inhabitants is not a large number.[45] But then this is not a complete list of all of the literates in the village, only of those peasants borrowing wheat seed who could write, out of an undoubtedly incomplete set of receipts. And those were written by village farmers who felt poor enough, or mean enough, to borrow wheat seed from the state granary.

Literacy, however crude its execution, had percolated down to the level of small Egyptian farmers. And what strikes me as even more interesting than the raw numbers is the bi-partite structure of the documents. As in the census documents, and in the auxiliary soldiers' receipts for hay-money discussed above (p.138), an official wrote the first part of the document. But there was a built-in expectation that the recipient would himself write, or get someone else to write, the second part of the document, which identified the size of his obligation to the state. And even if the peasant or soldier himself could not write, there was obviously a wide pool of literates to draw on, not only among auxiliary soldiers but also among peasants at Karanis.

And not at Karanis alone. From Tebtunis also, another village in the Fayum, we have résumés of contracts from one month in the year A.D. 42 (*P. Mich.* 121R). In this single month, illiterate villagers, who were participating as principals in contracts, called upon the services of 25 different literates to write an authentication or subscription on their behalf. Two points can be made quickly. First, these literate helpers were certainly not professional scribes; most authenticated only one

---

45 The wheat-seed receipts were published in *BGU* I-III, scattered between nos. 31 and 721, with a discussion by their editor P. Viereck, in "Quittungen aus dem Dorfe Karanis," *Hermes* 30 (1895) 107 ff. Those originally edited by E. J. Goodspeed as *P. Kar. Goodsp.* 1-91 (Chicago 1902) were republished as *Sammelbuch griechischen Urkunden aus Aegypten* Beiheft 2 (Wiesbaden 1961), and a further 8 were published as *P. Goodspeed* 16 and 18-24; 135 out of 142 were dated to A.D. 158. The small sizes of the loans reflected the modest size of the recipients' landholdings. On the population of Karanis, see A. E. R. Boak, "The population of Roman and Byzantine Karanis," *Historia* 4 (1955) 157 ff., and most recently R. S. Bagnall, "Agricultural productivity and taxation in later Roman Egypt," *TAPA* 115 (1985) 289, whose findings on falling tax yields are so dramatic that they must either be a fiction (e.g. a function of changing boundaries), or quite exceptional. The more probable multiplier from adult male to total population is about 3, not about 4 (see infra n.50).

contract in the month.[46] Secondly, the villagers at Tebtunis had a very wide pool of literates from which to draw. From very incomplete data we know of over 50 literate authenticators (*hypographeis* = subscribers) at work in the village in the period from 30 to 55. And we know of another 50 literates in the village during the same period who authenticated contracts by writing in Greek or demotic on their own behalf. In one village, therefore, we know that there were over 100 literate adult males living at the same time. That gives a picture of the density of literacy at the village level, a picture that somehow fails to emerge from Harris' study. Lots of people could write; and there was quite a lot to read, both in private houses and in the library belonging to the temple in the village.[47]

3. *Village schools*

The village of Tebtunis in the mid 1st c. A.D. contained certainly more than 100 literates, and probably over 200, however roughly or even generously defined.[48] It was an amazing concentration for a single village, and suggests a literacy rate well above 10%, since there were probably about 1000 adult males living in the village and its associated hamlets. It is difficult to explain these high literacy rates; but several

---

46 Youtie 1973 (supra n.15) 611 ff. argued for the general availability in Roman Egypt of public scribes for hire (cf. Harris 144). Of course, scribes were available for hire. But the detailed evidence from Tebtunis makes it clear that many other literates were also available, and were used by villagers to help them conduct formal business.

47 There is no convenient list of literary papyri found at Tebtunis, nor (as far as I know) any reconstruction of what there was available to be read in a village. For the temple library, see supra n.18. For other Tebtunis papyri, see for example W. J. Tait, *Papyri from Tebtunis* (London 1977); *P. Mil. Vogl.* vols. 1-2; *P. Tebt.* II 265 ff. Many more are yet to be published (some have only recently been rediscovered by that productive form of archaeology — looking hard inside a museum). See G. Avezzu, "Nuovi papiri ... [da] Tebtynis," *Bolletino dell'Istituto di filologia greca* (Padova) 4 (1977-78) 192-96.

48 Very complete records and scattered individual documents certainly attest over 100 literates in Tebtunis in A.D. 30-55. The actual number of literates was very probably at least double this. How can we tell? There are two arguments: first, a risky, statistical estimate of how much data is missing; secondly, since literates were asked to authenticate contracts only when they had reached social maturity, modally aged 30 or so, there very probably existed younger males aged 15+ who had learnt how to write but had not yet been called upon to exercise their skills as authenticators of contracts. QED.

factors should be listed, even though it seems difficult to assess their relative importance: they are, Egyptian religious and cultural traditions, which required at least some temple priests to read demotic and hieratic; the insistence by the Greek, and then by the Roman, administrations that commercial transactions were written down in formal contracts officially registered in the scribal office (*grapheion*); the overt status which literacy gave or enhanced — why else did many people struggle to write their own authentications to a contract, however slowly?[49] Literacy was often a public act of writing before witnesses either on one's own behalf, or to help out a relative, neighbour, or client. It gave some protection against exploitation, and some power to exploit others, and increased opportunities for employment. I must insist that all of these factors were at work, even at the level of a minor village at the edge of the Fayum.

How were literates produced at Tebtunis? We do not know. But there was a schoolmaster active in the village in the mid 1st c. (*P.Mich.* II 123 Recto 21.9). A single mention cannot tell us how long the school was active. But a school graduating 5 literate adolescents each year would, given probable death-rates, produce a pool of well over 100 adult literates.[50] The excavations of 1899-1900 in Tebtunis yielded several wooden writing tablets, including one carefully ruled into squares, and headed with the injunction:

> Good handwriting begins with well-formed
> letters and a straight line. Imitate me.

Various schoolchildren then copied the whole of this text several times underneath.[51]

---

49   *P. Tebt.* II 291 of A.D. 162 illustrates that at least some candidates for the priesthood at the temple to the Crocodile God in Tebtunis were required to show that they could read hieratic and other Egyptian writings. Twenty priests from the temple signed their names in demotic — *P. Mil. Vogl. Dem.* 2 (1st c. A.D.). The insistence by Greek rulers of Egypt that contracts written in Egyptian be summarised in Greek and officially registered in order to be legally effective in the 2nd c. B.C. is discussed by R. H. Pierce, *Three demotic papyri in the Brooklyn Museum* (Oslo 1972) 185-86.

50   Even with high mortality, if we assume an average expectation of life at birth of 23 years for males and a stationary population, the median life expectancy at ages 15-20 is another 30 years. Thus 5 graduating pupils per year, assuming no emigration, would yield 150 literates. Allow for error in such calculations. I use A. J. Coale and P. Demeny, *Regional model life tables* (Princeton 1966) level 3, model West, p.4.

51   There are several wooden school tablets from Tebtunis in the Lowie Museum at Berkeley, found by Grenfell and Hunt in 1899-1900. The one

Sometimes instruction apparently had a commercial slant. One papyrus contains an alphabetical list of tradesmen (baker, dyer, fuller) designed presumably to help children with learning Greek (*P. Tebt.* II 279). Another (not from Tebtunis) sets the following arithmetical problems:

> a. The freight charge on 100 *artabai* is 5 *artabai*. What is the freight charge on the whole cargo of 1000 *artabai*?
> b. The monthly interest on 100 drachmai is 2 *drachmai* 3 *obols*. In 4 months, if the principal is 200 *drachmai*, how much is the interest? (*P. Mich.* II 145).

It is a salutary and rare reminder that the village school aimed at the literacy of tradesmen, rather than, or as well as, at teaching the literary Greek which we find so often in other surviving school texts.[52]

Village schools were not merely training-grounds for literates and for the exercise of relative social privilege. They also served as a battleground for cultural conflict. After all, children had to choose between learning Greek or demotic. Some learnt demotic. Demotic texts from Tebtunis in the Roman period set uncommercial arithmetical problems ranging, for example, from the simple 13 x 17 to the more complex $(1/3 + 1/15) \times (2/3 + 1/2)$. The answer, of course, is $1/4 + 1/28$. From another Fayum village, Medinet Medi, we have a dump of well over 1000 pottery sherds, once used for school exercises and dating to the 2nd c. A.D. Roughly equal numbers of the texts were in Egyptian or in Greek, and a slightly smaller number were written in a mixture of both.[53]

Only a few of these texts have been published. They show ancient teachers pressing their pupils to work hard, and stressing the value of literacy: "Your instruction is in your own interest", "Five days journey on an ass equals one day in which you dedicate yourself to writing" (*O. Med.* 12 and 30). But some pupils were not entirely convinced of the

cited in the text is Museum no.6-21416. I am most grateful to Dave Herod and Frank Norick for generously showing me, and sharing their knowledge about, the Tebtunis finds in the Museum.

52   There is a catalogue of school-texts by G. Zalateo, "Papiri scolastici," *Aegyptus* 41 (1961) 160-235, which may include more than it should; and see also H. Harrauer and P. J. Sijpesteijn, *Neue Texte aus dem antiken Unterricht* (Wien 1985) for later additions, commentary, and bibliography.

53   Richard A. Parker, *Demotic mathematical papyri* (Providence 1972) on *P.B.M* 10520, problem 27 and plate 21. E. Bresciani (ed.), *Ostraka demotici da Narmuti* (Pisa 1983), which I have abbreviated as *O. Med.* I am grateful to Penny Glare for this reference.

value of learning demotic. One demotic sherd reads:

    I shall not write in Greek letters. I am obstinate. (*O. Med.* 5).

The joke is that the last word, 'obstinate', was written in Greek. My argument here is not statistical, but inevitably impressionistic. The impression that I get — and obviously such fragmentary evidence is open to several, competing interpretations — is that literacy in the Egyptian villages penetrated well below a social élite, and reached a variety of levels of competence, dispersed well above and below what one might call 'artisanal' or merely functional literacy.

4. Guild-rules and secretaries

Even in a village, there were jobs and positions which required literacy or in which literacy was an obvious and tempting advantage. For example, in Tebtunis alone there were about 20 associations of artisans, farmers or traders active in the mid 1st c. A.D.[54] One association, a monthly dining club, with provisions for mutual support and mourning, had a rather high monthly subscription; and 9 of its 15 members were literate (*P. Mich.* V 243; A.D. 14-37). The guild of salt-sellers, like other guilds, had written rules. They behaved as an active trade association: they fixed prices, they fixed penalties for transgressors, they drank together, and they allocated a monopoly for selling salt in the outlying villages by lot in return for a fee. Presumably demand there was too small to support competition (*P. Mich.* V 245, A.D. 47). This was conscious economic rationalism, and, on a small scale, economic planning. To be sure, such arrangements could have been fixed orally; the officially-registered written rules were perhaps never consulted. But written rules surely defined obligations rather more rigidly and more fixedly than purely oral agreements. One further point: several guilds or groups of farmers had an official secretary (*grammateus*), ranking second after the guild president. The very existence of a guild secretary is a striking index of the importance attached to writing in an Egyptian village, and to recording the decisions of the guild.

5. Tax statistics in the village

I began this essay with some tiny individual tax-receipts. I would like to end with the transformation of such individual receipts into

---

54   See conveniently *P. Mich.* V 243 ff. and A. E. R. Boak, "The organisation of gilds in Roman Egypt," *TAPA* 68 (1937) 212 ff. The price-fixing recorded in the rules of the guild of salt-sellers defeats the inherently implausible dictat by M. I. Finley, *The ancient economy* (2nd ed., London 1985) 138, that ancient guilds did not fix prices.

composite and well-organised tax statistics, sent from the Fayum
village of Karanis by a marginally literate farmer named Aurelios
Isidoros.[55] When it was his turn to be a village tax-collector for wheat
and barley, he was responsible for compiling and transmitting the
village tax-return for wheat and barley, which involved listing the
size of each land-holding in the village, the amount of tax due in
wheat and barley from each farmer and land-owner, the amount so far
paid, and the arrears (*P. Cair. Isid.* 9, 6 and 11). The clarity of the
summary statistics is very impressive. Their implications are also, I
think, quite interesting.

Aurelios Isidoros was responsible with all of his property for the
proper performance of his duty as tax-collector. It was only one of
several village offices which we know that he held during his life.
Knowing how to read, knowing what he was being made responsible for,
gave him a clear advantage over those who had to trust a relative, a
friend, patron, or paid employee. My first point is simple. Even in a
village, state intervention and the system of administration stimulated
literacy. Literacy was an expedient, an advantage, and a public status-
symbol, possessed by a significant minority.

Secondly, Aurelios Isidoros knew how much tax his village paid
every year, in wheat. It was a very sizeable amount. The collective
tax-return was a form of communication with the governor of Egypt,
perhaps even with the emperor. After all, it may well have crossed
the peasant's mind that the farmers of the village were paying an
awful lot for Roman peace and justice: did they wonder if they were
getting good value for their sweated labour? In the dossier of papers
which Aurelios Isidoros preserved, there is a preamble to an Edict of
the emperor Diocletian (A.D. 297) reforming taxation, and promising a
fairer distribution of the tax burden (*P. Cair. Isid.* 1). It is amazing and
unexpected that we find an imperial message percolating into the dossier of a modest villager. But from other papers we can also see how
very seriously Aurelios Isidoros took the spirit of the imperial mes-

---

55   See A. E. R. Boak and H. C. Youtie (edd.), *The archive of Aurelius Isidorus*
(Ann Arbor 1960), conveniently abbreviated as *P. Cair. Isid.* Isidorus was
explicitly called illiterate (ἀγράμματος), that is, he did not know how to
write his own letters to officials (*P. Cair. Isid.* 8, and Boak and Youtie ibid.
4). But we know several instances in which such categorisation as illiterate
was not true (see Youtie, n.15 infra); and I personally agree with Youtie's
earlier judgement that Isidorus could probably read; hence his dossier.
See H. Youtie, "A farmer under Diocletian and Constantine," *Byzantina-
Metabyzantina* 1 (1946) 42.

sage. During the course of his lifetime, he sent 20 petitions to various officials, including 2 to the governor of the province. And in these petitions, he reflected the government's own message: Roman law was meant to protect the poor against the unjust depredations of the rich.[56]

In this essay I have tried to argue, at the level of the general and the particular, that literacy and writing helped to integrate the Roman empire into a more unified political, administrative, economic, legal, and cultural system. Writing operated, in some ways, for example, like money. Just as money allows sellers and buyers to transcend face-to-face relationships — the seller can use the cash that he gets from the buyer to purchase other goods removed in time and space — so writing allows the writer to communicate with people he cannot see, and with people not yet born. But writing and money are not simply exemplary parallels: their use and operation, which we call literacy and monetization, were intertwined.

Money stored value, and helped foster the growth of long-distance markets. Writing stored rights and obligations, and helped create a larger store of knowledge, a system of laws, and a market in cultural skills and values. Their operation was mutually reinforcing, since both money and writing are systems of impersonal, symbolic exchange. Roman emperors, with their coins and edicts, could try to (and they occasionally succeeded in) communicating with simple peasants. Simple peasants could try to communicate via taxes and petitions with the emperor. Writing and money were two powerful agents of communication and control, which helped integrate the Roman empire into a single political system.[57]

Over four centuries, the Roman empire was increasingly integrated in several spheres — political, legal, economic, cultural, and religious. But it was in the field of religion that changes in integration were most remarkable. As before, humble believers tried to communicate with god(s) via prayers, dreams, and petitions; that was ancient practice. But for the first time in the 4th c., God communicated with all believers in the Roman empire by means of a single book. The empire was hooked

---

56 For example, "The laws forbid actions aimed at ruining us, the people of modest means, and driving us into flight. Now I myself, who am in every way a man of modest means ...." (a self-description which was not completely true) (*P. Cair. Isid.* 68); or "The laws have repeatedly enjoined that no one be made to suffer oppression or illegal executions..." (*P. Cair. Isid.* 69, A.D. 310).

57 See similar thoughts in H.-U. von Freyberg, *Kapitalverkehr und Handel im römischen Kaiserreich* (Freiburg in Bresgau 1988) 76-77.

into a single religious system, however diverse the interpretations of different sects and churches. The radical and subversive message of primitive Christianity could not have become initially established across the whole empire without significant sub-élite literacy. And it is the pervasiveness and effect of that sub-élite literacy that Harris has underplayed in his book.

King's College, Cambridge

Acknowledgements:

I should like to thank Mary Beard, Alan Bowman, Penny Glare, Wim Jongman, John Ray and Dorothy Thompson for help and advice.

Ancient illiteracy[1]

Ann Ellis Hanson

UNESCO, the educational organ of the United Nations, views illiteracy much as it once viewed smallpox — the sooner it can be permanently eradicated from earth's populations, the better. Models of accommodation, for example, might have been possible.[2] The emphasis on eliminating illiteracy stems, at least in part, from embarrassment over its uneven distribution among the world's population and its attendant economic consequences: although one-quarter is illiterate, there are few illiterates in North America and northern Europe; the highest concentrations are in Africa where many of the populations are also bi- or multilingual.[3] The drive to wipe out illiteracy thus combines political goals, such as the furthering of democracy; economic goals, such as the creation of worldwide appreciation of and markets for products of advanced technology; and social goals, such as the acculturation of the illiterate individual into the society of the fully literate. Such goals were, of course, inoperative in Graeco-Roman antiquity, and it is the merit of William Harris' *Ancient literacy*[4] that extravagant claims for widespread literacy at certain times and places in the Graeco-Roman world, offered in the past by enthusiastic students of a particular milieu, have been tempered by his thorough collections of the evidence. Literates made up only a small proportion of Graeco-

---

1   This paper is in memory of Beulah Wade of Trenton, N.J.
    I thank Alan K. Bowman, Ludwig Koenen, David Potter, and P. J. Sijpesteijn for discussing with me various aspects of literacy and illiteracy in Graeco-Roman antiquity; Bowman and Sijpesteijn also read earlier versions of this paper and improved it immeasurably. All dates are A.D. unless otherwise indicated.

2   Such as has come to the deaf and dumb in the second half of the twentieth century. More sophisticated evaluations have shifted emphasis from pathological deficiency and language deprivation to a linguistic-cultural view that sees the deaf as another minority population with its own language and culture.

3   For illiteracy, see *Unesco. Compendium of statistics on illiteracy* (Paris 1988) 8-16 and *Unesco. Towards a methodology for projecting rates of literacy and educational attainment* (Paris 1978). For bi- and multilingualism in areas where illiteracy is high, such as Africa and India, see J. F. Hamers and M. H. A. Blanc, *Bilinguality and bilingualism* (Cambridge and New York 1989) 31-59.

4   Harris *passim*, but esp. 7-24 and 323-37.

Roman populations at most times and in most places, and *Ancient literacy* tells their story. Harris promised occasional glances at semiliterates (p. 5), but they, together with the illiterates, disappear from view, even though they formed the greater proportion of Graeco-Roman populations.

Semiliterates and illiterates were unschooled and unlettered, but those of property were by no means undocumented. Papyri from the nearly 1000 years when Greek was the official language of Egypt afford a particularly full glimpse of those who are said "not to know letters" — a phrase conventionally applied to those who did not sign their name in Greek characters (see below, section 1). The literates and semiliterates who lived in Graeco-Roman Egypt collected documents that pertained to themselves and their families in the same manner as did literates. Illiterates assembled archives, and such figures as Tryphon the weaver, Soterichos and Kronion, farmers, Petaus the village scribe, Aurelius Sakaon and Aurelius Isidoros, wealthy landowners, are well-known through the documents they collected, in spite of the fact that they apparently were unable to write Greek.[5] These functional semiliterates and illiterates occupied a broad terrain between those illiterates, whose very lives poverty and the passage of time have obliterated, and those who were fully literate in every sense, the élites of cities whose literary productions and literary tastes

---

5   See "archives in papyri," with full bibliography, pp. 248-61 in O. Montevecchi, *La papirologia* (Turin 1973). The following individuals from that list did "not know letters": 20. Harthotes, son of Marres, priest and farmer of Theadelphia (early I A.D.); 22. Tryphon, son of Dionysios, weaver of Oxyrhynchos (I A.D.); 35. Petesouchos, s. of Eleis, weaver of Bacchias (d. in 139); 37. Segathis, daughter of Satabous, of Soknopaiou Nesos (II A.D.); 39. Kronion the elder, son of Pakebkis, landholder of Tebtynis (II A.D.); 40. Kronion, son of Cheos, priest and farmer of Tebtynis (II A.D.); 48. Petaus, son of Petaus, village scribe of Ptolemaios Hormou and other villages (late II A.D.); 58. Paniskos of Philadelphia (late III A.D.; cf. H. C. Youtie, *ZPE* 21 [1976] 193-96 = *Scriptiunculae posteriores* I [Bonn 1981] 307-310); 64. Aurelius Sakaon, son of Satabous, landholder and *komarch* of Theadelphia (late III/early IV A.D.); 65. Aurelius Isidoros, son of Ptolemaios, landholder, *komarch* and holder of other liturgic offices at Karanis (late III/early IV A.D.). To that list, add: Soterichos, son of Lykos, farmer of Theadelphia (late I/early II A.D. = S. Omar, *Das Archiv des Soterichos* [Opladen 1978] plus *ZPE* 86 [1991] 215-29); Babatha, daughter of Simeon, landholder in Judaea (late I/early II A.D. = N. Lewis, *The documents from the Bar Kokhba period in the cave of the letters: Greek Papyri* [Jerusalem 1989]. The archive is multilingual; one of the two guardians of Babatha's son Jesus was Julia Crispina, literate in Greek.).

continue to influence our own. The story of ancient illiteracy — with all its shadings of ability and deficiency; its pairing with bi- and multilingualism in much of the Graeco-Roman world of the historical period[6]; its perils and coping-mechanisms — was a facet of ancient literacy and its story has still to be told. I take this opportunity to present a few aspects of that story, as we know it from the evidence of Graeco-Roman Egypt (sections 1-6). I close with an examination of several papyri from the 1st c. A.D. tax archive from the Fayum village of Philadelphia, for I feel that these texts illustrate points raised in the discussion (section 7). The papyri and their photographs are published here for the first time.

1. Defining illiteracy

One of UNESCO's definitions for literacy — that "a person is literate who can with understanding both read and write a short simple statement on his everyday life," but the illiterate cannot[7] — offers parameters within which to place a discussion of ancient literacy. Harris mentions this definition for literates, because it emphasizes that the literate person can read and write, and, as he says, do so to a truly useful degree (p. 4). Such a definition looks upon writing as an act of composition, rather than, say, an act of reproducing an oral text from dictation or copying an exemplar. This definition is also more in keeping with Harris' project than ones that equate literacy with sophistication and urbanity.[8]

UNESCO offers a second definition, and this attracts me more. This definition better complements a discussion of ancient illiteracy through

---

6   Only the Greek peninsula was monolingual in any real sense, for the spread of Latin over the Italian peninsula followed centuries after the Roman legions. Cf. e.g. E. Campanile, G. R. Cardona, e R. Lazzeroni, (edd.), *Bilinguismo e biculturalismo nel mondo antico* (Pisa 1987), a collection of papers on bilingual inscriptions and other bilingual documents from the entire Mediterranean world.

7   *Unesco. Compendium* (supra note 3) 8. Some argue that with the advent of computers a new kind of literacy is developing — see e.g. R. P. Howell (ed.), *Beyond literacy: the second Gutenberg revolution* (San Francisco and Dallas 1989).

8   Much current work on literacy focuses on cognitive differences between literate and illiterate societies: e.g. J. Goody, *The logic of writing and the organization of society* (Cambridge and New York 1986) and id., *The interface between the written and the oral* (Cambridge and New York 1987); E. R. Kintgen, B. M. Kroll, M. Rose (edd.), *Perspectives on literacy* (Carbondale and Edwardsville 1988).

its ability to highlight differences between the ancient and modern literacies — namely, that "a person is functionally literate who can engage in all those activities in which literacy is required for effective functioning of his group and community and also for enabling him to continue to use reading, writing and calculation for his own and the community's development." The illiterate cannot so engage. This second definition emphasizes functionalism above all else; it also separates literacy into its component parts — reading, writing, and numeracy — and seems to allow for further refinements[9]; it acknowledges that literacy and illiteracy have implications for both individual and community and that these implications may be different.

Ancient literacy differed from modern literacy in that the stance of Greek and Roman governments toward illiteracy was one of casual indifference.[10] The governments reflected the attitudes of society at large, a society in which illiterates and those of restricted literacy functioned without prejudice in the company of literates in the pre-technological marketplace, as well as in the home. Essential skills were, for the most part, acquired orally through apprenticeship, not from books, and Graeco-Egyptian husbands who were literate found it no disgrace to write for illiterate wives. Literate women, on the other hand, seem less likely to have taken illiterate husbands.[11] Strategies were available to help illiterate and semi-literate Graeco-Egyptians ward off some of the perils attendant upon illiteracy, such as fraud and misrepresentation in both private and public documents. As a result, the successive Greek and Roman governments of Egypt were able to ignore for the most part the widespread illiteracy in their midst, for there were enough literates to carry the burdens of an essentially literate system and to aid illiterates in fulfilling the demands put upon them. The central government maintained offices in which public documents were housed and other offices in which archival, and therefore valid,

---

9   Impressive is the separating of reading and writing in medieval England that forms the underpinnings of the discussion by M. T. Clanchy, *From memory to written record: England 1066-1307* (London 1979); cf. also R. McKitterick (ed.), *The uses of literacy in early mediaeval Europe* (Cambridge and New York 1990).

10 H. C. Youtie, "ΑΓΡΑΜΜΑΤΟC. An aspect of Greek society in Egypt," *HSCPh* 75 (1971) 161-76 = *Scriptiunculae* II (Amsterdam 1973) 611-27.

11 For an example of a literate wife with an illiterate husband, see *P. Oxy.* XII 1463, 215 A.D.; the wife wrote for herself, but another man signed in behalf of her husband. For abbreviations of publications of papyri, see J. F. Oates et al., *Checklist of editions of Greek papyri and ostraka* = *B A S P* Supplements 4 (1985).

copies of private contracts and agreements were deposited. This system was firmly in place by 146 B.C.[12] The number of repositories increased during the Roman period, as did complaints about the poor condition of the documents contained therein. The governmental system of registration for private documents assumed literacy and it habituated illiterates and semiliterates to the use of Greek documents, even if they did not learn to read or write every word in their documents.

In a series of articles in the early 1970's Herbert C. Youtie examined the semiliterates and illiterates of Graeco-Roman Egypt. Although he made no attempt to quantify the numbers of illiterates, he argued persuasively that the majority in the countryside were likely to be illiterate and that some members of the privileged gymnasial class in the district capitals were only semiliterate.[13] Second, he demonstrated that those labeled illiterates in the papyri were men and women unable to append a signature in Greek to the bottom of a document, when asked to write as guarantee to the fact that they were responsible parties to a particular transaction. Instead, another wrote in their behalf. The custom of asking for a signature as a sign of acceptance was known already in the Ptolemaic period, but it became a widespread practice only under the Romans.[14] Some of those said "not to know letters" were capable of writing demotic, the native Egyptian language. Although the Greek-speaking central government set no legal or administrative objection on using demotic in documents, few

---

12   See especially *P. Par.* 65 (= *P. Select* II 415), and the comments of U. Wilcken, pp. 596-97 in *UPZ* I. For the official archives of Roman Egypt, see F. Burkhalter, "Archives locales et archives centrales en Egypte romaine," *Chiron* 20 (1990) 191-216; for the documents of a village *grapheion*, see E. M. Husselman, "Procedures of the record office of Tebtunis in the first century A.D.," pp. 223-38 in D. H. Samuel (ed.), *Proceedings of the XII international congress of papyrology* (Toronto 1970); for archives in Alexandria in the Roman period, W. E. H. Cockle, "State archives in Graeco-Roman Egypt from 30 B.C. to the reign of Septimius Severus," *JEA* 70 (1984) 106-22.

13   Cf. also Harris 10-11. Youtie first wrote about literacy because he and colleagues were editing documents that belonged to Petaus; first came "Pétaus, fils de Pétaus, ou le scribe qui ne savait pas écrire," *CE* 41 (1966) 127-43 = *Scriptiunculae* II 677-95. For the limited literacy of some members of the privileged gymnasial class, see Youtie, "ΑΓΡΑΜΜΑΤΟC" (supra n. 10) 174-75 = II 624-25.

14   E.g. P. W. Pestman, *The new papyrological primer* (Leiden 1990) 42-43.

Egyptians or Graeco-Egyptians ever did so.[15] The judgment that a man
or woman was semiliterate (rather than totally illiterate) was also
made on the basis of their ability to write Greek.[16] The abilities of
semiliterates were usually very limited and most were able to do no
more than append their name to a text in awkward Greek letters.
Third, since fraud and deception were easy for literates to perpetrate
against illiterates and semiliterates, these men and women habitually
turned to three main categories of writers in order to afford themselves
some degree of protection against the unscrupulous. They turned first to
literates among their close relatives and family members; next to
friends, business associates, and other colleagues; finally to professional scribes in government employ.[17] Common interests bound families,
friends, and even peripheral associates together into alliances of self-
interest and self-protection. This pattern of trust and reliance was
operative throughout the ancient world at all social levels and in many
different spheres of public and private activity.[18] The words of the
papyrus documents themselves guarantee the accuracy of Youtie's
meticulous descriptions.

The late 20th c. has brought, however, an increasing sophistication
in methods of approaching illiteracy, especially when it exists in
environments where two or more languages are in contact and two or
more cultures are interfacing. The bilingual and trilingual populations
of postcolonial Africa and India that also display high levels of
illiteracy suggest, for example, that language capacities of individual
Graeco-Egyptians are likely to have varied considerably, in accordance
with a large set of determiners — such as degree of self-containment
and isolation of their home community; their level of contact with
urban centers and their proximity to them; the prevailing patterns of
the commercial interchanges they encountered; the frequency of written
communication they maintained with the central government, and so

---

15 Youtie, "ΑΓΡΑΜΜΑΤΟC" (supra n.10) 162-63 = II 612-13; id., "Because they
    do not know letters," *ZPE* 19 (1975) 101-8 = *Scriptiunculae posteriores* I
    (Bonn 1981) 255-62.

16 Id., "Βραδέως γράφων: between literacy and illiteracy," *GRBS* 12 (1971) 161-
    76 = *Scriptiunculae* II 629-51.

17 Id., "ΥΠΟΓΡΑΦΕΥC: the social impact of illiteracy in Graeco-Roman
    Egypt," *ZPE* 17 (1975) 201-221 = *Scriptiunculae posteriores* I (Bonn 1981)
    179-99.

18 See, for example, the young boy Lysis, whom his mother and father asked
    to do their reading and writing for them first of all in the household (Plato,
    Lys. 209b).

forth.[19] In the postcolonial populations abilities in the first language, for example, usually outstripped those in the language acquired subsequently, especially if opportunities to use the second language were limited; competence in the skills of reading, writing, and numeracy in both languages was rare among the conquered populations, and the ability to communicate orally far exceeded other abilities; the conquered were more likely than their conquerors to become bi- or multilingual. Parallels from Graeco-Roman Egypt spring readily to mind, as, for example, the fact that the Ptolemaic rulers themselves were slow to learn the native Egyptian language, in contrast to those Egyptians ready and willing to hellenize in the wake of Alexander and his Macedonians. Only the last of the line of the Ptolemies, Cleopatra VII, was reputed to have spoken Egyptian, as well as other languages of the region.[20] The functional illiterates and semiliterates, known through their documents, show that illiteracy was also intertwined in their world with bilingualism. Thus recent scholarship, building on increased understanding of the mechanics of biculturalism, has called for new assessments of Egypt after Greek-speakers had come to rule the land.[21] The Egyptian language never lost its importance as the medium of oral communication, yet its final written form, Coptic, was a writing system that derived from the Greek alphabet. So habituated to Greek writing had Egypt become.

---

19 E.g. J. F. Hamers and M. H. A. Blanc, *Bilinguality and bilingualism* (Cambridge and New York 1989), 31-59; E. Perecman, "Language processing in the bilingual: evidence from language mixing," pp. 227-44 in K. Hyltenstam and L. K. Obler, *Bilingualism across the lifespan* (Cambridge and New York 1989); F. Grosjean, *Life with two languages* (Cambridge, Mass. 1982) 1-41 and 113-65; M. K. Adler, *Collective and individual bilingualism* (Hamburg 1977) 37-112. The literature on the phenomenon of bilingualism has begun to disentangle itself from anecdotal stories about the education of individual children that confronted bi- and multilingual situations.

20 Plutarch, *Ant.* 27.4-5, where he also credits Cleopatra with speaking to most barbarians of the region in their own tongue without an interpreter.

21 See J. Johnson (ed.), *Life in a multi-cultural society: Egypt from Cambyses to Constantine* (Chicago, forthcoming). D. J. Thompson, *Memphis under the Ptolemies* (Princeton 1988) 212-65, tells the story of Ptolemaios, son of Glaukias, II B.C. Glaukias was a soldier and a Macedonian who settled in the countryside; his son Ptolemaios, perhaps the child of an Egyptian mother, lived at the temple of Sarapis in Memphis, as follower of the god.

Egypt came early to the scribal habit and she developed traditions of scribal literacy in the millennia before the arrival of Alexander.[22] Professional writers had long served in the temples and central government of the pharaohs. The scribe was respected before Greek-speakers arrived and he remained an important figure in the successive bureaucracies of the Ptolemies and then the Romans. Under the new masters Egyptians and Greeks intermingled, as immigrant Greek soldiers married native wives. Already by the 2nd c. B.C. personal names were no longer a dependable guide to bloodlines, or even to linguistic capacities. Three centuries later and Romans were erecting a new governmental structure upon the Ptolemaic bureaucratic foundations and retaining the position of the Greek language. A new wave of soldiers came to Egypt without their womenfolk, and they too established bi- and multilingual households.[23] Graeco-Egyptians at all social levels continued to use professional scribes to do much of their writing for them. There were crucial moments, however, when those who could write were asked to do so and were expected to comply. Adding a greeting and date in one's own hand to the bottom of a letter was an epistolary courtesy, extended by the writer to the recipient, but the signing of one's name to public and private documents underscored the special rôle a signature played in demonstrating that the responsible party was aware of the provisions of the document and that he or she consented to them.[24] When the consenting party was said "not

22 J. Goody and I. Watt, "The consequences of literacy," pp. 27-68 in J. R. Goody (ed.), *Literacy in traditional societies* (Cambridge 1968), and reprinted in Kintgen, Kroll, and Rose (supra n.8) 3-27.

23 For personal names as a guide to ethnicity only in the III B.C., see introduction to *WChres.* 50, pp. 78-79, in L. Mitteis and U. Wilcken, *Grundzüge und Chrestomathie der Papyruskunde* I.ii (Leipzig and Berlin 1912); for a trilingual household, see J. N. Adams, *The vulgar Latin of the letters of Claudius Terentianus* (Manchester 1977) 1-6 and 84-87.

24 *Stud. Pal.* XX 128 (487 A.D.), in which Nilus, nephew of Sambas, signed an agreement of surety for his uncle, after his uncle had read the document and approved it; pain was what prevented Sambas from signing for himself; see also Youtie's comments, "Βραδέως γράφων" (supra n.16) 252 = *Scriptiunculae* II 642. Youtie, "ΥΠΟΓΡΑΦΕΥC" (supra n.17) 207 = *Scriptiunculae post.* I 185, also drew attention to a woman and her husband, against whom court proceedings had been initiated: the woman was represented as illiterate in an earlier contract of loan, but the couple's advocate countered with the fact that the woman was literate, because when instructed to write she had recently done so (*P. Oxy.* XVII 2111.1-12, 135 A.D.).

to know letters," and a personal signature of acceptance was felt to be an essential part of the document, another signed in his or her behalf. This substitute's name, and at times also his physical description, followed underneath the statement of acceptance he had written for the contracting party. Hence the personal statement was called an *hypographe* and the substitute called upon to write for others was an *hypographeus*.[25] It was largely in their resorting to the services of an *hypographeus* that we come to know the majority of the functional illiterates and semiliterates of Graeco-Roman Egypt.

For example, more than nine-tenths of the contracts and subscriptions drawn up at the *grapheion* in the agricultural village of Tebtynis in the 30's and 40's A.D. mention that at least one party to the transaction was unable to write the acknowledgment and to pen a signature[26]; over two-thirds of the cultivators of public lands at the village of Lagis were unable to sign a joint declaration that the lands for which they were responsible had not been inundated for cultivation in 164;[27] two-thirds of the cavalrymen in the squadron Veterana Gallica in 179 did not know letters, when asked to write an acknowledgement for receipt of their yearly hay allowance;[28] over two-thirds of the citizens who applied for distributions of grain in the district capital of Oxyrhynchos in the later 3rd c. asked others to write their applications for them.[29] The numbers are impressive in themselves, but the social dynamics, such as they were outlined by Youtie, demonstrate how an inherently literate system was manipulated by illiterates and semiliterates, compelled to live their lives with Greek documents.[30]

---

25 Youtie, "ΥΠΟΓΡΑΦΕΥΣ" (supra n. 17) 211 = *Scriptiunculae post.* I 189, argued that subscribers frequently marked the limit of their responsibility by specifying that they have written at the request of the principal and have done so in his presence. On the importance of a signature, see Harris 222.

26 *P. Mich.* V 249-355.

27 *P. Berl. Leihg.* II 29 (23 out of 33). The editor noted that only one of the ten who signed wrote in a hand that was badly formed (p. 25). For other but smaller groups of signers and illiterates in related texts, see also *P. Berl. Frisk* 23, 29, 30, 32, and 38.

28 R. O. Fink, *Roman military records on papyrus* (Cleveland 1971) no. 76 (= *P. Hamb.* I 39); Harris 254-55.

29 J. D. Thomas, *CR* 26 (1976) 111; R. Duncan-Jones, *Structure and scale in the Roman economy* (Cambridge and New York 1990) 80 and n. 1; Harris 214.

30 Cf. the similarities in the papers assembled by two roughly contemporary craftsmen in the district capital of Oxyrhynchos: Pausiris, son of Ammonios, master weaver and apparently literate (for relevant texts, see

Thus, in the village of Tebtynis, as the *grapheion* records make clear, many illiterates were female, and their guardians that were also kinsmen — fathers, husbands, sons, brothers — wrote subscriptions for their womenfolk. Men from two of the wealthier families in the village also wrote subscriptions for illiterate fellow villagers, and so did the professional scribes of the records office.[31] Literate friends not only wrote for their illiterate fellows, but they apparently came in company together to the place where such signatures were asked for. Thus, the illiterate cultivators of public lands in Lagis and the illiterate cavalrymen of Veterana Gallica came for their allotted portions in the company of a literate who wrote an acknowledgement of receipt for himself and then assisted his illiterate companion. The requirement for a signature revealed these private networks of trust that anticipated the need. And finally, in the town of Oxyrhynchos family and neighborhood not only supplied writers for illiterates, but neighborhood networks also communicated to literates and illiterates alike that a recipient of grain on their street had died and vacated a place on the lists of those who received the dole of wheat.

Illiterates engaged without prejudice in the same activities as literates, except that a special bond of trust between them and a literate relative, friend, or associate became visible at the point when the illiterate was asked to sign as responsible party to a transaction. Functional semiliterates and illiterates whose documents are preserved did not come to such moments of signing unprepared.

2. Semiliterates and illiterates in the documents

Some 75 years ago Ernst Majer-Leonhard catalogued the illiterates, literates, and semiliterates that had appeared in papyri published up to 1913.[32] He listed 488 documents relating to illiterates, the vast majority of whom were marked as such in their documents by specific terms or phrases; 749 texts involving literates who either said they

---

P. Mich X 598) and Tryphon, son of Dionysios, illiterate weaver (*P. Oxy.* I 38-39, 99; II 264-69, 275, 282, 288; *SB* X 10220-10249, with *BL* 7. Discussion by M. V. Biscottini, "L'archivio di Tryphon, tessitore di Oxyrhynchus," *Aegyptus* 46 [1966] 60-90 and 186-292, and R. L. B. Morris, "The economy of Oxyrhynchus in the first century," *BASP* 15 [1978] 263-73).

31   See e.g. E. M. Husselman, pp. 14-22 in Introduction, *P. Mich.* V, and Pestman, *Primer* (supra n. 14) 42-43 and 116.

32   *ΑΓΡΑΜΜΑΤΟΙ: in Aegypto qui litteras sciverint qui nesciverint ex papyris graecis quantum fieri potest exploratur* (Frankfort 1913).

wrote for themselves, or at least seemed to write for themselves;[33] 25 texts involving semiliterates, marked by a phrase indicating that they wrote (too) slowly.[34] Rita Calderini reviewed the illiterates in 1950 and found that the number of certifiables had climbed to 556.[35] As might be expected, the continued publication of papyri has nearly quadrupled the number of documents that mention illiterates.[36] That the number of certifiable illiterates continues to increase in proportion to the number of papyri published underscores and gives added resonance to my claim that ancient illiterates were not dysfunctional. On the other hand, the numbers of illiterates remain sufficiently small, such that detailed analyses of the data, as undertaken by Majer-Leonhard or Calderini, do not yield meaningful results.[37] There was a certain nexus between wealth and status on the one hand and literacy in Greek on the other, and Harris has documented this connection in the Graeco-Roman world. In the contracts and subscriptions registered in Julio-Claudian Tebtynis, for example, illiterates sold, borrowed, and leased more often than literates by a proportion of 4 to 3. At the same

---

33 Majer-Leonhard admitted that deciding a man was literate without an express statement to the fact was a subjective judgment.

34 See Youtie, "Βραδέως γράφων" (supra n. 16) 161-76 = *Scriptiunculae* II 629-51, and id., "ΥΠΟΓΡΑΦΕΥΣ" (supra n. 17) 201-221 = *Scriptiunculae posteriores* 179-99, for additional phrases that may mark a "slow writer."

35 "Gli ἀγράμματοι nell'Egitto greco-romano," *Aegyptus* 30, 1950, 14-41. Calderini did not, however, publish her catalogue, and her figures are difficult to build upon, since she does not always make it clear what is being counted — documents or illiterate individuals.

36 The Duke Data Bank (= DDB) CDRom3 contains 32,319 documents, and preliminary searches of phrases used by Majer-Leonhard and others have yielded more than 1400 Greek documents in which illiterates are mentioned. In order to yield data comparable to Majer-Leonhard's I have counted documents, not individuals. As of this writing I have not completed collations between my list and that of Majer-Leonhard in order to remove duplicate publications, nor have I identified all the illiterates that appear in more than a single text. By and large, however, the Majer-Leonhard data base of papyri is independent of that in the DDB, because both collections were assembled largely by date of first publication of a papyrus — i.e. papyri published before 1913 (M-L.) and papyri published published after 1926 (DDB). There are, however, exceptions, and DDB includes *P. Oxy.* I-LVI. Hence the total number of documents that refers to illiterates can only be said to approach 2000.
A new catalogue is a desideratum, and I hope to present revised results in the near future.

37 Cf. also the caveats from Calderini (supra n. 35) 24-26.

time, wealth and status were never a guarantee of literacy,[38] although wealth and status no doubt enabled an illiterate or semi-literate to function more easily in the literate systems.

The number of certifiable semiliterates remains very small, and the imprecision with which the term "slow writer," and its variant "too slow writer," were used suggests that the category not only lacked official status, but enjoyed only local popularity. That is, nearly 60% of the new testimonia for βραδέως (or βραδύτερον) γράφοντες occur in the first two centuries A.D. (21 out of 38),[39] and half of these earlier examples derives from only two archives — the registry office in 1st-c. Tebtynis and the leases the illiterate farmer Soterichos of the village Theadelphia held from a female landowner, Sentia Asklatarion, at the end of the century. Sentia was said to be a "slow writer" when her guardian Lucius Egnatius Crispus wrote three rent receipts in her behalf.[40] When Sentia acted for herself without a guardian, she hired a scribe to write the receipt, but wrote the subscription for herself. Sentia wrote the same, slow, and uneven hand in all four agreements she made with Soterichos, whether she was labeled a slow writer or not.

3. Public and private

The habit of looking to family members and to trusted friends and associates was a pattern that permeated ancient private life and frequently determined conduct in the public sphere as well. The Roman imperial system required that provincial administrators at all levels serve in communities and areas other than their native one; even an administrator in the lowest ranks of that bureaucracy, the "scribe of the village" (komogrammateus), functioned elsewhere than in his home village, in order to lessen his opportunities for favoritism and collusion.[41] Once arrived in the new community, those village scribes we

---

38 Thus, Duncan-Jones, *Structure and Society* (supra n. 29) 92, pointing to the case of the functional illiterate Aurelius Isidoros, argues that this is "... a warning against thinking that wealth always carried with it either numeracy or literacy" — but see below, section 6. There are also sufficient exceptions to the join between poverty and illiteracy to counsel caution in that regard: cf. e.g. the literate *ancilla* in the house of Barbatio, Amm. Marc. 18.3.2-4.

39 The only new example for III A.D. is *SB* XVII.12950 ii. 24, and the phrase "slow writer" occurs in lacuna.

40 *P. Soter.* 19-21 (with Crispus); *P. Soter.* 18 (Sentia acting alone).

41 D. Hagedorn, pp. 17-21 in Ursula and Dieter Hagedorn, L. C. and H. C. Youtie, *Das Archiv des Petaus* (= *P. Petaus*; Köln and Opladen 1969).

know best operated within a côterie of "like-minded" men, élite property owners in the new community who shared the bureaucrat's desire to preserve the existing power structure in the village and to keep the peace. If he expressed his gratitude in the proper fashion, the administrator could count upon such individuals for advice and support in the carrying out of his official duties, for these were "trustworthy" men. The personal fortunes of officials themselves, as well as their guarantors, ensured that what was owed to Rome was collected according to estimates filed during the previous year and was forwarded safely up along the bureaucratic chain of command.[42] Those at higher bureaucratic levels pledged larger amounts to guarantee the moneys from an entire district. The government investigated shortfalls with impressive thoroughness, safeguarding provincial revenues at the expense of propertied office holders.[43] The official, whether literate or not, protected himself and his personal fortune by aligning himself with others of the similar interests.

Petaus, son of Petaus, has gained a certain notoriety as "the scribe who could not write."[44] Although his home was Karanis, one of the larger villages in the Fayum, he served as scribe (*komogrammateus*) to a group of smaller farming villages, including Ptolemais Hormou, Syron kome, Kerkesucha Orous, toward the end of the 2nd c.[45] In Julio-Claudian Egypt men at this lowest level in the Roman bureaucracy were literate and they sometimes wrote in their own hand private communications, such as letters to friends and family members and personal accounts. On occasion they also drafted documents that concerned the on-going affairs of the bureaux under their direction. Nonetheless

---

42 Evidence for an unofficial circle of advisers for a *komogrammateus* is collected by H. C. Youtie, "P. Mich. inv. 855: letter from Herakleides to Nemesion," *ZPE* 27 (1977) 147-50 = *Scriptiunculae posteriores* I 429-32, and A. E. Hanson, "Village officials at Philadelphia," pp. 429-40 in L. Criscuolo and G. Geraci (edd.), *Egitto e storia antica dall' ellenismo all' età araba* (Bologna 1989). P. Mich. inv. 855 = *SB* XIV 12143.

  For a useful discussion of the financial requirements for eligibility to serve in government posts (*poros*), see J. D. Thomas, "Compulsory service in Roman Egypt," pp. 35-39 in G. Grimm, H. Heinen, and E. Winter, *Das römisch-byzantinische Ägypten* (Aegyptiaca treverensia 2, Mainz 1983).

43 See the discussion of *anachoresis* (flight from obligations to the government) with earlier bibliography in S. Strassi Zaccaria, *L'editto di M. Sempronius Liberalis* (Trieste 1988) and the appendix of documents concerned with *anachoresis* (76-91).

44 Cf. supra n. 13, and Harris 278-79.

45 See supra n. 41.

they too employed scribes to write for them, especially in the drawing up of public documents.[46] Petaus is the earliest example of an illiter-ate serving as chief administrator of a village or villages. In the years after Petaus illiterates became more common in the lower bureaucratic posts of Egypt and by the beginning of the 4th c. many village administrators, called *komarchs*, were said "not know to letters." Others signed their papers and reports on their behalf. There is nothing to suggest, however, that Petaus did not carry out his duties to the satisfaction of his superiors at the district level. On two separate occasions officials in the district capital asked Petaus to investigate charges of incompetence filed against colleagues serving as *komo-grammateis* in nearby villages. The specific complaints against the colleagues were insolvency, insufficient personal fortune to guarantee Rome's moneys, and, for one colleague, being illiterate. In answering the charges, Petaus first listed each man's property to show that it was the amount required to guarantee the moneys for which each was responsible.[47] In the case of the colleague accused of illiteracy, he laconically added — "he is not illiterate, for he affixes his name to the documents he submits to his superiors." As has been observed, this summary was an apt description of Petaus' own abilities.[48]

Petaus was never labeled an illiterate in his preserved papers, yet his documents make it clear that his ability to write Greek was severely limited. In the conducting of family business back in their

---

46 E.g. the *komogrammateis* Didymos the elder of Tebtynis (E. M. Husselman, p. 16 in Introduction, *P. Mich.* V, and *P. Mich.* V 267verso and recto 14-15) and Herakleides of Philadelphia, in P. Mich. inv. 855 (supra n. 42) and the list of men (γραφὴ ἀνδρῶν) Herakleides drafted in 50/51 A.D. (*P. Gen.* II 91), containing names and property of the three former collectors of poll tax he considered suitable for other official responsibilities. (Read in *P. Gen.* II 91.5-6: γραφὴ ἀνδρῶν ἐκ πρακτόρων κα[τοι-]/κίας τῆϲ προκειμένηϲ κώμηϲ.) Two ex-praktors are said to "know letters" (εἰδὼϲ γράμματα): Maron, son of Pylades, line 13, and Demetrios, son of Isidoros, line 30; cf. also the literate collector, Nemesion, son of Zoilos. He copied Claudius' letter to the Alexandrians (*P. Lond.* VI 1912) onto the back of a tax roll (*P. Brit. Lib.* inv. 2248; A. E. Hanson, "Caligulan month-names at Philadelphia," pp. 1107-1118 in *Atti del XVII congresso internazionale di papirologia* 3 [Naples 1984]); he wrote out accounts for the operation of his bureau, see ead., "*P. Princeton* I 13: Text and context revised," pp. 259-83 in M. Capasso, G. M. Savorelli, R. Pintaudi (edd.), *Miscellanea papyrologica:in occasione del bicentenario dell' edizione della charta borgiana* (Florence 1990).

47 *P. Petaus* 10 and 11.

48 *P. Petaus* 11.35 and note *ad loc.*; Harris 279.

home village of Karanis, Petaus' literate brother Theon wrote out a
contract of loan for himself and Petaus (*P. Petaus* 31). In his government
service Petaus presumably also relied on others, such as the
professional scribes in his employ, eleven of whom were known to have
written in the office when it was under Petaus' direction for some two
years.[49] Professional scribes that worked in the government bureaux
produced a cursive writing that flowed swiftly and smoothly over the
papyrus; individual letters seldom received full articulation, and the
scribe's nubbed pen remained in contact with the surface of the papyrus,
producing a chain of letters joined together in ligature (see figs.1 and 2
below). The scribe continued to write on until a shortage of ink impelled
him to lift his pen and refill. The hands of professional scribes seem to
account for the majority of business documents and many private letters
that have survived from Graeco-Roman Egypt; professional scribes also
copied texts of Greek literature, but they employed hands with few
ligatures in these copies they were making for the book trade.[50] A
writer capable of producing a fast cursive might, at times, write more
slowly and more legibly when a particular text was intended for eyes
other than his own.[51] Petaus' penmanship stood in sharp contrast to
that of professionals: he was not a skilful writer of Greek; his capital
letters were belabored and irregular; he slowly formed each letter
individually, as would a child who was just learning to write.[52] On
several occasions Petaus practiced his official subscription by copying it
either from an exemplar or from the memory of such an example.
Copying from an exemplar was an accepted method of learning in the

---

49 See U. Hagedorn, pp. 22-39, in Introduction *P. Petaus* (supra note 41). The
    largest of the villages under Petaus' authority may have had a total
    population approaching 3000 to 4000 inhabitants. For the population of
    larger Fayum villages, see D. Rathbone, "Villages, land and population in
    Graeco-Roman Egypt," *PCPS* 36 (1990) 103-42, a reevaluation of the
    evidence that replaces the earlier and widely cited account by A. E. R.
    Boak, "The population of Roman and Byzantine Karanis," *Historia* 4 (1955)
    157-62.

50 See E. G. Turner, *Greek manuscripts of the ancient world*[2] (Supplement
    BICS 46, 1987).

51 Compare, e.g., the description of Nemesion's hand in my republication of
    P. Princ. III 152 in "Egyptians, Greeks, Romans, *Arabes*, and *Ioudaioi* ... ,"
    forthcoming in Johnson (ed.), *Life in a multi-cultural society* (supra n. 21),
    with the description of his copying of Claudius' letter to the Alexandrians
    (= *P. Lond.* VI 1912) in Hanson, "Village officials" (supra n. 42) 437.

52 *P. Petaus* 121, 114.5, 122 d; he appended his signature to *P. Petaus* 46.34,
    47.54, 49.22, 60a + b.42, 77.18.

ancient school and it was suited to autodidacts as well.[53] In his most ambitious attempt Petaus enjoyed only limited success: he wrote twelve times in succession the sentence a *komogrammateus* needed to append to the documents that passed through his hands — his name, his title, and "I have submitted this" (ἐπιδέδωκα). He was able to correct himself when he made a slip in writing the initial letters of his name at his ninth try (he erased *Pte-* and replaced it with *Pet-*). He wrote the verb correctly, however, only four times and thereafter he omitted its initial epsilon.[54] Petaus' hand is known in the archive only in these unskillful practices and in the awkward subscriptions he appended to official documents. His hand appears ever the same in all texts but one. There his letters are larger, more experienced, and more elegant. Perhaps one of his scribes had written a different exemplar for him to copy or to trace.[55] Irregular and disjointed hands such as Petaus' are known in the papyri, found especially in private letters and among writers of subscriptions to their documents. Petaus did not expend the effort to become more skilled at writing Greek, apparently because the protection afforded his interests by his network of family, friends, and associates was sufficient when balanced against the effort to become more than a memorizer and a copier.

Hands said to belong to someone who was a "slow writer" are similar in appearance to Petaus' efforts. A woman such as Aurelia Charite of Hermoupolis in the early 4th c. also wrote an unpracticed and inelegant hand, even though her legal description included the fact that she "knew letters."[56] What differentiates Charite from Petaus was her ability to write in a variety of situations that involved drafting a text from the beginning. Her ability to write carried her far beyond those

---

53　H. Harrauer and P. J. Sijpesteijn, *Neue Texte aus dem antiken Unterricht* (Vienna 1985), 9-10; cf. also text 79 (*Iliad* II 244 written 19 times, with an error in line 18) in R. Pintaudi and P. J. Sijpesteijn, *Tavolette lignee e cerate da varie collezioni* (Florence 1989) 172-73.

54　*P. Petaus* 121.9: [[Πτε]] Πεταυϲ, but πιδεδωκα in lines 5-12. His other practice met with varying success (supra n. 52).

55　*P. Petaus* 115.4-5 and note *ad loc.*; cf. also p. 36.

56　K. A. Worp, *Das Aurelia Charite Archiv* (Zutphen 1980) 2; see texts 8.3 and 33.1-2 for the statement that she "knows letters"; for specimens of her writing, plates V (doc. 8.24-25), XXI (doc. 27), XXX (doc. 37.11), XXXI (doc. 36), and perhaps XXXII (doc. 41); cf. Harris 317 and also 280 for Aurelia Thaisous alias Lolliane, a woman who petitioned the prefect for the *ius trium liberorum* and in the course of her petition drew attention to her own ability to write with ease.

who could only copy from an exemplar, suggesting that her ability to read Greek outstripped the impression her penmanship conveys.

4. More speakers of Greek than writers or readers?

Two successive central governments in Egypt assumed that their peasant population could respond to official demands for Greek documents. The Ptolemies produced enough writers of Greek to satisfy the needs of their bureaucracy through the education available to the Greek community and increasingly to Graeco-Egyptian children, the products of intermarriage between immigrant Greek soldiers and native women.[57] The Romans, as successors to the Ptolemies, seem to have been satisfied with the quantity of writers already available, even though they demanded many more documents.[58] Other than sporadic exemptions from taxes and/or public service for a limited group of teachers of advanced students, Romans took no obvious and deliberate steps to augment the number of writers in the province.[59] Some professional writers who learned their Greek at schools worked in the various government bureaux;[60] those who drew up contracts or otherwise prepared or filed documents for private individuals charged the party that requested the document for their services. Scribes also made themselves available in public places for writing on private commissions. The Ptolemies charged holders of land allotments scribal fees to cover the additional paper work required on their holdings, while the Romans added surcharges to taxes in order to cover the cost of the receipts the government issued.[61] Tax receipts were usually referred to as *symbola*.

---

57   A. K. Bowman, *Egypt after the pharaohs* (Berkeley 1986) 122; see, in particular, the family of Dryton, son of Pamphilos a Cretan, and his wife Apollonia alias Senmonthis, who lived in Pathyris of Upper Egypt in the II B.C., S. B. Pomeroy, *Women in Hellenistic Egypt* (New York 1984) 103-24, with earlier bibliography in the notes *ad loc.*, esp. n. 49, pp. 197-98.

58   Harris 122, 206-218.

59   See the discussion of privileges and exemptions for *grammatici* and *rhetores* by P. Parsons, pp. 409-46 in *P. Coll. Youtie* II; for varying levels of bureaucratic activity in the first two centuries of the Roman period, see Duncan-Jones, *Structure and scale* (supra n. 29) 67-72.

60   H. C. Youtie, "Callimachus in the Tax Rolls," pp. 545-51 in Samuel (ed.), *Proceedings* (supra n. 12) = *Scriptiunculae* II 1035-41, and id., "ΑΓΡΑΜΜΑΤΟC" (supra n. 10) 174-75 = *Scriptiunculae* II 624-25.

61   For the *symbolikon*, "tax for a receipt," see S. L. Wallace, *Taxation in Egypt from Augustus to Diocletian* (Princeton 1938) 87-89, and for the *symbolikon* on poll tax, see J. C. Shelton, "The extra charges on poll tax in Roman

The professional scribes who wrote so many of the Greek documents from Egypt have left countless samples of their work. Some specialized in tachygraphy, while others specialized in the preparation of particular types of documents, such as the *katandragraphos*, who drew up large tax registers (see below, section 7). Copying was less demanding work than composing or drafting a new text and was left for the less skillful to carry out.[62]

Professional scribes, competent in Greek, were omnipresent, but those who translated from Greek to Egyptian or from Egyptian to Greek were mentioned relatively infrequently.[63] The majority of instances in which this act of translation was made explicit occurred in reports of court proceedings and hearings, where translators functioned for those unable to respond when questioned by government officials.[64] Translating between Greek and Egyptian in more relaxed circumstances was apparently taken for granted. Professional scribes and other practiced writers were able to turn Egyptian into Greek, but it is not always clear whether they were translating from a text written in demotic, or later in Coptic, or from the dictation of an Egyptian informant. G. Mussies has drawn attention to two Ptolemaic documents that were labeled Greek copies of demotic contracts and were said to have been translated

---

Egypt," *CE* 51 (1976) 178-84. For *grammatikon*, "tax on writing" in its Ptolemaic and Roman aspects, see Wallace, *Taxation* 236-37; cf. also E. M. Husselman, pp. 3-11 in Introduction, *P. Mich.* V.

62   For the important rôle that records of a previous year played, as basis for compilation of lists for the new year, as well as the notion that copying was considered routine scribal work, see *P. Mich.* XI 603, especially lines 5-13 and note *ad* 7.

63   References to an ἑρμηνεύς often intend the meaning "broker": see F. Preisigke, *Wörterbuch* (Berlin 1924) cols. 599-600, *s.v.* 3, and (e.g.) Wallace, *Taxation* (supra n. 61) 263 and 465, with regard to *P. Oxy.* XIV 1650.
W. Peremans, "Les EPMHNEIC dans l'Égypte gréco-romaine," pp. 11-17 in Grimm, Heinen, and Winter (supra n. 42), suggests that ἑρμηνεῖς are frequently encountered, but he has concerned himself with literary, as well as documentary evidence, with all functions of the ἑρμηνεύς, and with all translation activities, including that between Latin and Greek.

64   See Youtie, "ΑΓΡΑΜΜΑΤΟC" (supra n. 10) 205 = *Scriptiunculae* II 183, citing, in notes 9 and 10, *PSI* XIII 1326 (181-83 A.D.), *BGU* VII 1567B (III A.D.), *SB* XVI 12692 (as *P. Col.* inv. 181 (19) + 182, 339 A.D.), *P. Oxy.* II 237 ii.37-38. Add *P. Ant.* II 87 (III A.D.), *P. Sakaon* 32.23 (late III A.D.), *P. Vindob. Tand.* 8.2, *SB* XIV 11391 (II/III A.D.).

"to the best (of the scribe's) ability."[65] The body of these Greek agreements, however, were preserving Egyptian format when the parties to them were said to be making an oral declaration — e.g. "all four women speaking with one voice to the scribe Nexouthis, son of Patous." Panephremmis, son of Heron, resident in the village of Apias, probably dictated his census declaration in Egyptian to the interpreter at Theadelphia in 161 that subsequently set it down in Greek.[66] At the end of the 6th c. two women from Syene, Aurelia Tsone and her sister Aurelia Tsere, daughters of Apa Dios and Rachel, required that their contract of sale be read out for them and translated into Egyptian, but there is no indication that the contract had also been drawn up in Egyptian, despite the women's obvious unfamiliarity with Greek.[67] Learning to read and write the Egyptian language was part of training for the native priesthood, but even as some illiterates in Greek could write Egyptian, so too not all bilinguals read or wrote Egyptian, even if they could speak the language.[68] A section of a private letter in Greek from a man with a Greek name reinforces the notion. The text begins with the instructions that whoever reads it is to make an effort and translate the things written in the letter and impart the contents to the women.[69] The writer assumed easy availability of someone to read the Greek of his letter and then translate that Greek into Egyptian — wherever it was that this was to take place, since the letter's destination is unknown.

---

65 References to translations from Egyptian documents are explicit, esp. in Ptolemaic papyri — e.g. *UPZ* II 161.38-39, 162.3-4, 175.1, 177.1, 218.12; at other times it is less clear that a written Egyptian text lies behind a situation in which a translator was involved — e.g. *UPZ* II 227 (II/I B.C.), *P. Berl. Leihg.* I 16 A and B (161 A.D.), *SB* XVI 13071 (223-35 A.D.). For *P. Giss.* I 36 (cf. also *BL* I 169 [+ *P. Giss.* 108 = Meyer, *Jur. Pap.* 29] and III 64) and *BGU* IV 1002, see G. Mussies, "Egyptianisms in a late Ptolemaic document," pp. 70-76 in E. Boswinkel, B. A. van Groningen, and P. W. Pestman (edd.), *Antidoron Martino David* (Leiden 1968 = *P. Lugd. Bat.* XVII).
    For translating at the grapheion in Julio-Claudian Tebtynis, E. M. Husselman, pp. 54-55 in Introduction, *P. Mich.* V; Bowman, (supra n. 57) 122, lists those in the papyri known to write both Egyptian and Greek.

66 *P. Berl. Leihg.* I 16 A and B.

67 *P. Münch* I 13.71.

68 For the Egyptian priests, see e.g. *P. Tebt.* II 291 (162 A.D.) and *UPZ* I 148 (II B.C.); for a Graeco-Egyptian literate in Greek who seems only to speak Egyptian, but not to write demotic, see Hanson, "Egyptians, Greeks, Romans, *Arabes*, and *Ioudaioi*," (supra n. 51, and cf. n. 19).

69 *P. Haun.* II 14.

The importance of a document no doubt helped to determine the effort spent on its composition and its physical preparation. Careful attention was lavished, for example, on the Greek petitions destined for high officials, and efforts to present one's case in the best possible manner resulted in preliminary drafts never dispatched, with phrases rewritten and alternate wording tested.[70] Copies of supporting documents were collected with care to form extensive, accompanying dossiers. The less accomplished readers and writers of Greek — family members, friends, and business associates — surely assisted illiterates and semiliterates in preliminary preparations for the production of important documents, perhaps proffering written exemplars that had served on previous occasions and were stored among family papers. Professional scribes brought their familiarity with proper format, their linguistic skills, and their penmanship, to a project that was, in many instances, already in progress.[71]

The orthography employed in Greek papyri shows a considerable degree of bilingual interference from Egyptian to Greek, indicating that there was a substantial number of bilingual speakers among those who were writing the Greek.[72] Estimates regarding the extent of oral bilingualism must look, at least in part, to indirect evidence from antiquity, along lines suggested by studies of modern populations that are not only bi- or multilingual but also display high rates of illiteracy. Insofar as Graeco-Roman Egypt is concerned, a crucial question involves the extent of bilingualism in the agricultural villages of the Fayum, the source of many Greek and demotic papyri.[73] Preliminary work suggests that the villages need to be judged individually as to their potential for supporting a modest bilingual

70 See e.g. *P. Köln* V 222 and 223 (after 145 B.C.); A. E. Hanson, "The Archive of Isidoros of Psophthis and P. Ostorius Scapula, Praefectus Aegypti," *BASP* XXI, 1984, 76-87 (9 A.D.); *P. Mich.* X 582 (with the correction for line 1 in *ZPE* 10 [1973] 187).

71 There was a concern that an important document look attractive (*P. Sarap.* 84a ii.5-8); also Youtie, "P. Mich. inv. 855" (supra n. 42) 148 = I 430, who emphasizes that this was a letter of special importance in village affairs; the man who ordered it copied was, after all, himself competent in writing Greek. Cf. Harris 231 and n. 293.

72 F. T. Gignac, *A grammar of the Greek papyri of the Roman and Byzantine periods* I (Milan 1976) 46-48. See also Mussies, "Egyptianisms in late Ptolemaic documents" (supra n. 65) 70-76.

73 For the likelihood that the population of the larger villages was between 3000 and 4000, see supra n. 49.

population,[74] and that the following criteria would figure large in the assessment — if the village were large enough for its own government bureaux; if it were not an isolated and self-contained community, but maintained frequent contacts with the district capital and with Alexandria; if it were frequented by Greek-speaking visitors from outside; if the village's élite were speakers of Greek, and so forth.

Heads of peasant households became familiar with the process of securing the Greek documents that warded off harassment from government authorities. There were taxable items to report, as well as periodic changes in the taxables — changes with regard to land-holdings through sale or other transfer, or in productivity through poor inundations of the Nile; in the Roman period in particular, changes in flocks and in household through births, deaths, and migrations; there were tax payments in money and in kind for which receipts were taken. (For examples, see below, section 7.) The exchange of Greek documents between peasant and central government went on endlessly, reaching its peak in the 2nd c. of the Roman period.[75] Peasants grew accustomed to hearing and seeing Greek.[76]

5. More readers of Greek than writers?

The central government communicated with the population at large through Greek documents, beginning with royal commands of the Ptolemies and continuing with those from the emperor and his represen-tatives. These documents were displayed publicly, and it was expected that they be read and complied with. Sometimes placards were addressed to a limited audience. Nonetheless, they were written in large and clear letters so that those to whom the matter was of concern could readily grasp the sign's message — such as the order to a detachment of Alexander's troops, left behind at Memphis under the

---

74 E.g. D. H. Samuel, "Greeks and Romans at Socnopaiou Nesos," pp. 389-403 in R. S. Bagnall, Gerald M. Browne, A. E. Hanson, L. Koenen (edd.), *Proceedings of the XVI international congress of papyrology* (Chico 1981), arguing that while Karanis and Philadelphia had a considerable indigenous population that was at least partially hellenized, Soknopaiou Nesos did not.

75 See tables in Duncan-Jones, *Structure and scale* (supra n. 29) 67-72.

76 The practice of writing graffiti apparently became widespread only under Macedonian and Roman rule, as Greek-speakers scribbled their names on walls; pre-Greek examples of demotic graffiti occur less frequently, see V. Foertmeyer, *Tourism in Graeco-Roman Egypt* (Princeton University PhD diss. 1989) 11.

command of Peukestas, informing the troops that a ritual area was off-limits to military personnel, or the charter that granted a beer parlor (*zytopoleion*) in the Delta tax-exempt status during the reign of Augustus.[77] When a communication was intended for the entire populace, rather than a select audience, its postings were accordingly more numerous. The document was to be posted not only in the Greek cities and district capitals, but also throughout Egypt in peasant communities, regardless of size, in order to obviate claims of ignorance as to the document's provisions.[78] Some texts specified that the postings be displayed in clear and readable letters.[79] This system of communication envisages potential readers, even in settlements too small for their own government bureaux.

There were other government postings as well, such as the results of judicial hearings on petitions, but these were posted principally in the cities where the hearings took place — often Alexandria and its environs.[80] The purpose of postings was, as one announcement that judicial decisions would be displayed expressed it, so that "...those who ... wished would thus be able to get a copy of the judicial responses that pertained to them."[81] The supposition was that interested parties would be able to find the text which centered on their affairs and bore their names or the names of kin. A morass of other documents of similar

---

77   Peukestas' placard is the earliest sign thus far recovered, see Turner, *GMAW*[2] (supra n. 50) no. 79, and cf. Harris 205. For the inscription displayed at the beer parlor in the Menelaite nome, see P. J. Sijpesteijn, "Lucius Antonius Pedo: Prefect of Egypt," *ZPE* 65 (1986) 154-56, and esp. n. 7.

78   *P. Cair. Isid.* 1.9-10 and 15-17, with note to line 16; *P. Coll. Youtie* I 30, note *ad* 12-15, gives references for other public posting of government communiqués.

79   E.g. *SB* XIV 12144.13-14 (= *P. Coll. Youtie* I 30); *P.Oxy.* VIII 1100.2-3; XXXIV 2705.10-11.
      The statement by the freedman Hermeros that he could read *lapidariae litterae* (Petronius, *Sat.* 58.7) has always seemed to me to refer to public notices of this kind, whether on stone and commemorative, or on a variety of writing surfaces and therefore of current interest — cf. Harris 252 n. 408 and 258 n. 438 for other suggestions. The phrase *lapidariae litterae* is without parallel.

80   For a list of such postings, see A. E. Hanson, "A new affidavit formula for attestation of copies of prefectural *subscriptiones*: P. Mich. inv. 6554," *ZPE* 55 (1984) 191-99.

81   *P. Yale* I 61 (*c.* 209 A.D.; cf. *BL* VI 204 and *BL* VII 282); see also *P. Col.* VI, the responses of Septimius Severus and Caracalla to cases tried before them in Alexandria in 200 A.D. Cf. Harris 215 and n. 205.

nature presented themselves for viewing in the postings that covered the porticoes of the cities. It was left to the individual to discover his or her own text and to copy the response from the official to whom the document had been submitted, or to arrange for a copy to be made.

In a sense, magic texts in both Greek and demotic also presupposed an audience whose reading ability might extend to important words of placards and postings and whose writing ability was sufficient for copying clumsily from an exemplar.[82] The first reading out of a magic text could be done by a specialist, or anyone literate in the language of the document, in front of the petitioner, so that the petitioner might learn about its spells and its potencies. The implementation of the *praxis* — the actions which accompany the spell — and the recitation of its *logos* — the words that accomplish the spell — must, however, be carried out in some fashion by him or her who asked for the powers the spell promised.[83] If anyone but the petitioner performed the *praxis* or recited the *logos*, it would imperil the success of the spell by setting up confusion between the functional substitute and the dysfunctional petitioner. Infernal powers were expected to benefit the one who called upon them, and in the case of a love charm, for example, to whom should they send the beloved — to the substitute or to the petitioner?[84] The *praxis* often called for writing, but this was, in most cases, the copying out of the magic words and symbols presented in the exemplar. The writer did not have to draft or compose without a model. It was probably also sufficient for a writer merely to trace over magic words and symbols set down by a more practiced writer and a magic specialist, since precision was an important aspect. The recitation of the *logos* that brought the speaker the desired powers might likewise be no more than the recitation of a spell from memory, practiced many times to ensure that the final performance was meticulous. In the case of an illiterate the written *logos* did not serve as reminder to the words of the spell, but lay useless in his or her hand, as he or she recited what had earlier been memorized. Magic systems assumed readers and copiers, although memorizers and tracers were probably tolerated. Necessity created ability.

---

82   E.g. *PGM* I 15-37, 262-347, II 1-40, and *PDM* XIV 117-140, in H.-D. Betz, *The Greek magical papyri in translation* (Chicago 1986). Cf. Harris 27, 124, 299.

83   For recent discussion, see D. Martinez, *A Greek love charm from Egypt (P. Mich. XVI 757)* (Atlanta 1991) 8-20.

84   For the dynamics of love charms, see J. J. Winkler, *The constraints of desire* (New York and London 1990) 71-98.

The example of Petaus and other signers of severely limited
capacity show the importance of one's name as a configuration to hold
in the eye of the mind, a series of shapes to recognize and, if possible, to
reproduce, when asked to do so. It was a familiar symbol in the midst of
unintelligibility. Tax receipts written in Greek presented peasants
with a stylized text that included their official name. In the Roman
period peasants paid poll tax at the highest rate and were liable to
other capitation taxes from which more privileged elements of the
population were exempt. The harvest peasants gathered from the
fields and their animals were also taxed, and if craftsmen, they paid
trade duties.[85] The entirety of the rural population was also subject to
five days' compulsory labor each year on canal embankments to keep
the irrigation system in good order, and that labor was also receipted.
Tax payments and other obligations receipted by the government were
written on either an ostrakon or on a strip of papyrus by officials or
their scribes, and although the formulae of the receipts were quickly
written, it was not unusual for the first letter or so of individual words,
especially the initial letters of the taxpayer's name, to be given rather
careful articulation.[86] Busy officials occasionally used previously
prepared papyrus receipts, with introductory formulae already
written, to give to those who had completed their five days' work on
the embankments. All that was needed was one or more additional
items to individualize the receipts and give them validity. The first
scribe wrote the receipt's formulae to the point where only recipient's
name and the date were yet required, being careful to leave ample
blank space; the second scribe filled in the rest — the name of the
peasant who had done the work and the date.[87]

The receipt for work done or money paid (*symbolon*) was an *ad
hominem* guarantee of the individual's contribution, and his receipt
could be presented on demand to show that he had fulfilled a specific

---

85 In general, see Wallace (supra n. 61); cf. Harris 217. For compulsory labor
    on the dikes, see Thomas, "Compulsory service in Roman Egypt" (supra n.
    42) 37-39.

86 For ostraka, see Cl. Préaux, "Sur l'écriture des ostraca thébains d'époque
    romaine," *JEA* 40 (1954) 83-87; cf. also infra n. 91.

87 H. C. Youtie, "Diplomatic notes on Michigan ostraca," *CPh* 39 (1944) 28-29
    = *Scriptiunculae* II 830-31, and id., "Critical notes on documentary papyri,"
    TAPA 92 (1961) 553-54 = *Scriptiunculae* I (Amsterdam 1973) 359-60; also *P.
    Mich.* VI 418-420.

obligation.[88] Peasants kept their receipts as proof of payment, and these receipts could be compared with the cumulative records maintained in the local tax bureau. The receipt would have been especially useful to the peasant taxpayer when discrepancies arose in the records.[89] In the Roman period the large tax registers with records of payments in money or in kind were organized according to the peasants' names, arranged in a topographical sequence that reflected the provincial census, conducted "house by house" (κατ' οἰκίαν; for an example, see below, section 7). Accommodations were made in the geographical ordering to reflect collectors' routes, especially when collecting from villagers currently resident outside the village.[90] The lemmata of individual taxpayers' names, arranged in columns, gave a stylized appearance to the rolls: a man's name had special prominence at the beginning of each lemma, and the initial letters of the name were routinely given careful articulation; in some hands all the letters of the first name were well articulated; abbreviations were few, in contrast to the cursive character of the writing that followed, giving filiation, other personal information, and the payments (see below, section 7).[91] These habits in record-keeping were designed to serve the convenience of the tax bureau, without a thought for the peasant taxpayer. Nonetheless, the configuration of a peasant taxpayer's name, as it appeared in the master lists of the government offices, was repeated on the receipts that were in the man's possession. These receipts with his name in Greek were the symbols that the obligations charged against him as taxpayer had been fulfilled, at least for the time being.

6. Numeracy in Greek

UNESCO's second definition implies that in modern times dysfunctional illiterates are also deficient in numeracy. That distortions in

---

88 For the retaining of receipts, see e.g. *P. Mich.* VI, pp. 100-102; P. J. Sijpesteijn, *Customs duties in Graeco-Roman Egypt* (Zutphen 1987) 22. For ostraka blanks receipting one day's work on the embankments, to which the name was not added, see Youtie, "Diplomatic notes" (supra n. 87) 28 = *Scriptiunculae* II 831.

89 Petesouchos, son of Eleis (no. 35, supra n. 5), kept penthemeral certificates and receipts for weavers' tax and poll taxes for himself and his son Zoilos over many years.

90 J. C. Shelton, pp. 2-3 in *A tax list form Karanis (P. Cair. Mich.* 359), part 2 (Bonn 1977).

91 See also, e.g., the plate opposite p. 174 in *P. Col.* V (*c.*160 A.D.); plates I and III at the end of *P. Cair. Mich.* I (175 A.D.); plates I-III at the end of *P. Mich.* IV, part 1 (171/72 A.D.).

age-reporting, common in many traditional societies, and the tendency to round ages are characteristic of populations in which illiteracy rates are high is a commonplace.[92] Age-rounding in Graeco-Roman Egypt was no doubt a by-product of widespread illiteracy as well. At the same time, age-reckoning is a simple calculation in a system of era-dating, such as our own, where calculating one's age involves no more than subtraction of a birth year from the current year. In a system that employed regnal years of successive rulers by which to mark the passage of time, the calculation was progressively more difficult the older one became and the more rulers one survived. The impression of one's age sufficed in most instances. For example, the sister of a young man's grandfather and the villainess in the narrative of a petition was said to be "very old, for she appears to have lived more than sixty years."[93] An approximate statement of one's age was also accepted, however, in contexts where we would expect greater precision.

A well known example of distortion in age-reporting comes from the papers of Aurelius Isidoros of Karanis, a man who did "not know letters" and who used the services of an *hypographeus* to sign on his behalf. Isidoros' public and private papers contained conflicting statements about his age, as recorded in his signalments — the physical description that included his identifying marks, such as scars: in 12 years Isidoros aged only 10 years, but, more serious, he did so unevenly.[94] The editors argued persuasively that age-rounding accounted for the discrepancies and they linked the discrepancies to the fact that Isidoros was illiterate.[95]

Age-awareness among peasants in Roman Egypt does appear more precise, however, where young men's ages are linked with their liability for the poll tax. In the Roman period and up to 257/58 (the years in which the quattuordecennial census was in operation), all males of peasant status between the ages of 14 and 62 years were eligible for the poll tax at the full rate, and citizens of the district capitals paid a half rate. Aurelius Isidoros' declaration of persons belonged to the slightly later period of Diocletian and the early years

---

92   E.g. Duncan-Jones, *Structure and society* (supra n. 29) 79-92; Harris 271-72.
93   *P. Sakaon* 40.12-13.
94   *P. Cair. Isid.* 81.5 (about 35 in 297 A.D.); 97.6 (about 37 in 308 A.D.); 125.14 (about 40 in 308 A.D.); 91.2 (about 45 in 309 A.D.). In 8.9, a declaration of persons, the second figure of the numeral is illegible, although the first figure shows that Isidoros was then over 40.
95   A. E. R. Boak and H. C. Youtie, *The archive of Aurelius Isidorus* (Ann Arbor 1960) 4.

of the dominate; it was submitted according to Diocletian's reforms of the tax system in 297 that had created an equivalency among taxable items. Nonetheless, the age at which liability began for young men was still an important landmark. Isidoros listed the males in his household and their ages, noting that at age forty-plus[96] he, Isidoros, was taxable (ὑποτελής), but his three-year old son was not (ἀτελής). His male child's exempt status would presumably continue through ten more years and in the eleventh his name would join those of the taxables. Declarations of births were not required from the peasant population of Egypt, but under the quattuordecennial census under-age children and their ages were reported together with the adults in declarations from households. As in the case of Isidoros and his young son, the responsible adults kept track of how old the under-age male was, well aware that with each passing year the little boy was marching toward the age of liability. At a judicial hearing in about 181 a peasant whose name is lost spoke through an interpreter to answer the official's charge that he had never been registered for the census. He offered this excuse: "My parents died when I was little and they did not register me."[97]

Verifying the accuracy of the declarations for males and of the taxing lists prepared from the census declarations was left largely in the hands of village authorities, until disputes arose. During the time of the quattuordecennial census separate lists were kept of those who were approaching taxable age.[98] Their names were transferred from the list of minors to the taxing registers during the year they became fourteen years of age. Once a peasant's name had been entered onto the tax registers, a life of taxpaying loomed ahead of him. His grasp of his own age became less precise as the decades passed, and the need for precision appeared unimportant. Each year the tax collector visited the peasant's place of residence to gather tax contributions — they could be spread over eleven months in instalments of four drachmae each. Many more taxpayers left the registers through death than did so by reaching the age of exemption at 62 years.[99] Death notices were

---

96 See supra n. 94 on 8.9.

97 *PSI* XIII 1326.7-9.

98 I.e. "the 13-year olds in year 12"; "the 12-year olds in year 12"; "the 11-year olds in year 12"; the 10-year olds in year 12," and so forth, back to the last census. *P. Mich.* XI 603.9-10 labels such documents "lists of minors and of those excluded from the tax estimate" (ἀπολογιςμοὶ ἀφηλίκων καὶ ἐκτὸς / ϲυνόψεωϲ).

99 Although life-expectancy at birth was low, when compared with life-expectancies in the late 20th c., it rose appreciably for that segment of the population that survived to age 15 years. According to the tables in B. Frier,

submitted by family members in order to remove the name of the deceased from the taxing lists, if the dead man were still of taxable age (for examples see below, section 7).[100] Those who reached the age of exemption left the rolls, but we do not know what documents authorities required from the taxpayer in order to achieve that status. A few male villagers became "over-age 61" each year and thus brought their taxpaying lives to a close through exemption, rather than death.[101] Taxing authorities acknowledged that the liability for capitation taxes was now over, and there can be little doubt that those peasant taxpayers who perceived themselves as becoming very old and appearing to have lived more than sixty years would have been at pains to make this known to the local tax bureau.

Wealth did not guarantee numeracy in Greek any more than it did literacy in Greek, but wealth's preservation implies that a man of property in Graeco-Roman Egypt was functionally numerate according to some native system.[102] Aurelius Isidoros, although imprecise about his own age, was precise in reporting his son's age. He also brought precision to the reporting of his own landholdings in 299: they amounted to 53 and 59/64 arourae. By 310, however, he was paying taxes on more than 140 arourae, and this near tripling of his property

---

"Roman life expectancy: Ulpian's evidence," *HSCPh* 86 (1982) 213-51, for example, the average 15-year old could expect to live to about 46 years of age; the average 30-year old to about 53 years; the average 45-year old to about 60 years; the average 60-year old to about 69 years. The population declined most sharply between birth and age 15 years; only about 43% in a cohort of 100,000 births survived to age 15, and only 7.5% to age 65. Cf. also Duncan-Jones, *Structure and scale* (supra n. 29) 93-104.

100 Relatives and other associates of men who had abandoned their registered place of residence and disappeared, leaving behind no taxable assets, also submitted declarations in the Oxyrhynchite district during the Julio-Claudian period. The purpose was similar: to prevent tax authorities from forcing the relatives or associates to pay taxes in behalf of the man who had absconded. For a list of such declarations, see S. Zaccaria, *L'editto* (supra n. 43) nos. 1, 2, 3, 6, 11, 18 (cf. also 9, a similar document from the Arsinoite district), pp. 76-79 in the Appendix.

101 Cf. e.g. H. C. Youtie, "Notes on Papyri (IX)," *BICS* 11 (1964) 25-26 = *Scriptiunculae* II 1011-12.

102 Duncan-Jones, *Structure and scale* (supra n. 29) 92 gave the wrong impression about Isidoros' numeracy, when he deduced from Isidoros' age-rounding that "[t]he Egyptian landowner seen at the beginning of the chapter is a warning against thinking that wealth always carried with it either numeracy or literacy." There is no reason to impugn Isidoros' numeracy — he was simply unable to express calculations in Greek.

appears to have occurred after 309. The editors of his papers plausibly suggested that the additional land became his by inheritance.[103] By 324 Isidoros claimed only 80 arourae, and even after he had expended painstaking labor upon them, he had brought only seven of the 80 arourae under cultivation.[104] Isidoros also leased land for much of his life, no doubt because his own land was unproductive. He was apparently ever alert to the possibility of leasing small plots of well-watered, grain land that were easy to cultivate and almost certain to bring him a profitable crop. Isidoros also had an extensive public career at Karanis, including serving as a *komarch* and a *sitologos*, collector of grain belonging to the government. Others wrote Isidoros' reports for him. It was always possible for literates and illiterates alike to hire substitutes to manage the entirety of such operations, including making the collections, issuing the receipts, and submitting the necessary reports.[105] But the one to whom the duty belonged remained the party that was liable in the government's eyes for the funds owed to Rome, and his property guaranteed that the payment would be made.

Illiterates and semiliterates borrowed money, and rented, bought, sold, inherited and willed to family members complex fractions of their private property. Inability to express the transactions in Greek was a consequence of limited abilities in reading and writing Greek and not an indication that a functional numeracy was totally beyond the individual's competence. The same networks that protected those of limited abilities from having fraudulent words written in their Greek documents were likewise invoked to protect their calculations from misrepresentations when reported in Greek.

7. Texts from the Julio-Claudian tax archive from Philadelphia[106]

A. P. Mich. inv. 876 recto, col. ii: year ledger for A.D. 39/40

Five columns remain from what was once a much larger record — the collections of poll tax owed by taxpaying male peasants of the Fayum village of Philadelphia who were between the ages of 14 and 62 for the

---

103 For a summary of Isidoros' life and career, see Boak and Youtie (supra n. 95) 8-20.

104 For Isidoros' property, see *P. Cair. Isid.* 4.14 and 5.33-37 (299 A.D.); 68.12-13 and 69.17-19 (310 A.D.); 78.11-12 (324 A.D.).

105 E.g. *P. Mich.* XI 604 (223 A.D.).

106 For the archive, see A. E. Hanson, "Documents from Philadelphia drawn form the census registers," pp. 60-74 in J. Bingen and G. Nachtergael (edd.), *Actes du XV congrès international de papyrologie* II (Brussels 1979) 60-62, and ead., "Village officials" (supra n. 42) 429-40.

fourth regnal year of the emperor Gaius.[107] The ledger was one of about 150 papyri that were assembled by the collector of capitation taxes in the Fayum village of Philadelphia from late in the reign of Tiberius to the middle years of the reign of Nero. This year ledger was laid out by a *katandragraphos* (m. 1), a professional scribe whose specialty was to draft itemized tax records; he wrote out the names of the individual taxpayers together with patronymics and other pertinent information, such as profession (line 41) or current place of residence (line 27). He positioned the entries so that less space was allotted to men labelled *apolysimoi* (e.g. col. ii, line 44), because their entries routinely consisted of a single line. These more privileged villagers collected poll tax among themselves and were not visited by the tax collector month after month; hence no record of instalments followed under the names of *apolysimoi* and less space was left between an entry for an *apolysimos* and the following entry.[108]

The taxpayers mentioned in the surviving five columns of this year ledger for 39/40 have names beginning with the letter alpha, and the year ledger followed an alphabetical arrangement. Nonetheless, a geographical principle reflecting the "house-by-house" registration of the census also influenced this particular arrangement of the names beginning with alpha, for these same alpha-names appear in the same order in a non-alphabetical list drawn up a year earlier in 38/39.[109]

---

107 The name of the emperor Gaius does not, however, appear in the preserved portions of the text. Most entries are dated to year 4 of an unnamed emperor. That the unnamed emperor is Gaius is made likely by the use of three of the special, honorific month-names, introduced to honor the emperor Gaius: *Gaieios* (= Phamenoth) in lines 24, 31, 38, 43; *Drousilleios* (= Payni) in lines 25, 32, 35, 39, 46; *Drousieus* (= Epeiph) in lines 32, 36, 40, 47. Although two of the Caligulan, honorific month-names survived into the III A.D. (*Germanikeios* and *Kaisareios*), the other names did not survive long after the death of Gaius. Most disappeared in the early years of Claudius, strongly suggesting that the "year 4" in P. Mich. inv. 876 recto refers to "year 4 of Gaius," not "year 4 of Claudius." See Introduction to *P. Oxy.* LV 3780, a list of the Caligulan month-names.

108 Hanson, "Caligulan month-names at Philadelphia" (supra n. 46) 1107-18.

109 Cf. the ordering of alpha-names in the alphabetical *P. Mich.* inv. 876 recto col. ii, lines 22-48 with the ordering of alpha-names in the geographically arranged name list for 38/39 (*P. Harris* I 72 + *P. Mich.* inv. 890 + *P. Princ.* III 123 + *P. Mich.* inv. 791 + *P. Mich.* inv. 811), a text in which each name occupies a single line. Interspersed between the first and second names beginning with alpha in the name list for 38/39, Harphaesis, son of Ammoneus (line 47) and Harmaeis, son of Panetbeuis (line 60), are Pouoris, son of Agron; Pouoris, son of Ermias; Hermias, son of Pouoris;

After the *katandragraphos* laid out the ledger, he verified his work against his original list, drawing a short, thick stroke above the middle of each entry (in line 22, above the first alpha of Ἀρφαῆϲιϲ; in line 27, above the alpha in Πανετβεύιοϲ, κτλ.). Two other scribes (m. 2 and m. 3) then recorded the payments the individuals made in the course of the year 39/40. The two strokes extending toward and into the left margin below the taxpayer's name indicate that a taxpayer had paid in full for the year; seven of the taxpayers listed in col. ii had the strokes drawn in front of their names, while a single stroke was drawn in front of the name of the eighth, an *apolysimos* (line 44).

The poll taxes whose payments are recorded in this roll are for *syntaximon*, the *laographia* paid at its highest rate of 44 drachmae; the instalments were invariably 4 dr. or multiples of 4 dr., showing that the government's issue of tetradrachms was the currency required for such payments. A small surcharge (6 *chalkoi*) was usually paid with the final instalment for *syntaximon/ laographia*, together with pig tax (ὑική) of one drachma and one obol. Hareotes alias Arphaesis, son of Amonneus (lines 22-26), paid his poll tax for 39/40 in eight instalments of four or eight drachmae each; in a ninth instalment he paid surcharges and pig tax. By contrast Harmaeis, son of Panetbeuis (lines 27-29), currently resident in the Fayum village of Bacchias, paid his poll tax in only three instalments of tetradrachms and a final payment of surcharges and pig tax.

Patmoueis, son of Pnepheros; Paouetis, son of Patmoueis; Pouoris the younger, son of Hermias; Pylades, son of Herakles; Herakles, son of Herakles; Panetbeuis, son of Petesouchos; Panetbeuis, son of Harmaeis; Pnepheros, son of Panetbeuis. But the names beginning with alpha follow in the same order in the two documents:

Name list for 38/39	Year ledger for 39/40 (*P. Mich.* inv. 876 recto)
Harphaesis, son of Ammoneus (l.47)	Hareotes alias Harphaesis, son of Amonneus (876r.22)
Harmaeis, son of Panetbeuis (l. 60)	Harmaeis, son of Panetbeuis (l.27, rather than 29)
Hareotes, son of Leonides (l. 65)	Hareotes, son of Leonides (l.33)
Apollos, slave of Ision (l. 67)	Apollonis, slave of Ision (l.37)
Ambes, son of Ambes (l. 70)	Ambes, son of Ambes (l. 41)
Harpaesis, son of Mysthas (l. 73)	Harphaesis, son of Mysthas (l. 44)
Apollos, son of Mysthas (l. 75)	Apollonis, son of Mysthas (l. 45)

Philadelphia   81 x 28.5 cm.   39/40 (fig.1)

Col. ii, lines 22-48

(m. 1)   Ἀρεώτης ὃς κ(αὶ) Ἀρφαῆςις Ἀμόννεως

//   (m. 2) τρα(π.) (ἔτους) δ μη(νὸς) Νέο(υ) Ϲεβαϲτοῦ κδ̄ (δρ.) η,
            Χοιὰχ ἀλ(λ.) ιθ̄ (δρ.) η,

24   Τῦβι κβ̄ (δρ.) η, λ̄ με(τὰ λόγον) ζ̄ (δρ.) δ, ιζ̄ (δρ.) δ,
          μη(νὸς) Γαίου κγ̄ (δρ.) δ,

          Φαρμο(ῦθι) ιζ̄ (δρ.) δ, Παχ(ὼν) κη̄ (δρ.) δ, (m. 3) μη(νὸς)
          Δρουσιλλή(ου) κᾱ (ἡμιωβέλιον) (δίχαλκον)

          υἱ(κῆς) (δρ.) α (ὄβολος).

(m. 1) Ἀρμάεις Πανετβεύιος ἐν Βακχιάδι γι(νόμενος)

28   //(m. 2) Τῦβι κς (δρ.) κ, Φαρμο(ῦθι) δ̄ (δρ.) ιβ, Παχ(ὼν) κᾱ (δρ.) ιβ,
          Παχ(ὼν) κη̄ (ἡμιωβ.) (δίχαλκ.) υἱ(κῆς) (δρ.) α (ὄβ.)

      (m. 1) Ἀρμάεις Πανετβ(εύιος) νεώτε(ρος) (m. 2) τρα(π.) (ἔτους) δ μη(ν.)
//   Νέο(υ)

          Ϲεβαϲτοῦ λ̄ με(τὰ λόγον) γ̄ (δρ.) η, μη(ν.) Γαίου κγ̄ (δρ.)
          ιβ, Παχ(ὼν) κθ̄ (δρ.) ιβ,

32   μη(ν.) Δρουσιλλή(ου) λ̄ με(τὰ λόγον) δ̄ (δρ.) ιβ, μη(ν.)
          Δρουςέως ιθ̄ (ἡμιωβ.) (δίχαλκ.) α (ὄβ.).

      (m. 1) Ἀρεώτης Λεωνίδου (m. 2) τρα(π.) μη(ν.) Νέο(υ) Ϲεβαϲτοῦ

//   λ̄ με(τὰ λόγον) γ̄ (δρ.) η, Τῦβι ιη̄ (δρ.) η, Μεχ(εὶρ) κη̄
          (δρ.) δ, Φαρμοῦθ(ι) κγ̄

          (δρ.) δ, Παχ(ὼν) ιθ̄ (δρ.) δ, κᾱ (δρ.) η, μη(ν.)
          Δρουσιλλή(ου) κβ̄ (δρ.) η,

36   (m. 3) μη(ν.) Δρουσείο(υ) ιᾱ (ἡμιωβ.) (δίχαλκ.) α (ὄβ.).

      (m. 1) Ἀπολλῶνις δοῦλ(ος) Ἰσίωνος (m. 2) τρα(π.) (ἔτους) δ μη(ν.) Νέο(υ)

//   Ϲεβαϲτοῦ λ̄ με(τὰ λόγον) γ̄ (δρ.) η, μη(ν.) Γαίου κγ̄ (δρ.)
          ιβ,

          Παχ(ὼν) κη̄ (δρ.) ιβ, μη(ν.) Δρουσιλλή(ου) λ̄ με(τὰ λόγον)
          δ̄ (δρ.) ιβ,

40   μη(ν.) Δρουσείο(υ) ιθ̄ (ἡμιωβ.) (δίχαλκ.) α (ὄβ.).

      (m. 1) Ἀμβῆς Ἀμβήους γέρδ(ιος) (m. 2) μη(νὸς) Νέο(υ) Ϲεβαϲτοῦ κγ̄
//   (δρ.) η΄, Τῦβι ιη̄ (δρ.) δ, Χοιὰ(χ) ἀλ(λ.) ̔ιθ̄ ̓ (δρ.)
          η,

[[Τῦβι]] λ̄ με(τὰ λόγον) ι̅ϛ̅ (δρ.) δ, ῾Μεχ(εὶρ) λ̄ β̄ (δρ.)
δ´, Φαρμο(ῦθι) ι̅θ̅ (δρ.) δ, κ̅α̅ (δρ.) δ, δ (ἡμιωβ.)
(δίχαλκ.) α (ὄβ.)

μη(ν.) Γαΐου κ̅γ̅ (δρ.) δ.

44 (m. 1) Ἀρφαῆcιc Μύcθου ῎Αραβο(c) ῎Αραψ ἀπολ(ύcιμοc).

/

Ἀπολλῶνιc Μύcθ(ου) ῎Αραβο(c) (m. 2) Χοιὰχ ἀλ(λ.) ι̅θ̅ (δρ.) η,

// Τῦβι λ̄ με(τὰ λόγον) β̄ (δρ.) η, Μεχ(εὶρ) κ̅ε̅ (δρ.) δ,
Φαρμο(ῦθι) κ̅ε̅ (δρ.) η, Παχ(ὼν) (δρ.) η,

(m. 3) μη(ν.) Δρουcιλλή(ου) (δρ.) δ, (ἡμιωβ.) (δίχαλκ.) α (ὄβ.),
μη(ν.) Δρουcείο(υ) ι̅θ̅ (δρ.) δ.

48 (m. 2)   τη

NOTES:

22. ὃc κ(αὶ): written οc^κ.

23. τρα(π.)· probably to be understood as τρα(πέζῃ), "at the bank,"
indicating that the moneys from this individual were collected and
deposited locally. Note that τρα(π.) does not appear with Harmaeis,
son of Panetbeuis, currently resident in Bacchias (line 27), apparently
because his tax payments were collected at Bacchias and not returned to
Philadelphia. The omission of τρα(π.) from the entry for a weaver
(line 41) and for Apollonis (line 45) may have been accidental, since
these contributions figured into the total for poll tax (*laographia*)
collected in the entire column (see below, note *ad* 48).

Χοιὰχ ἀλ(λ.) ι̅θ̅ (δρ.) η: here ἀλ(λ.) indicates that the 8 dr. were
recorded in the second of two accounts, both bearing the same date — in
this case, "the second account dated to 19 Choiach." The use of ἀλ(λ.)
in this meaning can be seen elsewhere in the archive, and there can be
no question that its intention is to mark the second of two accounts, both
dated the same day: e.g. *P. Mich.* XII 639.6-7, 32-33, 43-44, although
the expansion offered there for α^λ is incorrect (α^λ =ἄλ(λαι) sc.
δραχμαί); *P. Corn.* I 21.115 (cf. line 99 for the first account dated to 5
Mesore) and 298 (cf. line 287 for the first account dated to 26 Mesore),
where α^λ is apparently thought by the editors to equal ἄλ(λοc) sc.
λόγοc. A 1st c. text from outside the archive, *P. Wisc.* II 38.1 and 43,
seems to add support to the explanation of α^λ as ἄλ(λοc λόγοc), since
λόγοc and ἄλλοc λόγοc function there as headings — but the records are
for different months and so the parallel breaks down. I shall argue that
α^λ = ἄλ(λου λήμματοc), "of" or "belonging to the second collection," on
the basis of *P. Mich.* inv. 876 recto.102 (reading Χοιὰχ α^λλλ^η ι̅θ̅ (δρ.) η)
and *P. Mich.* inv. 793 recto.14 (reading κα (ἔτουc) λήμ⟨μ⟩ατο(c), "of the
collection for year 21," to distinguish collections made for year 21 =
34/35 A.D. from those made for year 20 = 33/34 A.D.).

23-25. The month name Neos Sebastos (= Hathyr) was introduced in Egypt to honor the emperor Tiberius during his lifetime and was retained thereafter, even as the name Sebastos (= Thoth) honored Augustus during his lifetime and was retained thereafter. The remaining ten months of the Egyptian calendar were eventually renamed over a period of about two years to honor Gaius; of those ten names only *Gaieios* (= Phamenoth), *Drousilleios* (= Payni), and *Drousieus* (= Epeiph) appear in this year ledger for 39/40 (see *P. Oxy.* LV 3780 and introduction).

24. λ̄ με(τὰ λόγον) ζ̄ (δρ.) δ· "for the accounting on Tybi 30, but actually paid after that accounting on the 7th of the following month (Mecheir)." For such dating formulae, see *WO* I, pp. 814-15, and also below, line 42, for the omission of με(τὰ λόγον). For με(τὰ λόγον) written more fully in a dating phrase, see *P. Fay.* 53.2-3, [7], 8, 9; 54.3, 9, 11, 12, 14-15, 18.

Γαΐου· the correct orthography is uncertain, although on analogy with other formations, Γαϊείου seems likely to have been the academically correct form. See *P. Oxy.* LV 3780.7 and note *ad loc.*

32. μη(ν.) Δρουϲέωϲ: the first sigma was not given careful articulation, as also below in Δρουϲιλλή(ου) in line 47; Δρουϲείο(υ) seems to have been written in lines 36, 40, 47. This month-name does not appear in the preserved portions of *P. Oxy.* LV 3780, but the editor suggests that Δρουϲιεύϲ was the orthographically correct form.

α (ὄβ.): the abbreviation sign for δραχμαί was omitted before α, and elsewhere in the remainder of this column.

42. (δρ.) δ, δ· the two payments of 4 drachmae each were recorded as "δ, δ" (4 + 4 dr.), rather than the more usual "η" (8 dr.).

44. Apparently the scribe first wrote Μυϲου and, realizing his mistake, erased -ου and added a raised -θ- to produce Μυϲ⟨θ⟩[ου]⟧, that is, Μύϲθ(ου).

48. The total τη = 308 drachmae represents the 44 dr. paid in instalments to collectors from the Philadelphia tax office by the seven taxpayers whose tax contributions are itemized in this column. The amount paid by the *apolysimos* Harphaesis, son of Mysthas — (both father and son were *Arabes*[110]) — was not collected by the tax office and does not figure into the total farmed by the bureau in 39/40.

---

110   On the *Arabes* of the Philadelphia archive, see Hanson, "Egyptians, Greeks, Romans, *Arabes*, and *Ioudaioi* ..." (supra n. 51).

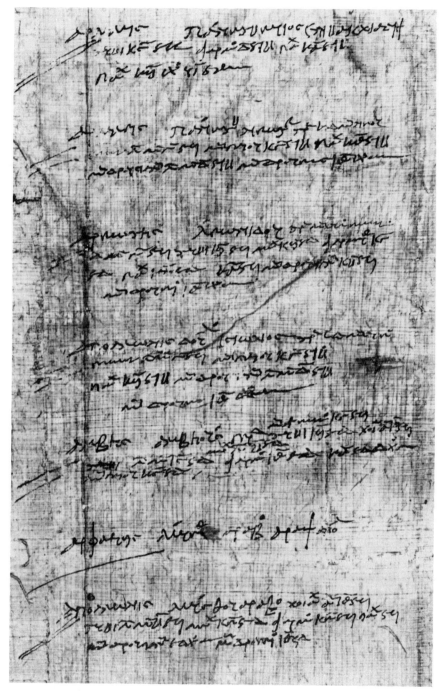

Fig.1. P. Mich. inv. 876 recto, column ii.

B. Two declarations of death: P. Mich. inv. 888 and P. Gen. inv. 213

Both death notices were written by practiced hands (see below, fig.2 for P. Gen. inv. 213). In each case it seems likely that the declarant approached an experienced writer, familiar with the format of such declarations, and enlisted his or her help in drafting the declaration of death for a brother who had died. The two texts are but fragments, passed over by earlier editors searching for publishable texts for themselves and their students. Many declarations of death, however, are known and an impression of the missing portions of each can be gained through comparison between the two contemporary declarations from Philadelphia and with similar texts. These two death notices augment the total number from Roman Egypt that has already been published.[111]

The two memoranda were found together in the same archive as the year ledger (above, *P. Mich.* inv. 876 recto), part of the papers assembled by the collector of poll tax and other capitation taxes in the Fayum village of Philadelphia during the Julio-Claudian period. Three other notifications of death, previously published, also derive from this same archive and they all announce the deaths of taxpayers from the village.[112]

For three of the five declarations of death the addressee is preserved: two were directed to the attention of the scribe of the village (*komogrammateus*)[113] and one was directed to a district official (*basilikogrammateus*),[114] resident in the capital of the nome. The fact that the five death notices were found among the papers of the local tax collector underscores the notion that their purpose was to remove defunct taxpayers from the list of those liable to poll tax and relieve

---

111 For a survey, see W. Brashear, "P.Sorb. inv. 2358 and the new statistics on death certificates," *BASP* 14 (1977) 1-10, and for a collection of the 82 texts published up to 1985 with accompanying plates, see L. Casarico, *Il controllo della popolazione dell' Egitto romano: 1. Le denunce di morte* (= *Corpora papyrorum graecarum* II; Azzate 1985). Eighteen are I A.D.; 47 are II A.D.; 17 are III A.D., not outlasting the cessation of the quattuordecennial census in 257/58.

112 For the three death notices from the archive already published, see *SB* XIV 11586 and 11587 = *CPG* II 5a) and 5b) and XII 11112 = *CPG* II 6.

113 *CPG* II 6 and P. Mich. inv. 888.

114 *CPG* II 5a.

the dead man's relatives from pressures by collectors.[115] The notifications are examples of the kind of documents, written in Greek, whose preparation peasants had to oversee and pass on to officials in the village bureaucracy. These fragmentary notifications take on added interest when juxtaposed with the larger archive of which they form a part.

(I.) P. Mich. inv. 888

Philadelphia   8 x 9.5 cm.   Reign of Claudius

Τρύφωνι κωμογραμματεῖ

Φιλαδελ(φείας)

παρὰ Πετάλου τοῦ Πασί-

4   ωνος τῶν ἀπὸ τῆς αὐ-

τῆς κώμης. ὁ ἀδελφός

μου Ἄδραστος λαο-

γραφούμενος περὶ τὴν

κώ[μη]ν ἐτελ[εύτησεν]

- - - - - - - - - - - - - - - - - -

NOTES:

1. Nemesion, the collector of poll tax and other capitation taxes at Philadelphia in these years, wrote in his own hand a business letter to a man named Tryphon (P. Mich. XII 656).[116] It is not impossible that he was the komogrammateus named here.

3-7. Petalos and Adrastos, sons of Pasion, are known elsewhere in the archive. The father Pasion was probably 49 years old in A.D. 21 (P. Mert. I 10), and the brothers both appear on the tax rolls of Philadelphia during the reigns of Gaius and Claudius.

---

115 The papers of Petaus the komogrammateus also included five death certificates, one in two copies for the same man (P. Petaus 3-8 = CPG II 59-63); some death notices from Oxyrhynchos were directed to collectors of trade taxes (CPG II, introduction 11).

116 For a correction to P. Mich. XII 656.7, see the discussion of journey-expenses for armed guards in Hanson, "P. Princeton I 13" (supra n. 46), note to line 36.

(II.) P. Gen. inv. 213 (fig.2)

Philadelphia   8.5 x 27 cm.   8 December 50

– – – – – – – – – – – – – – – – –

[παρ]ὰ . . [name and father's name]

τῶν ἀπὸ Φιλαδε[λφείας.]

ὁ ἀδελφός μου .[.]τ[...]..

4   λαογραφούμενος περὶ τὴν

κώμην ἐτελεύτησεν

τῇ δ̄ τοῦ Χοιὰχ τοῦ ἐν-

εcτῶτος ια (ἔτους) Τιβερίου

8   Κλαυδίου Καίcαρος

Cεβαcτοῦ Γερμανικοῦ

Αὐτοκράτορος. διὸ ἀξιῶ

ἐὰν φαίνηται cυντάξαι

12   τὸ αὐτοῦ ὄνομα περιαι-

ρεθῆναι καὶ ἀνενεχθῆ-

ναι ἐν τῇ τῶν τετελευ-

[τ]ηκότων τάξει ἵν' ὦ

16   [ἀ]ναίτιος, καθάπερ καί εἰμι.

εὐτύχει.

– – – – – – – –

(ἔτους) ια Τιβερίου Κλαυδίου

Καίcαρο(c) Cεβαcτοῦ Γερμανικοῦ

20   Αὐτοκράτορος Χοιὰχ ιβ̄.

NOTES:

1-3. The name of both declarant and deceased are mutilated. In line 1 would have come the name of the declarant, the deceased's brother, followed by their father's name; in line 3, the name under which the deceased was registered for poll tax — but only about 9 letter-spaces are available and the 3rd letter in the deceased's name should be a *tau*. Since the men were brothers and the father's name presumably appeared in line 1, it might be heavily abbreviated in line 3, or even omitted, although in parallel instances some other indication that the men were sons of the same father usually occurred instead.

P. Mich. inv. 876 verso.77-78 lists three taxpayers of the village as dead in the month of Choiach in regnal year 11 of Claudius (= 50/51): Psenobastis, son of Petermouthis; Petermouthis, son of Psenobastis; and Herakles, son of Horos. Psenobastis had a brother also named Psenobastis; Herakles had a brother Herakleides, but no brother is known in the tax registers for Petermouthis up to now. The fact that Petermouthis' name absorbs the somewhat clear *tau* in line 3 at the proper position and the fact that Πετερμοῦθ(ις) is the conventional abbreviation for this name in the majority of the tax documents make him at present the most attractive candidate for the deceased. Petermouthis was 51 years old in 46/47 and had two sons aged 24 and 19.

6. Because the death occurred in the fourth month of the Egyptian year, the deceased's estate was liable for only half the poll tax of the year.

15-16. ἵν' ὦ / [ἀ]ναίτιος, καθάπερ καί εἰμι: for the phrase — it also occurs in *CPG* II 6.18-19 — which is no doubt parallel to ὑπὲρ τοῦ ἀπαρενόχλητόν με γενέσθαι in the roughly contemporary *CPG* II 2.14-16, see *CPG* II, pp. 18-19, with earlier bibliography. The phrase has been used to support the claim that notifications of death were obligatory and required by the Roman bureaucracy, but it seems to me more likely that the more important function of the notification was to relieve relatives of the deceased from further attempts to collect the tax and from harassment by officials.

Composite translation:

(P. Mich. 888) To Tryphon, *komogrammateus* of Philadelphia from Petalos, son of Pasion of the same village. My brother Adrastos, paying the poll tax at the village, died... (P. Gen. inv. 213) on the 4th of Choiach (= 30 November) of the current 11th year of Tiberius Claudius Caesar Germanicus Imperator (=50 A.D.). I therefore ask, if you approve, that you order his name to be removed and entered in the register of the dead so that I may be without liability, as in fact I am. Farewell.

Year 11 of Tiberius Claudius Caesar Augustus Germanicus Imperator Choiach 12.

Department of Classical Studies, University of Michigan

Fig.2. P. Geneva. inv. 213.